David Potter has lived in Kirkcaldy since 1971
when he began his teaching career in nearby
Glenrothes, He is interested in football, cricket,
drama and history, and he was at one point an Elder
in Kirkcaldy Old Kirk and has acted for a drama
group called the Auld Kirk Players for over 40
years.

Dedicated to all who have ever lived in Kirkcaldy, but particularly to my wife Rosemary who has done so much to keep the history of Kirkcaldy alive in the Civic Society and the Kirkcaldy Old Kirk Trust.

David Potter

FAMOUS KIRKCALDY MEN

AUSTIN MACAULEY
PUBLISHERS LTD.

A CIP catalogue record for this title is available from the British Library.

ISBN 9781785549823 (Paperback)
ISBN 9781785549830 (Hardback)
ISBN 9781785549847 (E-Book)

www.austinmacauley.com

First Published (2016)
Austin Macauley Publishers Ltd.
25 Canada Square
Canary Wharf
London
E14 5LQ

I would like to acknowledge the help given to me by the Civic Society, the Old Kirk Trust and the hard working staff of Kirkcaldy Galleries. In addition, many Langtonians (the name given to those who live in the "Lang Toun" of Kirkcaldy) who have helped me in so many ways by giving me the odd snippet of information about one or other of the nine people chosen.

In particular I would like to single out George Grant, Derek Allan, Eunice Cameron, Regina Janas, Iain Hirschfeld and David Muncey.

Introduction

It is often said that Kirkcaldy is a town which undersells itself in terms of its cultural achievements. A visit to the once thriving and bustling High Street can be a depressing experience, and there often seems every appearance that the hub of the town has in fact relocated itself as if by magic to the Retail Park. This is of course a shame because the High Street area of the town simply breathes history, and it is often said that a community that ignores its own past has no future.

This book is an attempt to keep Kirkcaldy's rich history very much alive. Nine famous Langtonians (inhabitants of the "lang toun" as Kirkcaldy was once known) have been chosen. Some like Adam Smith and Gordon Brown are world famous; others like Michael Nairn have had worldwide influence, and others like Robert Adam had an influence that did not really spread all that widely beyond the town itself.

Possibly only three of those chosen were actually born in the town. The others are arrivistes but made such a great contribution to the town that they are properly considered to be Langtonians. There are others whose ghosts might find themselves annoyed at being denied a place in this book – one thinks of Sandford Fleming and Robert Adam the architect (not to be confused with

Robert Adam the Headteacher who is indeed included) – but the author has attempted to be as broad as possible with two clerics, two footballers, two politicians, a headmaster, an industrialist and an economist.

Five centuries are represented from the 17th to the 21st, and naturally there have been mighty changes in these times. Industrialisation has come and gone, religion has declined, football has arrived, politics have remained and economics have wobbled capriciously, but the town still remains. The Old Kirk tower is a symbol of permanence, and it has been here since well before the first character mentioned in this book. Kirkcaldy, in spite of everything, has been, still is and in the future always will be Kirkcaldy.

The author has one final plea. He has lived in Kirkcaldy since 1971, but was not born here. Can he now be considered to be a Langtonian?

Adam Smith
1723-1790

The life and achievements of Adam Smith are well known, and Kirkcaldy is rightly proud of what he did. Many books have been written on him (some of them rather tough and difficult) but there is a distinct lack of information on the sort of man he was.

His "The Wealth of Nations" is of course, very famous and was (reportedly) carried in the handbag of Margaret Thatcher – an uncomfortable fact perhaps for the town of Kirkcaldy in which it is not easy to find many lovers of the Conservative party! But then again, there is a strong argument for saying that Adam Smith was Kirkcaldy's first capitalist. In summer 2014 ex Labour Prime Minister Gordon Brown and distinguished History Professor and author Tom Devine appeared at the Adam Smith theatre for a symposium in which they were asked various questions. One of them was "Was Adam Smith Kirkcaldy's first and most famous capitalist?" The answers were amusing!

Kirkcaldy boasts of Adam Smith with its theatre named after him and various foundations and trusts in place. There is the Adam Smith Close off the High Street where he may at one point have lived (although the house is long demolished and replaced by another, if indeed that is the correct spot!) and there is a garden where the local Civic Society have been known to have a few Strawberry Teas on hot, lazy July days.

Kirkcaldy has Adam Smith as its answer to Dunfermline's Andrew Carnegie. In the land of the Pars, it is similarly difficult to avoid a reference to Andrew Carnegie. Ironically, both towns vote solidly Labour or SNP (sometimes Liberal, never Conservative!) yet both their heroes were undeniably exponents of the capitalist system. Carnegie was an out and out money maker who in later years, (to salve his conscience, perhaps) bestowed his largesse in the shape of theatres, clinics and baths to the families of those he had exploited, whereas Smith was more of a theorist – an enlightened capitalist, perhaps, who encouraged the belief that well-paid and well-fed workers would probably do a better job in producing inordinate wealth for the moneyed classes, rather than those who were being ground into the dust. There is also a hint now and again in the writings of Smith that he appreciated what is now known as Keynesian economics – namely that the richer the working classes are, the more money they will have to spend on goods. In the twentieth century, it took a long time for that particular penny to drop!

Adam Smith was born sometime in early summer of 1723. We know that he was baptised in the Parish Church (Kirkcaldy Old Kirk as it now is) on June 5 of that year, and some authorities put that date forward as the date of his birth as well. It was indeed not uncommon for children to be baptised on the day of their birth, but the more likely explanation is that he was born a few days previously. He was a posthumous child, and he never knew his father who died on January 25 1723, several months before his birth. His mother would therefore have an inordinate influence over young Adam.

His father, also called Adam, had been of the legal profession. He originated from Aberdeen and was a Scottish Writer to the Signet which meant that he was high up in the law, prosecuting criminals, defending clients and even becoming Comptroller of the Customs, which was presumably what brought him to Kirkcaldy. We do not know to what extent there would have been smuggling on the Fife coast, but the guess is that it would have been not unknown, if not perhaps the wholesome and thrilling adventure that Boys Own and other magazines and books would have made us believe. We know little about what caused the death of Adam senior, but we do know that in 1720 he had married Margaret Douglas, daughter of Robert Douglas of Strathendry, an estate not far from Leslie.

Adam's father was a widower, whose first wife had died in 1717, and when he married Margaret in 1720, he had a boy called Hugh who was about 8 or 9. Thus Adam had a half-brother, and as far as we can ascertain, Adam's mother brought up Hugh as her own, even after Adam's father had died. We know little about Hugh, other than that, like Adam, he was a sickly child and died in about 1750 when he would have been about 40. There is no indication that he and Adam did not get along

Adam was thus a child of a one-parent family, but by no means a poor one. He spent his youth alternating between his house on Kirkcaldy High Street and his grandfather's estate at Strathendry. It was on one of these occasions at Strathendry when young Adam suffered an alarming experience at the age of three years old. He had wandered away from his family and was abducted by gypsies (or "tinkies" as they are sometimes called in Scotland)! The alarm was raised and he was returned safely to his anxious mother, whether by a rescue, the paying of a ransom or simply because a kind-hearted gypsy woman returned him of her own free will, having found the boy when he was lost. In any case, no harm was done, but it did show up a facet of Adam's character which would become all the more apparent in later years, namely his tendency to become absorbed in something that he was doing and to lose all track of time and place. Sometimes the word "autism" is used in this context. "Away with the fairies" was a common phrase to describe children of this ilk. In Adam's case, he was nearly "away with the gypsies".

Presumably when he was living in Kirkcaldy, he would on occasion, possibly in the company of Hugh, wander down to the sea, a very short distance from his house, and look at ships and boats of all kinds. The traffic, of course, on the River Forth in the 1720s would be considerably more than it is today, and the young Adam would sit on the beach transfixed by these vessels, and being an intelligent boy, he would ask and keep asking what was in these ships, where they were going and what was the purpose of their journey. The answer was, of course, trade and it would be possibly from his early years in Kirkcaldy that the young Adam developed his interest in commerce.

Kirkcaldy in the early 18th century was by no means a poor town. The harbour in itself ensured that there would be a reasonable amount of prosperity. The town had declared itself pro-Hannoverian at the time of the first Jacobite rebellion, itself an indication that it is happy with the status quo and is not tempted by poverty to try anything revolutionary – there are records too warning about the dangers of "ane Popish pretender" – and the town had done well to avoid any serious action in what history has come to record as "the 15". The rebellion had fizzled out piteously after the indecisive battle of Sheriffmuir near Dunblane, but for several years after that, Scotland seethed with "spies" and "rebels" on the one hand, and "government agents" on the other.

Sensible people, by the time that Adam was born in 1723, were a great deal less bothered about who the King was, or of what religion or tradition he was, than they were about the desirability of providing a good standard of living and a good quality of life. There was of course a certain amount of resentment about the King being a German, but the Scottish Kirk was considerably less upset about that than it would have been if the King had been a Roman Catholic. Germans, not yet demonised as they would be in the 20th century, were preferable to Catholics! But there is also a certain amount of evidence that people wanted to move on. Two years after Adam was born, for example, in 1725 we find that the Councill (sic) among other things was setting up a Committee to "provide materials, agree (sic) with workmen and do everything necessary towards building a school". On the other hand, we also find mention of the menace of beggars, and the desirability of removing the dunghills which had gathered in the High Street!

The political situation, though always volatile and potentially able to flare up at any moment in time, had settled down a little. Either the Government repression was very effective or (more likely) the rebels withdrew to the Highlands where the power of any Government was limited. Some soldiers were billeted in the town in case there was going to be trouble – there would of course be no police force for well over 100 years – but there are few records of any disturbances. George I, though seldom seen in England, let alone Scotland, had a toast drunk to his health frequently, and behind the scenes, Parliament, taking advantage of the King's obvious preference for living in Germany and of his inability to speak English fluently, was gradually and with subtlety taking over more and more, and now at last beginning to exploit its victory in the Civil War of last century. Power was passing more and more into the hands of politicians like Robert Walpole, the man whom history has recorded as the first Prime Minister, although he was never, of course, called that in his time.

And Scotland had settled down, accepting (but not without some complaints) that it was part of Great Britain, now that its Crown and Parliament had been united with that of England. There was an element of

Scotland wanting its independence in the Jacobite Rebellions, but apart from that, any serious attempt at Scottish Nationalism would have to wait for the best part of 300 years. Other things now began to seem to be more important.

Adam Smith would have attended the Parish Church. Indeed, the Old Kirk Tower (not the Old Kirk itself, for that was rebuilt in the early 1800s) is the only building extant in the town that we can say with any degree of certainty that he was probably in, or, at least passed through on his way into the Church where the Minister was one John Drysdale. Indeed, it is more than likely that Adam climbed the steps to the top of the tower, as indeed one can still do today, to enjoy the lovely view of the river Forth and Edinburgh Castle as well as the view of the rest of the town and its hinterland. Once again, he would have had the opportunity to view the ships which were to play such a huge part in his thinking.

Adam thus grew up in Kirkcaldy. He was always a quiet, thoughtful boy, not particularly sociable nor interested in the games that his peers indulged in. He was also a sickly child. To what extent this was caused and encouraged by his pampering mother we cannot be sure, but we are told by Dugald Stewart whose father was a friend of Adam's that "The weakness of his bodily constitution prevented him from partaking in the more active amusements; but he was much beloved by them on account of his temper, which, though warm, was to an uncommon degree friendly and generous".

From about 1729 onwards, he went to the Burgh School. Where that was, no-one can say with any degree of exactitude but it would almost certainly have been in the Kirk Wynd area of town, (and the consensus of opinion is that it was where the Fife Free Press offices are now, as Kirk Wynd joins with Hill Street). Even then Kirkcaldy enjoyed a reputation, since proudly maintained and fiercely guarded, for high standards in education. Adam was certainly very fortunate in that he came under the influence of an excellent Scottish dominie under the name of David Miller. Adam learned to read and write there, and then went on to study the two subjects that were the *sine qua non* of a good Scottish education (because of the rigour necessary to learn them), Latin and Mathematics. What else he learned, we can but speculate upon but there would have been a little history and geography perhaps. He also may have studied music and art, but if he did, they would have been looked upon as less important than the "real" subjects of Latin and Maths.

It may be that from the distant perspective of almost 300 years later some psychologists may deduce that the young Adam suffered from what is now called "autism" or as it is more tactfully and euphemistically put, he was "on the spectrum". Such children are of course highly intelligent with remarkable powers of concentration, but lack the social skills to deal with their peers. Adam certainly would "tick some of these boxes" (to use another horrible modern expression) as far as this condition was concerned, but as we are talking about such a loosely defined set of symptoms, no one could really say for certain. But he was certainly very intelligent, and was certainly far from gregarious, as far as other children were concerned. He was certainly not "one of the boys" but that does not mean that he was unpopular.

Throughout his life, stories are told by his friends about his absent mindedness. One Sunday morning he went for a stroll before going to Church but forgot to put his clothes on, became involved in some mental problem or conundrum and ended up near Dunfermline until Church bells brought him back to reality. He then walked back to Kirkcaldy still in his night clothes! Possibly slightly more believable is the story of how he put bread and butter into a tea pot, then declared that it was the worst cup of tea he had ever tasted! And of course there are myriads of slightly more credible but less spectacular stories of him being found wandering around the streets of Edinburgh because he was lost, and him being late for appointments etc.

In 1737 at the age of 14, he went to the University of Glasgow. In the 18th century entering University at that age was by no means unusual, but even so it must have been a wrench for the delicate, sheltered, possibly naïve young man to leave his fretful and over-protective mother. There is no evidence to prove or disprove this, of course, but it would have been possible in the financial sense of the word for his mother to move temporarily to Glasgow to stay with him. Certainly, moving between Glasgow and Kirkcaldy would have been by no means easy or cheap. The most likely method of travel would have been to sail up the Forth as far as possible, then a coach from someplace like Stirling.

But Adam would certainly have had some problems settling in the still comparatively young town called Glasgow. It was not yet a mighty city, but it was already a prosperous town on the banks of the Clyde. It benefitted from the tobacco and indeed, to a lesser extent, the slave trade with the Americas, although its heyday would not be until the Industrial Revolution of a hundred years later. Adam had few problems dealing with the academic work. He studied Latin, Greek,

Mathematics, Natural Philosophy, Moral Philosophy and Logic and Metaphysics.

One of his teachers was a man called Francis Hutcheson, an inspiring character and it was from him that Smith inherited his passion for such alien and (to 18th century eyes) subversive concepts like freedom of speech and freedom of religion, as well as his ability to reason and argue logically and cogently. It was probably at this point too that he began to question the contribution of the Church to society. He was not necessarily a godless character – and certainly retained strong views on what was right and wrong – but the Church, whether Catholic or Protestant, began to appear to him as a power group, led by a few dictators. Rumours abounded throughout Glasgow in the late 1730s that the Stuarts were on the point of having another go at unseating the Hannoverians (George II had now replaced his father George I since 1727) – and religion certainly did play a large part in determining on whose side any individual would range himself (Catholics would tend to side with the Stuarts, to a large but not exclusive extent, and Protestants with the Hannoverians). This to the young Smith seemed dangerous, and frankly irrelevant to other and more important issues.

Hutcheson, Smith's beloved teacher, was well known throughout Glasgow. Such was his belief that education should be free to all, that he frequently opened the doors of his lecture hall to allow members of the public to attend, should they so wish. He was a brilliant orator, thoroughly enjoyed teaching and Smith would often admit to being spellbound just listening to him. So much did he learn from Hutcheson that after three years he won what was called the Snell Exhibition which allowed him to go to Balliol College, Oxford to study at what we would now call a post-graduate level.

Perhaps no teacher on earth could have been as good as Hutcheson, in the eyes of the 17 year old Adam Smith, but Adam was a great less impressed by the quality of teaching at Oxford University in the early 1740s. Such lectures as there were failed to interest him, for there was little or no control over lecturers and Professors, so he very soon lost any sense of direction as far as his further degree was concerned (a phenomenon still by no means unheard of in the 21st century!), but unlike other young men in different circumstances, he refused to become depressed or dissolute. But he did not spare the lazy teachers in his letters to his relatives "In the University of Oxford, the greater part of the publick (sic) professors have for these many years, given up altogether even the pretence of teaching" and in one letter to his cousin at Strathendry who was in charge of his financial arrangements, Adam complains of "the extraordinary and most extravagant fees we are obliged to pay the College and University on our admittance" and states that "it will be his own fault if anyone should endanger his health at Oxford by excessive study, our only business here being to go to prayers twice a day and to lectures twice a week".

One might from this infer that Adam was toying with the idea of returning home, but instead, realising that he was in Oxford with loads of libraries, the Bodleian in particular, and study opportunities in abundance, he embarked on a self-directed course of studying everything – classical and (unusually for the 18th century) modern languages, more philosophy and logic, public speaking (at which he was, as yet, no great success) and more and more this new subject which was beginning to absorb his interest – trading and political economics. He stayed in Oxford until 1746, his stay in southern parts perhaps prolonged by the news of the rebellion in Scotland in late 1745. Edinburgh had fallen to the rebels, Sir John Cope had been defeated at Prestonpans, and the country was in an uproar. The peace loving Adam would have preferred to stay in England rather than travel north towards the fighting and bloodshed.

Yet he was homesick. He had stayed for a few years in Oxford and was longing for home to see his mother again, and he was beginning to develop symptoms of illness. His shaking fits became all the more pronounced and he was more and more susceptible to chills and colds – clear signs of a man who had been away for far too long and who was pining for home, for Kirkcaldy, or at least for Scotland, a country which, in any case, encased a far more rigorous and indeed vigorous intellectual climate in the 1740s than England did.

Eventually in April 1746, to the relief of Smith, one imagines, the Jacobites were defeated at Culloden, and Smith felt able to return to Scotland. He arrived back in Kirkcaldy sometime in summer 1746 to discover that the town of Kirkcaldy had played little part in the rebellion, and if anything, had sided with the Hannoverians, (as indeed they had in 1715) although there was a tale that the Town Council had bribed the Jacobite army to leave them alone. If this story is true, it was probably a wise use of the "thirty five pound sterling", for it saved the town a great deal of bother.

Lowland Scotland now began to look forward. Highland Scotland was a totally different matter for the repression of the Highlanders and their families went on for many years afterwards, but the dreadful outrages perpetrated by Cumberland and his thugs (men who, in another age, would have fitted seamlessly into the SS or the Gestapo), passed Kirkcaldy by, and if the locals knew anything about this, they chose not to hear. Once again, one sees the parallel in 1940s Germany of those "who knew nothing about it" or even worse "it's nothing to do with me".

Adam was now in his 20s. Clearly a very intelligent young man, but a rather unprepossessing one. By no means a handsome man – his portraits and statues do him more than justice, one feels – and also a man who, though genial and pleasant, was far from gregarious and emphatically would not join in excessive drinking or other sorts of merrymaking. In company he was gauche, awkward and prone to long embarrassing silences in which he was totally absorbed in his own thoughts. He also had a stammer, or at least a speech impediment, and sometimes found it difficult to control his arms and legs which would unaccountably convulse.

These problems need not be any major sort of impediment. The Roman Emperor Claudius was remarkably similar to Adam Smith in such ways, yet he reigned from 41 to 54 AD and was by no means the worst of the Roman Emperors in sharp contrast to his immediate predecessor Gaius Caligula and his successor Nero. In more recent times, we have the parallel of King George VI who served the country wonderfully well in difficult times in spite of all sorts of neurotic problems.

No woman ever seemed to enter his life. For 20th and 21st century psychologists this is a dream, for they can point to his close relationship with his mother, nod sagely, talk about Oedipus and sum everything up in a simplistic fashion. The truth may be more complex. He may have been homosexual – and that would never have been mentioned in the 18th century, even though it was a phenomenon of those times just as much as it is of the 21st century – or he may simply have been one of those many people with a low sexual drive. Nor does the lack of mention of a woman in his life necessarily mean that there wasn't one! That would be a classic case of an "argumentum ex silentio".

Be that as it may, Smith spent two years in Kirkcaldy until 1748 living with his mother, until in that year he obtained a job at Edinburgh University, on the strength of some of the treatises he had written, as a lecturer in Rhetoric. It seems odd that such a socially awkward man should now be teaching public speaking, a subject that he himself had no great skill in, but it is important to realise that "Rhetoric" may in 1748 not necessarily have meant what we in the 21st century consider it to have been, nor indeed what the ancient Greeks and Romans may have meant by the term.

Possibly "Philosophy" might have been a better description of what he taught, but what, in turn, does that word mean? "Love of wisdom" "the meaning of life" "practical precepts for life" – all these descriptions might well have been valid, but the emphasis that Smith was putting on it more and more was an economic one, and he felt, increasingly, that without a solid economic base, i.e. everyone having a reasonable standard of living, any discussion about values in life was pointless. After all the great civilizations of the ancient world with their massive contribution to drama, architecture, sculpture and indeed philosophy, flourished only because of wealth, and indeed wealth based on an Empire at that.

It is of course a very small step from this position to begin to think that the making of money was the ONLY important thing in life. This smacks of Thatcherite economics, and is rightly denounced in the Bible ("the love of money is the root of all evils" in 1st Timothy 6.10, for example) and elsewhere, but there is no evidence to suggest that Adam Smith takes up such an extreme position. Money, he believed, was the base of everything.

It was while he was in Edinburgh that Smith met David Hume, a great philosopher of his day and a leading figure in what has come to be known as the Scottish Enlightenment. He was slightly older than Smith and both of them became great friends although possibly not, as has been suggested, homosexual lovers. They shared a great deal in common for many years and contributed a great deal to l8th century Scottish thought, but there is nothing to make one think that the relationship was as close as that.

In 1751 Adam Smith was appointed Professor of Logic (later Professor of Moral Philosophy) at Glasgow University. These two subjects, traditionally nebulous and intangible, possibly owe their definitions, such as they are, to Adam Smith, for it was under him that they really became accessible for most students. This was an age, more than most, in which teaching could be dull and it will be remembered that Smith himself had no high opinion of the lecturing at Oxford. Smith had now developed into a good teacher of his subjects, having created his own particular style of lecturing, and it was an attractive and appealing one, if we may believe the following assessment from a contemporary historian of Glasgow University.

"He did not content himself with merely reading to his students a set of lectures fashioned in his study. He rather chose to think out the subject afresh in their presence, setting out with a number of leading statements or ideas, which he explained, illustrated and exhibited in relation to each other. He was sometimes rather slow and hesitant at first, but became more fluent and animated as he went on, defending his tenets, combating objections to them and pouring forth illustrations – somewhat diffuse but with the main doctrines still discernible through all the mazes of his oratory."

And it was somehow appropriate that these ideas of philosophy merging into economics and producing the answer that wealth was worth pursuing, were being aired in the town of Glasgow, for it was in this town that things were really beginning to happen with the building of ships and the import of tobacco. Glasgow was now young and vibrant, not yet as huge as it would become with the arrival of the Irish, and commerce was very much the order of the day with the Glasgow Merchants, for example, already exercising a great influence over civil life, as can be seen today in the architecture of what is called the Merchants City area of Glasgow. Glasgow, like Kirkcaldy, had been little affected by the Jacobite rebellion – more Glaswegians and more Scotsmen in general had fought on the side of the Hannoverians than had fought on the Jacobite side, an uncomfortable truth for some, perhaps, but undeniably true – and now Glasgow was making great strides forward, as the Americas became more and more a factor of British life.

Smith taught for about 12 years at Glasgow University from 1751 until 1763, during which time Robert Burns was born in Ayrshire in 1759 and George II died in 1760 to be replaced by his grandson George III. It was now a time for Scotland to redefine itself. The wars against England (several centuries of them, all bloody and really rather pointless) were now behind

Scotland, and the time had come for Scotland to forge a partnership with England and create the greatest Empire that the world had ever seen. Enlightened English politicians began to realise that the repression of the Highlander was not in the best interests of anyone – far better, surely, to channel their fighting and aggressive instincts into the British Army, even to the extent of allowing them to form Highland regiments and even on occasion, allowing them, under controlled conditions to wear the proscribed kilt, a garment outlawed after Culloden in 1746.

There was an Empire to be built. This involved expansion into places like Canada, America and India but also of course necessarily embroiled them in other wars against other European powers, mainly the French who had similar ideas. For this, tough heroes were required. The Scots, both Lowland and Highland, with their tough, cold, wet climate and severe poverty with which they nevertheless coped, were ideal recruits for this.

But other things were happening as well. Adam Smith now resident in Glasgow could hardly have been unaware, even if he were not already pre-disposed to such things, of the possibilities of trade with the New World which seemed to offer limitless opportunities on account of its size. Smith realised that what made a people great was not so much its military might (although that was necessary and essential to defend its interests) as its ability to trade. Influenced as he was by people like the Mercantilists who believed that there was a limited amount of wealth in the world (Smith now began to question whether it really was "limited", in view of what he was hearing about the Americas) and that the strongest nations would get the biggest share,

Smith began to realise more and more the importance of trade and commerce.

At this point, he began to see a connection between economics and philosophy. It was incumbent upon those who created the wealth to make sure that the wealth filtered down to all sections of society. A happy, contented, prosperous working force would surely work all the harder. There was no real point in exploiting the poor. The poor had to be made less so, and thus being better fed, fitter and healthier, they would be all the more able to join the partnership necessary to create wealth. A parallel may be drawn with slavery in Greece and Rome. A wise owner treated his slave well and fairly, and reaped the rewards in hard work and loyalty; a bad owner had multiple and constant problems with slaves running away and rebelling, and was constantly in fear of his own life.

As for the current manifestation of slavery in 18th century in Great Britain, Smith was genuinely appalled by the slave trade. Glasgow did not base its wealth on the slave trade to the extent that English cities like Liverpool and Bristol did, but Smith cannot but have been aware of why some of the ships on the Clyde were now being built. As to most intelligent men, the idea of people in chains and the appalling suffering as men, women and children were captured and forcibly transported to another continent was totally repugnant. The Church may have seen nothing wrong with it, but Smith did.

There was also growing up at this time the movement called the Scottish Enlightenment. It was to a very large extent centred on Edinburgh and featured his friend David Hume, and Smith, even though based in Glasgow, would certainly be part of it, being prepared, now and again, to give up a day in his life to travel on horseback or coach to the capital. Scotland, of course, in the 18th century was far ahead of England or indeed anyplace else in the world in its education system (John Knox and his "school in every parish" policy had given Scotland a head start!) and men of vision and intelligence flocked to Edinburgh. As a result, we can see in architecture and general culture, the effects on Edinburgh even today.

Yet it was not all as simple as that. Edinburgh also had some appalling poverty as well, as indeed did Glasgow, and Smith, like all members of his urbane and civilised circle of friends, would have been concerned about this. It was a problem however that almost defied solution. Even today in the early years of the 21st century, there are areas of Scotland that still appal by their deprivation, poverty and despair.

"The monarch's hindmost year but ane

Was five and twenty years begun

Twas then that a blast o' January wind

Blew hansel in on Robin"

Thus does Robert Burns describe his own birth in 1759. Burns was, of course, a visionary but so too was Adam Smith, and in that same year of 1759, Smith published his first book "The Theory of Moral Sentiments". It is of course a great deal less well known than "The Wealth of Nations", but arguably is the better book. There is a school of thought that believed that Smith himself was of that opinion that his first "magnum opus" was better than his second and better known one. The title gives little idea of its contents, but its basic tenet is that there should be more "sympathy", possible even "empathy" between rich and poor, between nobles and peasants, between those who own the means of creating wealth and those who work hard in order to create such wealth.

What it emphatically does not say (possibly disappointingly to modern socialist eyes) is that there should be any kind of equal distribution of wealth, or even that there should be any kind of social mobility, so that one can, as it were, move up a class. But it does say that every social class should make every effort to understand each other; that they should all work together and in this way everyone should benefit. It was in no way any kind of rebellious, seditious or subversive document, although there were those who thought so at the time. It was more like Cicero's ideal in Ancient Rome of a "concordia ordinum" – an "agreement of all the social classes" and an ability to understand each other. It was certainly not any attempt to redefine the social order.

Smith's view was that man is naturally inclined to selfishness. He would have to be, because otherwise he would never be able to survive childhood. He must make sure that he is well fed, clad and able to look after his family. What Smith seems to be suggesting is that man should perhaps see more and more people, possibly society itself, as part of his family and that the natural feelings of protecting his family and providing them with nourishment should be extended towards all of society. In this respect, perhaps, we can see a parallel with the Christian ideal of loving one's neighbour as oneself. Jesus never said "*more* than oneself"; he said "*as* oneself". In other words, society's welfare depends to a very large extent on everyone being happy, and that it was up to everyone to ensure that this was the case for everyone.

There is also a certain emphasis on spectating someone else and his behaviour. This will enable the observer, perhaps, to be able to clarify and evaluate certain aspects of his own behaviour, and therefore improve it. Rather than be judgemental of others, the natural "sympathy" that Smith craves will enable the spectator to understand where the other person is coming from. Thieves, perhaps, are only thieves because they have no money or resources in the first place. People who commit violent crimes only do so because someone has committed similar outrages on them in the past. We should appreciate and understand that, and if necessary, refer them to oneself. Once again there are Christian echoes here where Jesus tells people not to be concerned about a speck in someone else's eye (meaning bad behaviour of some kind) when there is a plank in one's own.

Not unnaturally, Smith's views were described by some as utopian and impossible, but this did not deter him. It was rare for such sentiments to be expressed in the 18th century in a world where slavery was still practised, where there was barely such a thing as a prisoner of war (they would normally be enslaved or butchered on the spot) and where the iron, cold rule of the Church – whether Catholic or reformed - still influenced everyone and did not often brook any argument. Religious tolerance was not generally practised, nor indeed was political diversity, although Britain was better than most in this regard, or was at least beginning to become so.

"The Theory of Moral Sentiments" written in the 1750s, and published in 1759 throughout the land and in Europe brought Smith great popularity and renown, with even a reported increase in numbers of students wanting to enrol at Glasgow University to hear more and to learn from this great man. Such claims are of course difficult to substantiate two and a half centuries down the line, but what is indisputable is that Glasgow University decided in 1762 to offer him the Honorary Degree of Doctor of Laws.

Smith stayed at the University of Glasgow until 1763 when he suddenly felt that a career change was in order. He received an invitation to become the tutor of the young Duke of Buccleuch. This invitation came from a man called Townshend who was the stepfather of Henry Scott, the young Duke. It was a full time job and Smith had to resign from his post at Glasgow, a move that caused him no little distress, so much so that he was reputed to have offered to refund fees of students who had already signed up on the promise of hearing him.

But the offer of the new job was totally irresistible. Not only was there a massive increase in salary – some £300, an enormous amount in the mid18th century – but he had felt for some time that, much as he enjoyed Glasgow and teaching, he was now 40 years old and could do with a change. This job would indeed involve a change, notably some travel on the continent of Europe, for the young Duke was about to undergo what was called The Grand Tour of Europe, whereby a young man would travel to large cities in Europe and complete his education. For this he needed a tutor.

What exactly Smith's role was, we cannot be sure. In some ways, he was like the paedagogus of ancient Rome, a slave who escorted the son of a rich man to school, making sure that the young man got up to no mischief, and similarly to ensure that no-one kidnapped or murdered him. But the unworldly, 40 year old and not particularly tough Adam Smith was hardly suited to this job, and one would presume that there was someone else in the party as well, specifically for the strong-arm stuff. The paedagogus, however, would also sit with the boy at school, and when he came home at night would do his academic work with him. Adam of course did more than that. He actually was the teacher, teaching the young Duke all sorts of things including, reputedly, Polish.

As to where they went from 1763 to 1766, we cannot be sure, but we do know that they spent some time, eighteen months according to one account, in Toulouse, Geneva and Paris. Toulouse he found to be rather boring, and apparently Adam said to his friend David Hume that he had begun to write a book in order to pass the time. This may or may not have been the origin of "The Wealth of Nations" but we cannot be sure.

At some point the party moved on to Geneva where Smith met Francois Marie Arouet, more commonly known as Voltaire. Voltaire was living in Geneva because he was not "persona grata" in his native France because of his persistent polemical attacks on the French Establishment and the Church. He is often regarded as the father of the French Revolution which happened a year after his death, and he was certainly one of the best brains of the 18th century. A humanitarian, thinker and philosopher, it is easy to see why the oppressive Church and State of France did not like him. He was a believer in God, but despised any attempt by the Church to say what was acceptable religious practice, and he and Smith easily formed a warm relationship, for they had a great deal in common.

Voltaire was a prolific writer of poetry, of plays and of other books. He had been to Great Britain as a young man, and was very interested in the British constitutional monarchy which he said was an excellent example of tolerance and acceptance of other strands of government. Not everyone in Great Britain would have agreed with that, of course, and it is certainly not the verdict of history, but the British monarchy of George III was considerably more advanced and enlightened than that of the French. It was for this reason of course that the British monarchy survived the various trends towards "freedom" in that late 18th century whereas its French equivalent headed inexorably towards disaster in 1789, along with its greatest ally, the Church.

Satire and sarcasm were Voltaire's main weapons, for he reckoned that if he made people laugh, they would be more likely to remember the objects of his attack. It was not only Christianity that was the object of his attacks and score; he also denounced Islam and Judaism with equal ferocity, and the story goes that on his death bed in 1778, many years after his floruit, when he was asked by a Roman Catholic priest if he would denounce Satan, he demurred, saying that "Now is not the time to make new enemies".

Voltaire was particularly keen to talk to Smith about Scotland, a country with a dreadfully bloody past but which seemed to be picking itself up again and moving forward. Smith for his part, with all his ideas about trade and the development of a bourgeoisie but with the emphasis on humane treatment of everyone, was a ready talker and listener to the great Frenchman, and the relationship was a pleasant, urbane and civilised one, proving to Smith, if he had not realised it before, that international barriers were superficial ones and that the problems of one nation were remarkably similar to those of another.

It was in Paris however that Smith really met famous people. Paris, even in the 18th century when it was the epicentre of the most repressive and incompetent regime on earth and continually losing wars to the British in various parts of the globe, was still looked upon as a centre of culture and intellectual activity. There was also the phenomenon known as the French Enlightenment. He is reputed to have met Benjamin Franklin there – and if this is true, he would have learned a great deal from the remarkable American – but he certainly met Anne-Robert-Jacques Turgot, the famous economist and Francois Quesney, the head of the Physiocratic school of economics, who would have a tremendous influence on his thinking as he began to write The Wealth of Nations.

The Physiocrats were the opposite of the Mercantilists. Their doctrine, in a vastly different social and economic set-up in comparison to what obtains today, is difficult for us moderns to understand, but there was an emphasis on agriculture rather than trade. Trade was of course important too, but what really counted was the nation's ability to feed itself, and not to allow itself to be dictated to by the Church and the nobility who basically considered the interests of no-one but themselves. As for everything else, the motto seemed to be "Laissez faire et laisez passer. Le monde va de lui meme" – meaning that one should let things happen, for the world looks after itself.

This last statement was not perhaps as brutal or as callous as it seemed. It did not mean that one should simple ignore the way that wealth was produced. Rather, it meant that as there always would be people who were to produce wealth because it was in their own interests, they should be allowed to do so without any great interference from the state in terms of taxation or restrictions. "Laissez faire" was adopted by Adam Smith, and very soon became a central tenet of 19th century capitalism and remains to this day something that is not entirely unfavourable to or unsupported by right wing economists.

To most of us, the idea of allowing anyone to collect and amass as much wealth as he wanted to without any kind of restriction is anathema. We are far more likely to subscribe to the thinking of John Locke who, when asked if anyone had a right to gather as many apples and acorns for himself as he wanted, would say emphatically "Not So!" It was, however, quite different in the 18th century, and in any case, Smith surely did not want to imply or involve any sort of unsympathetic disregard for those at the bottom of the heap. Yet Smith probably did subscribe, perhaps unconsciously or subconsciously, to what has been called in Scotland the "Protestant work ethic", whereby some parts of the Bible can be distorted by those who are good at such things to mean that there were the "deserving" poor and the "undeserving" poor, and that anyone who did not work hard enough was quite worthy of starvation!

Smith was thus influenced by all sorts of things when his contract terminated in October 1766. He was possibly glad to leave Paris, and he decided that he was going to return home to Kirkcaldy, not Glasgow and not Edinburgh but to his house in the High Street, Kirkcaldy. He had sufficient wealth from his family and indeed from what he had earned as tutor to the Duke of Buccleuch to lead a life of comparative leisure in his home town, studying and applying himself to write his magnum opus "The Wealth of Nations". But he summed up his life in the ten years from 1766 until 1776 by telling his friend David Hume "My business here is study in which I have been very deeply engaged. My amusements are long solitary walks by the seaside. You may judge how I spend my time. I feel myself, however, extremely happy, comfortable and contented. I never was, perhaps, more so in my life".

And he was also staying again with his mother. Margaret Douglas was now ageing, and possibly needed some help and support, and this of course Smith was able to supply. There had never been any problem with finance in that family, and she would have had loads of maids and servants to supply her bodily and worldly needs, but emotionally she perked up considerably when Smith returned to live with her. The image is of Smith, with his mother on his arm, taking the short walk down from his house to the sea, or up to the Church on a Sunday, greeting passers-by and passing the time of day with them. Kirkcaldy then being a very small place, everyone would have known who everyone was, and would have been impressed by "Maister Smith's" travels around the continent and the fact that he was a writer of books.

He seems between 1766 and 1776 to have done little other, on the literary or any other front, than write "The Wealth of Nations". There would, no doubt have been the occasional trip to Edinburgh to see David Hume or other friends, although, given the fact that railways were still 50 years away and the Forth Bridge more than 100 years in the future, that voyage on a rickety wooden boat across the river would have presented a few problems, given that Smith was notoriously prone to seasickness even on a short, and normally calm, voyage like that.

"The Wealth of Nations" or to give it its proper title "An Enquiry into the Nature and Causes of the Wealth of Nations" is indeed a mighty tome. It was originally in two volumes and was published in March 1776 by Strachan and Cadell of London, and was sold out within six months. Another four editions appeared in Smith's lifetime, but the work itself was substantially unaltered other than the correction of a few misprints and the occasional rephrasing of a sentence to make the meaning clearer. After Smith's death in 1790, more editions appeared, and very soon Smith was being given titles like "the father of economics" and his book described as "the Bible of economic theory".

It was critically well received, including in the important market of the United States of America, not least because Smith had been one of the many prescient and wise people in Great Britain who had sympathised with the American colonists in their prolonged struggle for fair play in the first instance and then independence in the long run. Smith did not like excessive taxation, something that struck a very sympathetic chord with the Americans whose slogan had, of course, been "No taxation without representation".

Yet to a modern reader, the book can be tedious. Not everyone is interested in political economy, of course, but even those who are so inclined, find that Smith's tome tends to be somewhat obvious and trite. But this "criticism" is in fact a huge compliment to the work, because one must apply a certain amount of historical perspective here. Such observations about the employment of labour and other things were far from trite and banal in 1776; that they have become so now is because economists and politicians have to a large extent copied and picked up on Smith's analysis.

Possibly aware that the subject matter can, by its very nature, be dull, Smith made a conscious effort to make it readable using homely and easily comprehensible imagery like "It is not from the benevolence of the butcher, the brewer or the baker that we expect our dinner, but from their regard to their own interest", which seems to mean that you have to find a way of making everything suitable for everyone before any deal can be done. He even used a local analogy from a pin factory in Pathhead, Kirkcaldy, which he had visited to tell everyone that 10 men on 18 "operations" (machines, possibly?) can produce 50,000 pins per day, whereas one unskilled man can make only a very few a day. This is a clear vindication and encouragement given to the movement towards industrialisation which was beginning to pick up momentum.

Sadly, it has to be said that Smith's exegesis of world economic problems was, to a very large extent, overtaken by events. In the first place, the French Revolution occurred in 1789, a year before Smith's death, and only 13 years after the publication of "The Wealth of Nations". This momentous event, which Smith, if he had not actually foreseen from his sojourn in

France, would not have been entirely surprised at when it happened, had worldwide ramifications in the shape of the collapse of the French market, dreadful wars, the rise of Napoleon, then another war which finished at Waterloo in 1815, followed by a prolonged slump in trade which did not really pick up for many decades.

But there was another alteration to the economic position of the world. This was the Industrial Revolution which had not quite begun in Smith's lifetime, but which was in full swing by the 1820s and 1830s. The Agricultural Revolution began a little earlier and did, as we know have an enormous impact on the Industrial Revolution, but it was the Industrial Revolution which brought large factories, railways, the growth of cities and horrendous social and living conditions. Great Britain, of course, experienced the Industrial Revolution first, and was able to exploit its new industrial wealth into expanding and consolidating its Empire. The only potential rival, France, had now been defeated, totally it would seem after the fall of Napoleon, and there was no other obvious obstacle to Britain ruling the world. Germany was not yet even a nation, Russia was large but backward and corrupt and the United States of America, Britain's wayward offspring, now with an intense loathing for the mother country, was content to contain itself to the continent of America. But as far as Europe, Africa, Asia and the High Seas, there was only one superpower and that was Great Britain.

In these changed circumstances, a manual of trade, however excellent, published in 1776 was of limited value. Yet it is remarkable how much of it does still apply to today's much changed world. It was given a great critical review when it was published, and although the work has its detractors (inevitably, perhaps, given that we are talking about a subject which, even today, is notoriously imprecise and prone to be riven by the different "schools" of thought), it has been translated into almost every language of the world, including, surprisingly, Russian where it was read even in the Communist era, and still sells in reasonable numbers on Amazon, with even a Kindle edition available. It may be disagreed with, it is certainly a little out of date (inevitably when it was written almost 250 years ago) but it is still a work that is highly respected.

After the publication of "The Wealth of Nations" in 1776, Smith found himself travelling more and more to

Edinburgh where most of his friends lived, particularly of course David Hume. Then in 1778, he and his mother left Kirkcaldy for good, when he took a job (not that he needed the money and to a large extent it was an honorary post in any case) as Comptroller of Customs at an enormous salary of £900 per year. This was of course the job that his father had done in different circumstances some 60 years earlier, and he possibly took this post as a tribute to his father whom he had never known, while the Customs for their part were glad to have the distinguished economist working for them.

His wealth allowed him to buy a mansion called Panmure House not far from Calton Hill, and it was there that he was able to entertain all the literati who were or soon became his friends, for he was a man well known for his generosity (to beggars in the street, for example) and his benign disposition to all who met him. He became a bit of an eccentric, and particularly after his mother died in 1784 at an advanced age, people began to question whether he too was beginning to lose some of his mental powers and to show the early signs of what is nowadays known as senile dementia. Carlyle of Inveresk in his own Autobiography, for example, has this to say about Smith. "His voice was harsh and his enunciation thick, approaching to stammering. His conversation was not colloquial, more like lecturing. He was the most absent-minded man in company I ever saw, moving his lips and talking to himself and smiling, in the midst of large companies. If you awaked him from his reverie and made him attend to the subject of conversation, he immediately began a harangue and never stopped till he told you all he knew about it with the utmost philosophical ingenuity. But when you checked him, or doubted, he retracted with the utmost ease and contradicted all he had been saying!"

He was also famous for his huge collection on books. Adam would frequently say in a comment about his lack of handsomeness "I am a beau in nothing but my books". He was reputed to have over 3,000 books, a huge amount by 18th century (or any century) standards and they contained works of literature, Greek and Latin classics, philosophy, law, architecture and of course of the new subject that he had done so much to popularise, economics.

He died of some unspecified illness on 17 July 1790 at the age of 67, and was buried in the Canongate Kirkyard in Edinburgh. It was a pity that he was not moved to Kirkcaldy, the town in which he was born and which he loved so much, and which in the 21st century is doing so much to keep his memory alive.

Dr John Smith

Very few Kirkcaldy people now will have heard of Dr
John Smith of Brycehall, a man who practised medicine
in Kirkcaldy with great distinction for over 40 years, and
that was after he had made his mark as a football player
with Queen's Park, and was capped 10 times for
Scotland between 1887 and 1884, was a reserve for the
Scotland rugby team and in later years became the
President of the Scottish Bowling Association.

He was 6 foot 2 in height, and even in his later years was a singularly robust man, ceasing from active practice in medicine only a few months before his death at the age of 79 in November 1934. Clearly an all-round sportsman of some repute, and for those who knew him, a thorough gentleman.

He retained until his death a reputation for benign eccentricity. He despised modern appliances like motor cars, and was seen visiting his patients in his "Victoria" – an open carriage pulled by his equally well known and loved white horse, a beast that had been retired after active service in the First World War, but was still able to do its bit in taking the kindly doctor to tend his sick patients. He both lived in and practised from a house called Brycehall at 33 Kirk Wynd, now the offices of Charles Wood, the lawyer. He had no children, and on his death in 1934 he was survived by his wife, one Beatrix (sometimes called Beatrice) Whitle whom he had married sometime in the early 1900s. Beatrix herself died in January 1947.

John Smith was born in Mauchline in Ayrshire on August 12 1855. Mauchline of course had been immortalised in the poetry of Robert Burns who had lived there during the 1780s, and most of his best poems were written in the time of his residence there with his dealings with the Church and local women well documented. Arguably, one of Burns best verse epistles was to a man called James Smith who, for all we know, could have been an ancestor. John Smith, in later life, like a surprising amount of Ayrshire men, did not identify himself to any great extent with Burns. He would attend Burns Suppers from time to time, and we know enough about him to be sure that he accepted, to a large extent, the Burns philosophy, but he was never, as far as we can make out, a great fan of his fellow Ayrshireman.

His father, William Smith, is described as a Manufacturer on John's birth certificate, and his mother's maiden name was Miller – something that Smith would use in his footballing career as we shall see. Smith attended Ayr Academy, and was a member of its first ever football team, thus playing the game that had really taken off in the 1860s and was threatening to revolutionise sport. Team games generally had developed in an organised form throughout the early 1800s (although, in a disorganised form, a ball had of course been kicked about on grass or on streets for many centuries) and Scotland's first football team had been formed at Queen's Park in 1867, followed by Kilmarnock as early as 1869. Thus football was anchored in Ayrshire at an early stage.

There still exists uncertainty in the minds of footballing historians about what exactly is meant by "football" at that time. The game that we now call "rugby" started at about the same time and was sometimes referred to as the "handling" game as distinct from the "kicking" one. To young men like Smith, it made little difference, for he enjoyed playing both, and there are times when there was a certain confusion even in teams who travelled to a game without any clear idea in their mind about what code they were actually meant to be playing! Often they would decide to play both, one perhaps in the morning, the other in the afternoon.

Indeed, Smith himself told the story about his first ever game of football. Ayr Academy specialised in rugby or "the Union game" or "the handling game". They had invited a Glasgow school team to come down to Ayr to play "football", but did not specify which form. The Glasgow team travelled with only 11 men – not enough for the 20 then necessary for "rugby", so they decided to play the "Association game" or the "dribbling game" instead. From them on, Smith preferred what we now call "football", although he excelled at both games.

In the early 1870s Smith went to Edinburgh University to study Medicine. It was there that his footballing career developed, but he enjoyed rugby as well, so much so that he was chosen as reserve for Scotland in a rugby International in 1876. He did not play in that 20 per side game on March 6 1876 (the following year, the numbers in a team would be reduced to 15), but would have enjoyed his trip to Kennington Oval, (now the home of Surrey Cricket Club) a venue to which he would return many times.

In season 1876/77 he was offered the captaincy of the Edinburgh University Rugby Football club, but declined, because he had promised someone in a football team called the Edinburgh 3rd Royal Volunteers that he would create a football team in the University. This was to provide opposition in the new sport that was burgeoning in the capital with teams called the Heart of Midlothian, a club which had been formed from a dancing organisation and the Hibernians, a team created to give the young Irish immigrants something to do. Rumour had it that other teams were being founded – very soon Stockbridge in the north of Edinburgh would have its own team to be called St Bernards - and games would be played on the Meadows.

Smith, a natural leader, went around the University persuading young men to join his new University side (sometimes provoking the ire of the rugby people, but Smith was bright enough to realise that with the reduction of teams from 20 to 15, there would be at least 5 frustrated rugby players who might want to try football instead!) and very soon, in the words of whoever wrote Smith's obituary in *The Fifeshire Advertiser* in 1934, the University team frequently beat Hearts, Hibs and St Bernards who "all fell victims to the slashing onslaughts" of Smith's young and enthusiastic side.

But it was Smith himself who attracted most attention. His height and strength were in themselves a great asset, particularly for a goal scorer. "Barging" and "charging" were recognised as skills of the game, and the 6 feet 2 inches youngster, with a background in rugby, from Ayrshire had a clear advantage here. But there was more to him than that. Being a physical fitness fanatic, and generally abstaining from the dubious pleasures of the flesh and the strong drink available to other more gullible students in Edinburgh, Smith became very fast. He may have done some athletics as well in his spare time, but on the football field his speed and movement were sights to behold.

But he was also very intelligent. It is probably true in most sports that, other things being equal ie. fitness and ability, intelligence will win through. Smith did research on his opponents, worked out weak spots, had a look at the pitch the night before and began to think about tactics, about dribbling and in particular passing the ball. Smith is described in *A Scottish Soccer Internationalists Who's Who* by Douglas Lamming as "gifted in dribbling and shooting" and "superb in distribution and cool judgement". Clearly, reports of his prowess had spread to the Scottish authorities, for as early as 1877, when he was just 21, he was offered his first Scottish cap against England at the Kennington Oval.

Football has of course come a long way since the 1870s when Smith started to play, but one is struck more by the similarities to the modern game than its differences. Things like substitutes, goalkeepers wearing different coloured jerseys from the others, lines on pitches, penalty boxes and other things would come later, but the basics were in 1877 as they are now. The idea was to score goals, and the game was both exciting and thrilling. Its essence was its simplicity, for as long as you have a ball, you can play football. Interest in the game grew rapidly, although at the time that Smith started to play, the game was to a large extent, middle class and, of course, amateur.

International football was of course in its infancy, and the idea of Scotland playing England at anything other than war was a new and novel one. The two countries had co-existed peacefully in a grudging sort of tolerance for several centuries now (give or take the odd scrap like the Jacobites, for example) but there still existed a certain animosity. Now organised sport provided a channel for aggression and competition, but it was only a last minute decision by Queen's Park before they played a team of Englishmen at Hamilton Crescent in 1872 to call themselves "Scotland" and the other team "England" that International football was born. Thus Smith arrived on the footballing scene just at the very birth of what we can call "football".

On his International debut in 1877 Smith is described, surprisingly, as a Mauchline player rather than one of Edinburgh University. It was with the students that he was making his name, but of course there was nothing to prevent him from playing for his home town team as well now and again. The game being totally amateur, there were no registrations or signing forms or anything like that, and in any case, even if a team had decided to play a "ringer" from another club, what would there have been to prevent them? There were few photographs of players, and very few people could have said with any degree of certainty "Heh! That fellow plays for Edinburgh University!" In any case, it seems to have been perfectly legal.

The Glasgow Herald gives an account of the game in which Smith made his International debut, telling us that there were a large number of spectators (about 2,000) at the Kennington Oval in London and that Scotland were well served by Smith although the goals in the 3-1 win were scored by John Ferguson of Vale of Leven (twice) and William Richmond of Clydesdale. "The cheering was tumultuous" when England scored, and we learn a few interesting asides that Scotland won the toss "for choice of goals and had to kick off" in a clear difference between the Victorian game and the modern one. But the jerseys were the same with Scotland wearing a dark blue vest with a white lion on it.

This was the third time that Scotland had beaten England, but the first time in London and we can imagine the celebrations among the players and Scottish population of London. Then on the way home – such was the excellence of the modern railway system, regarded not without cause as the envy of the world – the "Scotch men" were able to "call in", as it were, to Wrexham and play a game against Wales on the Monday. The first Monday in Wales was traditionally a Welsh holiday because of St David and what was meant to be the start of spring.

Conditions of wind and rain belied the arrival of the Welsh spring, however, as Smith again donned the blue jersey and played a fine part in the 2-0 defeat of the

Welshmen. "The Scottish team are so well known that to say they played well is superfluous" is the way that *The Glasgow Herald* sums things up, but there are also good things to be said about the Welsh, for whom a 0-2 defeat was an improvement on the 0-4 defeat in Glasgow last year.

The teams had a meal together at night and when the Scotland party returned to Glasgow on the Tuesday, there was a crowd to cheer them, for they were now undeniably the champions of the United Kingdom, and effectively, the world. Mauchline too had heard about the exploits and Smith's return to his village provoked great scenes of celebration there as well. Football had clearly taken a hold of the Scottish population. At long last there was something that we in Scotland were good at.

Smith wasn't chosen for either of the Internationals in 1878 – perhaps he was injured, or more likely, his face simply did not fit with the Queen's Park establishment – but reappeared in 1879, again at Kennington Oval. This time it was a very exciting, if ultimately heart breaking game for Scotland and for Smith. The game kicked off at four o'clock, the later time possibly because most of the 4,500 crowd had been at the Oxford v Cambridge boat race earlier in the day. *The Glasgow Herald*, nothing if not snobby, tells that a great deal of "fashionable" people were there, including "a fair number of clergymen". This is of course significant to the Scottish readership because football had for a while struggled in Presbyterian Scotland, because it involved enjoying oneself, but in England there seemed to be less of a problem. It would be a decade or so yet, before the Scottish Kirk realised that if its young men were playing football, it meant that they weren't doing anything worse, like visiting alehouses and whorehouses. "Muscular Christianity" and playing sports was possibly the least of quite a few evils.

Using the wind to great advantage, Scotland went in at half time 4-1 up, with Smith having scored one of the goals. But this England team was made of sterner stuff than some of their predecessors and levelled the score at 4-4. In "conditions of the greatest excitement" Scotland "charged forward" and Smith managed to get the ball "between the sticks" – but the English side appealed for offside and "the appeal was sustained by the Umpires". This was a bad blow to Smith – and in later years in Kirkcaldy, at a quiet moment at the Bowling Club or in one of his chats to a terminally ill patient - he would insist that he was never offside, for the English Umpire simply did not understand the rule! It meant that he was deprived of the kudos of being Scotland's match winner, but worse came a few minutes after that when William Mosforth scored a winner for England!

Scotland vented their frustration at this unfortunate loss when they visited Wales at Wrexham on the Monday, and Smith, now described as of Edinburgh University rather than Mauchline, scored a couple of goals in the 3-0 victory. The game was played on heavy ground for the rain in the morning had been absolutely torrential, and the win went a certain way to mollifying heavy hearts from the Kennington Oval defeat. It can readily be understood why the superbly fit John Smith revelled on the heavy ground which slowed down defenders but did not prevent the long legs of Smith (with the ball sometimes "glued to his shinpads" in an eccentric but graphic description) rampaging through the middle.

But if 1879 was a disappointment as far as England was concerned, the following 5 years made up for it, for between 1880 and 1884, Scotland beat England a record five times in a row. Those of us who were alive in 1964 will recall the tremendous excitement in the country when Scotland, thanks to an Alan Gilzean header at Hampden, registered three wins in a row with "Scots Wha Hae A Hat-Trick" among the headlines in *The Evening Times*. 80 years earlier, in totally different circumstances, the triumph was no less, and the boost to the game in this country was something that remained permanently on the national psyche. Those who say that Scotland is obsessed with football (to the detriment of other sports, perhaps) possibly have a point. The obsession owes its genesis to the years between 1880 and 1884.

SEASON 1880-81.

Top Row—Thomas Lawrie, Andrew Watson, Charles Campbell, Dr. John Smith, J. J. Gow, J. T. Richmond
Middle Row—Harry M'Neil, John L. Kay, David Davidson, Wm. Anderson.
Bottom Row—Archibald Rowan, Andrew H. Holm, M. J. Eadie Fraser, George Ker.

Smith in the Queen's Park team of 1880/81

The big difference that it made was the social one. Gradually through the 1880s, more and more employers began to see the advantages of giving their workers a Saturday afternoon off, on the grounds that what production was lost was compensated by having their workers a little happier and more contented, and it helped to put a spoke in the wheels of the annoying "combinations" or "unions" which could potentially cause a great deal of trouble. Some workers, sadly, headed straight to the alehouse when the whistle blew at 12.00 pm, but others, younger and more active, perhaps headed to a park or a piece of waste ground to hear another whistle, that of a referee.

Smith is in the centre (arms over the chair) in this picture of the 1884 Scotland team which beat England 1-0

In addition, the effects of the 1872 Education Act (Scotland) were beginning, slowly, to have an effect. By 19th century standards, literacy had always been higher in Scotland than elsewhere, but now more and more people could read and were able to hear about and enjoy the exploits of men like John Smith of Mauchline as Scotland regularly took on the English (and the Welsh) and beat them. A whole collection of sporting newspapers like *Scottish Sport* and *The Referee* began to appear in newsagents.

Smith played in all of Scotland's 5 triumphs over England except 1882, where it appears he was injured (not that he was much missed, for Scotland won 5-1) and he scored a famous hat-trick at his favourite ground Kennington Oval in 1881 (which must be his "annus mirabilis", for he had another great moment that year), two goals (or possibly three, for evidence is unclear) at Bramall Lane in 1883 and also the one and only goal at Cathkin in 1884 (before a massive crowd of 10,000) in the famous game which established Scotland's supremacy over England for five years in a row.

The 1883 game has an unresolved argument about Smith's contribution. *The Glasgow Herald* is curiously emphatic that Smith scored all three goals, whereas most journals and books say only 2 and the other was scored by Malcolm Fraser. *The Glasgow Herald*'s report, which seems to have been lifted from an English report, for it keeps taking about the "Scotch" and the "Caledonians" states quite clearly at the end that "it will be noticed that Smith scored all three goals for Scotland." The game played at Bramall Lane, Sheffield, was a thrilling affair, played on a frosty but thawing pitch and Smith, whether he scored 2 goals or 3 in the 3-2 victory, was the hero of the hour.

The first goal came from a free kick which McPherson sent over the heads of the defenders and "Smith came rushing in to score the first goal for the Caledonians amidst vociferous cheering". The second was a more mundane tap in by Smith from a good run and cross from John Kay, but then with time running out and the teams locked at 2-2, "the Scotch got up in a body", Kay once again got the cross over and Smith put the ball "between the sticks" to "deafening plaudits" from the astonishing crowd of nearly 10,000 "eager enthusiasts".

Smith, thus, may or may not have scored hat-tricks on two successive trips to England in 1881 and 1883 but the 1884 game was the more famous. This game, played at Old Cathkin in Govanhill, Glasgow on 15 March 1884 was the first game to provide any strong indication that interest in football was spreading geographically. Tales are told of trains arriving from Edinburgh and Dundee, and people asking at the station for a cab to take them to "the International". Up to that point, football (at least organised football) had been confined to the Glasgow middle class, the Dunbartonshire villages and towns of Renton, Alexandra and Dumbarton itself, and of course Smith's Ayrshire. Now more and more people were flocking to football matches, all eager to see the famous John Smith, variously described as of Mauchline, Edinburgh University or Queen's Park.

All football fans love a goal scoring personality. Smith, tall and angular, hard-working and "clever with the football in his distribution and speed" was just that. The genteel ladies who attended football in large numbers in those days (compelling the SFA to erect a "Ladies Rest Room" at International matches in case they needed a respite from some of the coarser language or sexual approaches of the lower orders!) were known to swoon at this tall, well-built man with his rugged features, now a general medical practitioner, who had the ability to score goals against the English. He was also famously sociable and genial, being seen frequently talking to supporters as he walked to and from the games, discussing the game and indeed more general topics of conversation. A couple of days after this game in 1884, everyone in Scotland had heard of the man with the ordinary name of John Smith and he was to all intents and purposes an ordinary man, but whose achievements had been anything but ordinary.

He was sometimes called "Doctor John" or "Scotland's Doctor". His latter name owes its genesis as a riposte to "England's Doctor", the famous cricketing WG Grace of Gloucestershire and England. Stories abounded about Grace's cricketing abilities and quirky eccentricities including how an "amateur" managed to make so much money out of cricket! "Scotland's Doctor" however had no such baggage, he just had the ability to score the goals that beat England.

Let us talk about 1881. It had been the year in which he had made his name. His hat-trick that he scored at the Kennington Oval was not the first for Scotland, but it was the first against England and various journals have accounts of Smith's goals in the 6-1 triumph. His first and third were scored by charging through on his own (a recognised skill of Victorian football being the ability to charge opponents off the ball) and his second was a "crisp drive" from a Charlie Campbell pass. These goals were scored to "wild applause", something which indicates that there was a sizeable amount of Scottish supporters in the 8,500 crowd, or that English supporters were a great deal less partisan than they are now. That was on March 12 and Smith also played in the game at Wrexham on the way home, but although cheered every time he kicked the ball, Smith did not score that day. The return to Scotland was one of a hero, with "bagpipes skirling" and the authorities having to erect a few "fences and barriers at Glasgow Station" to control the widely excited crowd.

In truth, they had little else to cheer about in many cases. Smith, a humanitarian man and far too intelligent a man to believe the traditional Presbyterian nonsense coming from Churches that it was all either predestined or their own fault, was appalled to see the poverty and deprivation of Glasgow with these bedraggled, thin, ill-clad but happy urchins cheering the return of the train and stretching out their arms to welcome the team home. But all that society could do was shrug their shoulders and take refuge in the clichés of "someone should do something about that"! Smith however felt a thrill of satisfaction that he had given them, temporarily at least, something to be happy about.

Smith was also very much involved in the Scottish Cup final that year. He had now joined Queen's Park (one hesitates to say "signed for", for football in 1881 was, theoretically, a gentlemanly, amateur pursuit in which one's word was one's bond). Playing for Queen's Park in the 1880s was like playing for Real Madrid today. They were big in every sense of the word, the founders of the game in Scotland, and even prepared to play games in England. Their ground, Hampden Park (there have been three Hampdens, and this one was the first), was the centre of the game in Scotland, and they had won the Scottish Cup for its first three seasons, had lost out, to their extreme distress, to the Vale of Leven side for the next three seasons, but had won the Cup back in 1880.

Impressed by the Mauchline man's performances for Scotland, they had persuaded him to join them. Whether there was any money offered to Smith we cannot say. It would have been hotly denied, for it was indeed illegal, but one might suspect that there may have been some "expenses", money changing hands, and certainly payment in kind in the shape of meals at the best hotels etc. To reach the final Queen's first disposed of a team with the unlikely name of "John Elder", then Possilpark, Pilgrims, Beith, Smith's old team Mauchline, and Campsie. We cannot be sure whether Smith played for them in the earlier rounds, but he certainly did in the Scottish Cup final against Dumbarton at Kinning Park. This was on March 26, and Queen's Park won, but then Dumbarton protested on the grounds of crowd encroachment (a recurrent motif of Victorian football) and the game had to be replayed on April 9.

Contemporary newspapers sometimes give the impression of being more interested in the peripherals of the game rather than the game itself. We have accounts of platforms being erected for the spectators to stand on, old railway stock being deployed for the same purpose and enterprising householders in the vicinity of Kinning Park leasing out their front rooms with a view to the field at 1 shilling per head. Such was the enthusiasm of "upwards of 10,000 people" to see the mighty Queen's Park, and the man who had set all Scotland alight with his London hat-trick a month earlier, the "second greatest man to come from Ayrshire" (as one journal described him) John Smith.

Queen's Park again won 3-1, and some people claim that Smith scored all three, which would have made him the first hat-trick scorer in a Scottish Cup final. Sadly, the evidence, scant and unclear as it is, certainly in *The Glasgow Herald's* account, does not support this contention. Smith certainly scored two, but it seems that a man called George Ker scored the other. Possibly the idea of a hat-trick in the Scottish Cup final arises from confusion with the Scotland v England international of that year, at the end of which he certainly was presented with a hat for his achievement. One feels that if he had scored a hat-trick in the final as well, there would have been more fuss about it. As it is, conventional wisdom states that the first Scottish Cup final hat-trick was not scored until 1904 when the great Jimmy Quinn of Celtic completed that feat.

He didn't seem to play in 1882 – injury presumably, or perhaps too busy with his medical commitments – but 1883 saw his two goals (or possibly three) against England at Bramall Lane, Sheffield. They were good ones too, "the fruits of good Scotch running and passing" and Smith is given the added compliment of being called "Dr Smith" in *The Glasgow Herald's* account of the game. Queen's Park however had a less happy season, losing to Dumbarton in the Scottish Cup at an early stage in February, with Smith, for some reason or other, (another injury?) conspicuously absent.

He was not exactly "playing" for Queen's Park either in the 1884 Scottish Cup final, but he won a winners' medal for them! The game was scheduled for February 23 at Cathkin and the finalists were Queen's Park and Vale of Leven. Vale of Leven suffered an injury crisis on the Wednesday before the game. They asked for a postponement but neither Queen's Park nor the SFA would consent. Vale of Leven, alleging collusion between the "establishment" of Queen's Park and the

SFA, (indeed there were quite a few men on the committee of both) failed to turn up, and the Cup was awarded by default to Smith and Queen's Park, who proved the point by playing a friendly against Third Lanark instead and winning 4-0. It was not incidentally the first time that the Scottish Cup had been won that way, for Vale of Leven themselves had benefitted in 1879 when Rangers, having drawn the final on April 19 when they felt they would have won but for a wrongly disallowed offside goal, simply refused to turn up for the replay! John Fairgrieve in this book "The Rangers, Scotland's Greatest Football Club" (sic) states laconically that the "affair did not reflect well on Rangers". Nor did 1884 do Vale of Leven a great deal of favours. They never won the Scottish Cup again.

Smith had several other big games in 1884. One was the game against England, already referred to, in 1884 at Cathkin in which he scored the only goal of the game. In scoring that goal, he was fortunate in that Cathkin had modern cross bars rather than the rope which still had to suffice on other, less well-appointed grounds. The goal is well described in the contemporary press. Wattie Arnott punted a long ball forward, it was headed on by another forward to Smith (or "Doctor John" as the fans now called him) who beat a few men and crashed an unsaveable shot above the head of goalkeeper William Rose. The ball then hit the bar and bounced into the goal. Had there simply been a rope, the ball would have kept soaring upwards! As it was, the goal was given and the cheering and clapping continued for minutes afterwards!

A couple of weeks after that, Smith returned to Kennington Oval to play in the FA Cup final. We in Scotland are prone (incorrectly) to name this trophy "the English Cup", but the correct name is indeed the

Football Association Cup and it was certainly not "the English Cup" in 1884, when Queen's Park participated. (They would do so in future years as well, as did Rangers). Queen's Park had had a great run to the final, the most famous game being the 6-1 defeat of Aston Villa on January 19 at First Hampden in which a "goodly concourse" of about 12,000 crammed the primitive enclosure to see a great Queen's Park performance in which Smith scored at least twice. (Reports, as always, are obscure). Amazingly to 1884 eyes, many trains of Birmingham supporters came to see this game – such was the effect of football! The "Brummies" were all very friendly and left impressed with Scotland, Glasgow and Dr John Smith.

The town of Blackburn, like Glasgow, Birmingham and Dunbartonshire, a famous centre of football provided opposition to Queen's Park in the latter stages of the FA Cup. First Queen's Park disposed of Blackburn Olympic at the neutral venue of the Trent Bridge cricket ground on March 1. They won 4-1 and one of the goals was scored by "Dr Smith" who ran through and scored with a shot that the "goalkeeper could not possibly have stopped" In the final at Kennington Oval on March 29, Queen's Park were less successful. The opponents were Blackburn Rovers, a fine side, who won 2-1. Smith, although "conspicuous among the Scotch forwards" was well policed and failed to score.

In spite of this reverse, Smith in 1884 was on top of the footballing world. But then things get rather murky. But before we can begin to understand the passions involved, we must appreciate the difference between professional and amateur. Being paid for playing sport was considered in polite, genteel, Glasgow society (and in the 1880s it was exactly this breed of people who controlled both Queen's Park and Scotland) to be, if not totally beyond the pale, certainly "infra dig". You would not, if you could help it, allow your daughter to marry a professional football player, in the same way as you would move heaven and earth to prevent your son marrying an actress!

Fortunately, the situation in Scottish football was resolved as early as 1893, but in other sports, notably cricket and rugby, problems associated with this issue lasted a great deal longer. But in the 1880s, of course, Smith was an amateur. In the absence of any system or registration, he could play for whomsoever he wanted to and there was little or nothing that Queen's Park or the SFA could do to stop it.

Along with his good friend, Andrew Watson a West Indian half caste from British Guyana, Smith would go to England and play for several teams like the Corinthians, the London Swifts and the Liverpool Ramblers. Often he would play openly as Dr John Smith, the famous Scottish goal scorer, and would attract a large crowd to see this famous man of whom much was known, notably the hat-tricks in 1881 and 1883 against England.

Other times, however, a man looking remarkably like him called JC Miller would play. This immediately rouses our suspicions. Miller was, of course, Smith's mother's maiden name and there is the possibility that Smith was using this device for sinister reasons. Perhaps he was in fact being paid as a professional, and did not want the very amateur Queen's Park to know about it, lest it prejudiced his chances of playing another game for Scotland, something that was very important to him.

Now, Smith did not need the money. He was of a wealthy family, had a job as a doctor in any case, and was certainly not the type of "professional footballer" who aroused such contempt in Victorian society – a working class ragamuffin who really should have been earning his money in some factory, mine or shipyard.

This is not to say that he would say "no" to filthy lucre when it was offered. It may be that he was actually playing as a professional for some teams, and using the pseudonym JC Miller as a cover, lest it prejudice his chances of more caps for Scotland. Certainly JC Miller and Dr John Smith looked very like each other, and scored the same sort of goals! Yet such things are hard to prove.

Using one's mother's maiden name has a distinguished parallel. In the 1890s, (even after professionalism had been legalised in 1893) a player called Willie Montgomery played for Celtic. This was no less a person than Willie Maley who would become Celtic's manager in 1897 but was then working for an accountancy firm at that time, and simply did not want his employers to know that he was also earning money for playing football for Celtic.

In England, it would very soon be no problem in any case, for in 1885 professionalism was recognised and in 1886 legalised. But Scotland and Queen's Park in particular, backed up by *The Glasgow Herald,* persisted in pursuing their absurd policy of persecuting professionals. They would eventually themselves be the losers, for the rise of Celtic brought the legalisation of professionalism in 1893, but Queen's Park eventually were able in 1885 to get Smith banned, not because he played professional football (they could never prove that) but because he had played a few games for the

Corinthians who did play a few games against an openly professional team! This was petty and vindictive but it effectively brought an end to Smith's international football playing career. He had played 10 games for Scotland and scored (although the evidence is sometimes contradictory) 10 goals.

Perhaps there were a few other issues at stake, other than "playing football against a professional team". The trouble with being a national hero is, of course, that there is often a reaction. Jealousy is often a terrible thing, and possibly quite a few in the Glasgow "mafia" that was Queen's Park felt that the jumped-up Ayrshire doctor was getting a disproportionate share of the glory that had been heaped upon Scotland, with even the English Press wholesome in their praise and admiration of Scotland and of Dr John Smith, the idol of so many people. Therefore, the less than heinous charge of "playing football against a professional team" might have been a peg on which to hang a great deal of grievances.

Smith, of course, by no means an unintelligent or insensitive man, realised what was going on, and in any case, now that he was nearly 30, may have realised that the good days had gone. He accepted that he could not go for ever. It did not however bring an end to his interest in the sport, nor did it curtail his involvement in another sport. He had played rugby concurrently with football (as did many players) and although he was never chosen to play for Scotland at rugby, he was at one point nominated as reserve in 1876. Now that he was banned from playing football, he took up rugby, but also in football, bizarrely for a man who had been banned, he became more interested in refereeing or umpiring the game.

His contribution to football was enormous. Football is all about scoring goals, and a player who can do just that will be very popular and rapidly become a cult hero. In later years, men like Jimmy Quinn, Hughie Gallagher, Jimmy McGrory, Denis Law, Joe Jordan and Ally McCoist would become great Scottish cult heroes for doing just that. But the prototype was John Smith.

He still had other sporting fields to plough, however. In 1888 Alfred Shaw and Arthur Shrewbury, two professional cricketers who had seen various cricketing teams from 1877 onwards visit Australia and New Zealand, thought it would be a good idea to try a similar thing in rugby. They obtained a reluctant blessing from the Rugby Football Union, who feared that it might open the doors to professionalism (that old obsession, again!) but could find no real reason to stop it, which they couldn't have done anyway. But a bigger problem turned out to be the recruiting of players who would need to be away from March until November. Smith was approached and agreed. He was a valuable recruit, for he could perform several functions. He could play, referee (the Australian and New Zealanders might not know the rules!), could be the tour doctor, but his main attraction was that he was a well-known sportsman who could lend an air of respectability to this somewhat dubious idea.

The tour could only be said to be a moderate success. They played 35 games of rugby, won most of them and a few games of Australian Rules Football, but the crowds were poor, accommodation was not always great and a major catastrophe hit the tour when tour captain Robert Seddon was drowned in a sculling accident on the Hunter River in West Maitland, Smith's attempts at reviving him, having failed. It was probable that at least some of the players were paid – hence the reason for the financial failure of the tour – and many of the players would in a few years' time defect to the Rugby League code of rules in the north of England, an avowedly and self-confessed professional sport. Nevertheless, this tour is often regarded as the forerunner of the British Lions tours of the southern hemisphere.

On his return home, Smith, now 33, decided that with all his degrees and qualifications, (he was an MA, MD and a MRCS) it was time to start working and to practise at last the medicine that he had loved studying. In about 1890, the Brycehall practice in Kirk Wynd needed a partner for Dr Proudfoot. Smith, already a celebrity, applied and got the job, and a long relationship with Kirkcaldy began. One can imagine the excitement in the town at the arrival of such a personality.

But he had not, by any manner of means, given up sport. He seems to have refereed rugby matches, but also football matches as well, and we find him refereeing the Scotland v England football match at Ibrox on April 2 1892. The appointment of referees for even big games like International matches was a haphazard quixotic affair, and we are surprised, for several reasons, to find the Kirkcaldy doctor (as he now was referred to) appointed to take this game. *The Glasgow Herald* says he was appointed "by mutual consent", as if England had agreed that he was a man of such status that he was the best referee around. It certainly seems to have been a late decision, because when the Scottish team was announced a week before the game, Mr Sneddon was appointed as linesman (in 1892 each team would supply a linesman), but no announcement of a referee!

It is not unparalleled (indeed it was common practice) for a Scotsman to referee Scotland games, but it was more common for a Scotsman to referee the game when it was played in England and vice versa. Moreover, it was not all that long ago that Smith's conduct as a player and his dealings with the world of professionalism had led to severe disapproval and effectively a ban. Yet here he was, clearly very much in favour and handling a game of this magnitude. Ironically, he was refereeing a game between an amateur team and a professional team, for England were now professional, and Scotland were still amateur - at least in theory.

Amateurism did not last long, and a clear indication of the way in which things were heading was the formation in 1890 of a Scottish League, whereby each team had to play each other twice, rather than the gentleman's agreement to play friendlies on the days when there was no Scottish Cup. Queen's Park, fearing that this would lead to professionalism, stayed aloof but everyone else joined the Scottish League and, under the counter, paid their players. The crowds that came to football were more than enough to allow teams to do this, and the official recognition of professionalism in 1893 was merely an official acknowledgement of what had gone on for some time. Stopping professionalism was like "trying to stop Niagara with a kitchen chair" was the graphic description of John H McLaughlin of Celtic, one of the leading proponents of professional football.

Clearly the persistence with amateurism was not doing Scotland much good, for in the game that the worthy Kirkcaldy doctor refereed in 1892, they lost 1-4! Smith disallowed two Scottish goals, one for offside and one because he did not think that the ball had crossed the line, but no-one in the Press blamed the referee for the defeat (some of the disgusted crowd did!), the Press centring their criticism on the Scotland team who were 0-4 down at half time and described them as "spineless" and "feckless". Some of the crowd showed their disgust by not coming back after half-time, and *The Scotsman* in an attempt to cheer up its readers, concentrates on a detailed description of the Highland Fling exhibition at half-time, the music of the Dumfries Industrial Band and full credit being paid to Rangers for the fine job they had made in decking out their ground!

Scottish Sport says "Dr Smith who refereed, represented Scotland against England on six different occasions. In spite of the demonstrations which he occasionally met with, he showed he could manipulate the whistle as well as he used to manipulate the ball. We wish we had more of his kind on the referee list". *Athletic News* is even more complimentary "Dr Smith was a wideawake (sic) referee and did his duty bravely despite the hostility displayed towards him in the second half. I am sure he will appreciate the compliment of being selected to officiate on such an auspicious day and England's trust in his honesty was thoroughly justified" while *The Fife Free Press* purrs its satisfaction that a Kirkcaldy man has been so honoured "…no greater honour can be conferred in the football world than that of refereeing the International…".

It was his one and only International appointment, and he never refereed a Scottish Cup final, but presumably he kept refereeing lesser games. He refereed at Scott's Park, Pathhead a couple of days later (the Holiday Monday) a friendly between Kirkcaldy and the mighty Queen's Park, and it was through Smith's influence that the fixture was arranged. This game attracted a crowd of 2,000 to see the pioneers of the sport, Queen's Park, but whether it was wise of the

Glasgow Amateurs to play this game is open to question, for they lost the Scottish Cup final to Celtic the following Saturday.

Smith played other sports as well, and was a great believer in keeping himself fit by running and cycling. Having taken up his residence in Brycehall in Kirk Wynd, as an assistant to Dr Proudfoot, he soon made himself a well-known character, (if he was not before) being seen running round the town in a way which would have shocked, one imagines, some of the genteel Victorian ladies of the Old Kirk. Bits of his body might have been showing! Other ladies perhaps looked at him with slightly different thoughts, for he was still a bachelor and, not yet 40 when he first came to Kirkcaldy, a fine figure of a man. Being intimately examined by such a man would be no unpleasant experience.

But hero of Scotland though he had been a decade previously, and now on paper at least an eminent physician, he now had to re-train, as it were, to deal with the mundane practice of dispensing medicine in Kirkcaldy. He would have been reasonably un-shockable as far as diseases and their treatments were concerned. Medicine degrees in Victorian Scotland were not easy to come by, especially at Edinburgh which had a deserved reputation for turning out the best doctors in the world. They did not do so by making life easy for their students.

So we may safely assume that Smith could cope with blood, gore, operations, deformities and everything else that would come his way in a medicinal capacity. What he would not have been prepared for, one imagines, would have been the extent of the poverty, deprivation, filth, neglect and all the evils of a society which had industrialised too quickly over the past 100 years, and in which those who made a colossal amount of money did not see the need to spread it around for the benefit of those who had produced the wealth.

Smith, of course, was a very humane man. In politics it is difficult to imagine him being anything other than a Gladstonian Liberal. He went to Church, but never became sufficiently involved in it to become an Elder, as far as we can see, and was probably still too obsessed with his varying sporting activities to be too interested in religion or politics to any great extent. But he must have been shocked at some of the things that he saw in Kirkcaldy in places like the Links, Rose Street, Pathhead and other areas of the town. Possibly the biggest problem for a man like Smith would have been the sheer filth and the stench in which so many families had to live.

The alienation of the working class was something else that he would have found difficult to comprehend. "Doctors are no' for the likes of us" was a common opinion expressed in working class circles, and of course there was the undeniable fact, that with the National Health Service still 50 years away and only the tiniest gleam in the eye of a few luminaries like Keir Hardie or Ramsay MacDonald, people had to pay for the attentions of a doctor. For this reason, a visit to a doctor would be a very rare event indeed, and the doctor would only be summoned in the direst of emergencies.

There were insurance schemes of sorts, but this involved paperwork and bureaucracy and most working class people simply had no cover at all, and relied on the good will of the doctor to attend a patient in dire emergencies without any guarantee that he would ever be paid. Often a case of something like scarlet fever would be allowed to happen by a family unable to pay a doctor, the fever would naturally spread to other members of the family, and before anyone realised what was happening, there was an epidemic involving such an unnecessary loss of life.

This all comes as a shock to us more than 100 years later and after several generations of the National Health Service which has gone such a long way to improve the quality of life for everyone, but to someone like Dr Smith, it must have been a real shock. He must have realised that something was wrong about this way of life, yet what could be do? He would write various learned papers to medical bodies on subjects like obstetrics and ophthalmology – and he very soon became a respected doctor in the area, but the basic problem needed a political solution, and this was still a long way in the future. Victorians are often described as "the great improvers" and one recent Prime Minister once talked about the excellence of "Victorian values". One must beg to differ.

There was also the "sinful" diseases and conditions. It was hardly surprising that so many people took to the ever present alcohol. Churches were right to rail against this evil, but it was a symptom, not the cause. And there were the sexual diseases picked up from prostitution, a phenomenon which (although no-one seems prepared to accept this) has actually declined in modern times! In Victorian times, no-one would even mention it or if they did, they used euphemisms like "ladies of the night" or "fallen women", but everyone knew that it happened. It was indeed very common, and Smith would have definitely seen the effects of this.

There would have been another kind of woman in Victorian and Edwardian Kirkcaldy that Smith would have seen an awful lot of. These were the middle class ladies, usually spinsters, who suffered from what would be described euphemistically as "the vapours" or other disorders. In fact, they were suffering from nothing at all. It might have been called depression but it came about from not having enough to do. They were wealthy, their fathers and brothers would have been appalled at any idea of "work" for them, and being unmarried, they had no children. Smith would have realised what the real problem or need was, but what could he do about it?

For relief from what would have been undeniably a difficult job, Smith turned more and more to sports. In Kirkcaldy, he had the occasional round of golf, indulged in the "roaring game" (curling) but his main interest became bowls. In 1900 we find that he was president of the Kirkcaldy Bowling Club, and was good enough to play several times for the unofficial Scotland bowling team from 1903 until 1905 before becoming President of the Scottish Bowling Association in 1925. In 1948, sometime after his death and that of his widow Beatrice, a couple of trophies were donated to be played for, one to be called the Dr Smith Cup and one to be called the Beatrice Smith Cup.

His wife Beatrix Alice Whitle was 12 years younger than John. He is listed in the 1901 Census as living in Bryce Hall, a bachelor, with two lady servants. (No doubt there were the customary nudges and winks, even in Edwardian society about that!). But by the 1911 census when John is 55, Beatrix has appeared, aged 43 and with the other description of "wife" and born in "England". In fact, she may have been Welsh, for other sources tell us that her father was a Colonel and that he came from Old Colwyn in North Wales. They had no children, but had a long and happy marriage with Beatrice seeming to live the genteel and (to modern eyes) somewhat boring life of drinking tea with other doctors' wives in the winter afternoons and possibly a "spot of gardening" in the summer.

It was the fortune of Dr John Smith to live in Kirkcaldy through interesting times from 1891 until 1934. He saw the introduction of things like the National Insurance Act in the era of the Liberal Reforms of the Edwardian era, something that did a great deal to improve health, in that poor families would now be less reluctant to summon doctors when someone was ill. He saw a gradual improvement in medical techniques, a few more hospitals appearing on the scene and he was always well to the fore in urging the authorities to improve housing. Gradually, he felt that things were improving, but he knew that there was a long way to go. Possibly towards the end of his life, he began to feel that men like Ramsay MacDonald and Tom Kennedy (whom he met several times and who impressed him by his sincerity), dangerous radicals though they were in some ways, might yet have some solution to the awful health problems which prevailed in the town.

He must have had mixed feelings about the Great War. Yes, it was perhaps necessary if the Kaiser was hell bent on taking over Belgium and France, but Smith (now nearly 60 in 1914 and too old for any active part in the conflict, even as a medical officer) would see soldiers after they came home on leave or if they had been invalided out. He would, at first hand, see the results of wounds and gas, and the perhaps less obvious but possibly more insidious effects of shellshock and stress. He would see the stress of the grieving widows, and the lack of support offered by a so-called triumphant nation.

The end of the war would see a dramatic increase in trade, as it were, for there was the Spanish flu outbreak to deal with. It developed in the last year of the war – and little wonder with all that poisonous gas in the atmosphere – and ravaged the civilian population throughout 1919 as soldiers came home to spread the illness to wives and children who hadn't necessarily been starved or under-nourished in the war but had certainly been lacking in the proper vitamins of a balanced and healthy diet. Smith, himself still a strong and robust man, was tireless in his attention to his patients, but there was little that he could do in circumstances like, for example, the story of Sapper Dryburgh who came home on leave in February 1919, played football with his friends in the Beveridge Park, then died of flu 12 hours later!

Medical science did eventually get the better of the flu epidemic, and to an extent society settled down in the 1920s but then came the General Strike and all its problems. Smith, now 70 and still in practice but now with a younger doctor called Dr Beveridge with him, was distressed by all this, particularly when the miners themselves continued their strike long after the General Strike had collapsed. In this context, we might consider the words of Philip Hodge, one-time agent of the Miners' Union "I always found him (Dr Smith) a true sportsman; he had developed the spirit and letter of fair play and justice to a very high degree, and when examining my miners and reporting (on their condition), he was patient, tolerant and sympathetic. He was independent and incorruptible, and in my opinion, he was the ideal medical referee". Smith was clearly looked upon as the doctor who would spot a malingerer, as distinct from the miner who was ill and needed to go "on the sick". There were of course a huge number of such cases, for mining was a dreadful job, and one suspects that Smith sympathised with the militant miners as distinct from the "fat cats" of the Wemyss Coal Company.

Smith's barely legible tombstone in the Bennochy Cemetery

In his old age, Smith continued to practice, feeling that he still had something to offer. He was a frequent sight in his horse-drawn carriage going round the town, often pipe in mouth, nodding genially to all he met, and a few of the older people in Kirkcaldy would tell their grandchildren that that man scored goals for Scotland against England just like Jimmy McGrory and Hughie Gallacher did now. He still played his bowls and went every week to see Raith Rovers, even in the early 1930s when things were not so good. On a Sunday morning he would take the short walk across the road to the Parish Church.

In early 1934, his beloved Beatrix became distressed at his cough which was more than just a winter cold, but Smith kept going all through the spring and summer of 1934 until he was forced to take to his bed sometime in early October. His colleague Dr Beveridge diagnosed "pulmonary congestion" probably caused by heavy smoking, and hard though he fought it, Smith became worse and worse, eventually dying in his house on 16 November.

The Fife Free Press tells us about his funeral held on the Monday. The Old Kirk was full as Reverend Evelyn Gall took the service. All the town dignitaries were there from the Provost downwards, and the streets were lined with mourners as he was conveyed to the Bennochy Cemetery. Various people from the world of football were there, and Mr Hamilton from the Scottish Bowling Association. Reverend Gall described him as "A skillful doctor, a man with a deep understanding of human nature and with the geniality and frankness born of such, Dr Smith added to these qualities that of sportsmanship in the highest sense. He loved sport for its own sake and he realised all that it meant".

The town was clearly a worse place for his passing. He was 79, and had helped with the birth of babies, stuck needles in bottoms, gave people good and bad news of relatives, and had been there at the end so often – but always with a sincere, gentle, sympathetic expression. The fact that he had been such a hero of Scotland was never mentioned by himself, but if anyone wanted to talk to him about it, he would be more than willing to do so. In fact, it was a good and therapeutic thing for seriously ill patients to talk about. The tributes that were paid to him were indeed deserved.

Beatrice moved to 51 Townsend Place, and being the brave woman that she was, rallied and remained a good friend to many people in the difficult days of the Second World War. Like her husband, she too was 79 when she passed away on January 12 1947. They had no family. Their tombstone is a simple one near the top of the west wall of the eastern section of Bennochy Cemetery. It is in danger of falling into disrepair. This is a shame, for now very few people know how great a man Dr John Smith was.

Gordon Brown

Quite a few British Prime Ministers were educated at Eton. This one was educated at Kirkcaldy High School. He is in some ways still a Kirkcaldy man. He makes no bones about the fact that he supports Raith Rovers, is very proud of his origins and frequently appears in Kirkcaldy which, of course, he represented as MP until 2015.

He is not a Langtonian by birth. He was born on 20 February 1951 in Giffnock, but by 1954 his father John Ebenezer Brown had been appointed Minister of St Brycedale Church in Kirkcaldy, and thus Gordon, the middle of three boys, was brought up in Kirkcaldy, going to the West Primary School and then Kirkcaldy High School.

His father, John Ebenezer Brown or "Johnnie Broon" as he was affectionately known to some of his congregation, was a fine man and Gordon remains fully appreciative of the effect that he had on him. St Brycedale Church, a fine example of Victorian architecture, built in the early 1880s and financed to a very large extent, it must be said, from the profits of Michael Barker Nairn and his linoleum factory, was originally the "Free" Church of Kirkcaldy. It was well endowed, and well attended. Possibly the reputation of "snobbiness" was a little misplaced by the mid 1950s, but there was little doubt that St Brycedale Church had a high percentage of middle-class and wealthy members. This might have put a brake on John Brown's "radicalism" (as it would have been called a century earlier), but Brown senior preserved his integrity and earned a deserved reputation for good preaching, never being afraid to shirk the uncomfortable questions of why some people seemed to have more money than others.

Back Row—H. Johnstone, C. McAndrew, G. Brown, J. Robertson, J. Sharp, M. Piotrowicz.
Front Row—J. Holmes, G. McFarlane, S. Halley, E. Brooks.

Brown the Prefect at Kirkcaldy High School

It was of course from these origins that Gordon Brown was attracted to the Labour Party. Kirkcaldy was by nature a Labour stronghold. Since the legendary Tom Kennedy, the town and the Labour Party had been well served by Tom Hubbard as MP until 1959, then Harry Gourlay in the 1960s and 1970s, but there was a sterility and predictability about local politics, and Brown never to any great extent involved himself in this area.

But he was like quite a few young men who attained manhood in the 1960s. He may or may not have been affected by the Beatles (as sociologists love to claim about that generation, the "baby boomers" as they were called), but he began to object to the Conservative squirearchy where one scion of the upper class succeeded another − Churchill gave way to Eden, Eden to McMillan, McMillan to Douglas-Home, none of them even remotely middle class, let alone working class! − and he also began to see that something was wrong about apartheid in South Africa, the Protestants in Northern Ireland were getting away with murder (sometimes quite literally) and that the Americans had no business in Vietnam. Indeed, they had their own problems of racial intolerance to sort out.

Gordon's education at Kirkcaldy High School, however, was unusual in at least one respect. It was the very antithesis of the Labour ideal of comprehensive education, an idea that was only beginning to gain ground in the early 1960s. He was part of an experimental fast-track experiment whereby a year was missed out, and these very intelligent pupils were given special attention in order to concentrate on their studies. They were indeed singled out, and almost deliberately created as an elite.

Brown himself in later years was absolutely appalled by this experiment, and indeed it was never really persevered with. Educationalists generally think it was a bad idea, but it could nevertheless be defended. Kirkcaldy High School, at that time, had a reputation for excellence in academic standards. It took the best pupils from all the primary schools in the whole town and in places like Kinghorn and Burntisland as well, and taught them intensively with no other end in view than to produce pupils to win Bursaries at University. The idea of missing out a year by intelligent pupils was merely a development of this ethos.

It was probably however a step too far. It did of course cause resentment among those who were not selected, and this could happen even within families if one sibling was chosen for special treatment and the other not. Moreover, the pupils themselves had a year less time in which to develop their social skills (Brown himself went to University when he was 16) as well as feeling perpetually under pressure to perform well. On the other hand, anyone who has seen or observed the slow progress made in most subjects in first year mixed ability courses will sympathise and even empathise with the frustrations felt by so many intelligent pupils, some of whom can very easily be seduced into lazy, non-academic ways of life from which they never recover. Clearly there is a happy medium to be found here, but academics have as yet to come up with an answer.

Be that as it may, Brown enjoyed Kirkcaldy High School under the stern, occasionally dictatorial regime of R M Adam, commonly referred to as "the Bod". The dictatorship, on at least one occasion, might well have landed Adam in trouble, if a story concerning Brown is correct. It was December 1965, and Scotland had a vital

World Cup tie against Italy to be played in the early afternoon. Adam, suspecting that attendance might dip somewhat that particular Tuesday afternoon, told the Assembly that dire consequences would be visited on absentees. Fair enough, so far, but he then invited all those senior pupils who wanted to see the game to appear in his room. Thinking that Adam was about to make a concession, or even a negotiated settlement about letting them watch the second half, perhaps, Brown and a few others went along. Adam belted them all!

But for all that, Brown benefitted greatly from Kirkcaldy High School. But there was one unfortunate incident. Playing rugby one day, as a result of a blow to the head, he suffered a detached retina which caused him to lose the sight of his left eye, and caused severe problems for his right – fortunately the sight in his right eye was saved after an intensive course of hospitalisation – and, apart from anything else, Brown deserves our admiration for the way in which he has overcome this fairly serious handicap and has been an example for so many partially sighted people.

He went to Edinburgh University to study History, graduating with First Class Honours in 1972, and going on to complete a Ph.D. some ten years later on "The Labour Party and Political Change in Scotland 1918-1929". This highlights another and less heralded aspect of Gordon. He was and remains a very fine writer. He was particularly interested in this time of history and in the mid-1980s he published a book "Maxton - A Biography" on the famous Red Clydeside MP called Jimmy Maxton. Maxton, a gaunt, unconventional, chain smoking, cadaverous looking man, is a great character for a political biography and Brown clearly relished writing about him.

In 1972 while still a student, Gordon was elected by his fellow students as the Rector of the University of Edinburgh. This post, somewhat nebulous and ill defined, was nevertheless a great honour for the young man, and involved him in the necessity to Chair the University Court, putting cloistered academics and Professors in their place when necessary. It is perhaps interesting to note who the Rectors of the other Scottish Universities were at the time. Dundee had Peter Ustinov, the famous actor, Glasgow had Jimmy Reid the man who had done so much to organise the Upper Clyde Shipbuilders movement against the Conservative Government and St Andrews had John Cleese, already famous for his Monty Python programmes and soon to become a veritable television legend as Basil Fawlty in Fawlty Towers, arguably the funniest TV programme of them all.

Brown stayed as Rector until 1975, then took up a job at Glasgow College of Technology, lecturing in politics, which had clearly by now become his main interest. He was also a Tutor for the Open University, but he clearly showed interest in standing for Parliament, and in 1979, Labour adopted him for the Edinburgh South constituency to stand against Michael Ancram, a man who would star in the Thatcher Government.

There was of course by this time a new dimension to politics in Scotland, which would have been unfamiliar to Brown in his youth. The Scottish National Party had won 7 seats in February 1974 and 11 in October of that year. Although most of their ideas at that time played to the emotions (their slogan was "It's Scotland's Oil") and included unrealistic campaigns to remove Scotland from the Common Market, (as the European Union was then called), they nevertheless persuaded a half-hearted

Government to allow a referendum on Scottish devolution. Half-hearted was the Government and half-hearted was the support of the Scottish people, and the idea failed to the disappointment of Brown who had led a group called "Labour Movement Yes". The 1980s however would see any Scottish Home Rule movements definitely put on the back burner, at least temporarily. It was from this period of time however that comes Brown's dislike and distrust of Scottish Nationalism. Devolution, yes, and he was a prime mover in the establishment of a Scottish Assembly, but the Nationalists of the 1970s were naïve, simplistic and played too much to emotion and anti-English sentiment.

The young Gordon Brown with his family. Gordon is at the front on the left

1979 was perhaps an unfortunate year to cut one's political teeth. The Labour Government of James Callaghan, a competent but inferior man in comparison with his predecessor Harold Wilson, had clearly run out of steam, blatantly unable to solve the problems of inflation, capitalist greed, and the bloody-mindedness of Trade Union militancy. It was in fact the Trade Unions who let Labour down in 1979 with their traditional inability to see the wood for the trees, and to think no further than their next selfish pay rise. The winter of 1978/79, a cold severe winter, saw many strikes to add to people's general misery, including the infamous one where militants actually picketed a graveyard! Not without cause, it was called "the winter of discontent" and it was difficult to support Labour in such circumstances, especially as Callaghan himself, a benign but none too aggressive politician, seemed to have given up the ghost.

Margaret Thatcher on the other hand, had been elected as Leader of the Conservatives a few years earlier with no other end in view than to beat the Unions and create unemployment to tame them. The Conservatives under Edward Heath had been twice beaten by the miners in 1972 and 1974, and elected Mrs Thatcher for no other purpose than to gain revenge and reclaim the country for the upper and middle classes. It was a naked class war but she did seem to have the determination and the political will to do what she was asked. She won the 1979 General Election comfortably. One would have to concede that she succeeded in doing what she was elected to do – the Unions have not been a significant force since - but with dreadful collateral damage to large areas of society, particularly in Scotland.

On May 3 1979, Brown did well to increase the Labour share of the vote in his constituency, mainly at the expense of the Liberals and the Scottish Nationalists, but he was still more than 2,000 short of Michael Ancram. Nevertheless, eyebrows had been raised by this performance, and by the next election of 1983, he was given a far more likely Labour seat in Dunfermline East to contest.

By this time, he had worked for a few years on Scottish Television, doing current affairs and had ended up as Editor when the events of June 1983 compelled him to concentrate entirely on his own political career. 1983 was, of course, the year of one of the Labour Party's greatest electoral disasters. The Thatcher Revolution, at least in England, was obviously working, the Unions which had for so long crippled the credibility of the Labour movement by their constant militancy were now beginning to crack, and in addition Mrs Thatcher was a war hero, the highly competent and professional British Army having with some ease driven the reluctant Argentinian conscripts from the Falkland Islands the previous year.

Labour were now led by Michael Foot, an old Left winger, who, fatally, with his stick and his thick glasses, did not LOOK like a leader. He had often been described as "the darling of the Left", and went down well with pacifists and old-style socialists, but not with the general public. In addition to a perceived failure to back the Falklands War with as much enthusiasm as the British people would have liked, he latched on to the policy of unilateral nuclear disarmament, something that is always a loser in General Elections, however praiseworthy it might be to thinking people. Labour's Election Manifesto has been described as "the longest suicide note in history" and Labour was absolutely smashed, although noticeably, not in Scotland.

Brown was always likely to win in Dunfermline East, and did so, earning more votes than all the other candidates put together. Yet in 1983, there was no such thing as a foregone conclusion for Labour, and it was to his credit that he did so well. He thus entered the House of Commons, as indeed did at the same election a young man from Sedgefield. He had been to Fettes Academy in Edinburgh and was called Anthony Blair. Thus, even at this early stage of their political careers, their lives became intertwined.

Following the euphoria of being elected to the House of Commons, there is often a period of quiet in which disillusion can set in, as a conscientious MP has to sift through all the constituents' letters about anything and everything, but often centring on someone not getting as much pension and housing benefits as they feel entitled to, while someone else down the road does. There is also of course the jockeying for position, the boring meetings to sit through and the necessity to travel up and down to Scotland most weekends. It can of course become an easy, routine-driven life as well – it is no secret that some MPs do next to nothing other than drink in the House of Commons bar - but Gordon was determined that this was not going to be the case with him.

It is an inevitable and universal truth that any political party, in the wake of a heavy election defeat and doomed to a long period of opposition, will indulge in a fair amount of navel gazing. "The long hard look at themselves" as the Press will invariably call it, will probably contain its fair share of back-stabbings and resignations. The Labour Party, which nominally believes in the brotherhood of man, is usually the world's worst for internecine strife. The 1950s saw the prolonged power struggle between Bevan on the Left and Gaitskell on the Right, a struggle only really resolved by Harold Wilson after both men had died.

The 1980s, even before the 1983 disaster, had seen its split when a group of Social Democrats (led by the "Gang of Four") left the Party and eventually lined up with the Liberals. There was thus the common perception that the "broad Church" ideal of the Labour Party was no longer in place and that the Labour Party was the prisoner of the militants on the Left, while at the same time, the Conservatives, with clear and obvious electoral success to prove their point, were moving steadily to the Right, the general direction in which, it would appear, the British public wanted to go, particularly in England where prosperity was the order of the day. It was the age of the YUPPY – young, upwardly mobile professional people – and the DINKY – double income no kids, as distinct from the NILKY – no income loads of kids!

No easy task then faced the Labour class of 1983, as they entered Westminster. Michael Foot was soon replaced and returned to become the darling of the Left wing once again as the leadership passed to a Welshman called Neil Kinnock. Very soon the name "New Labour" began to be heard, and new boys like Blair and Brown began to align themselves with that. The key plank in all this was to recapture the old Wilsonian ideal of making Labour the natural party of Government. This inevitably led to a few necessary concessions to the centre ground, including for example, in economic terms, no increases in taxation.

Tony Blair and Gordon Brown

It was in economics that Brown specialised, becoming in the mid 1980s an Opposition Spokesmen on economic affairs, then on to Trade and Industry on his way to becoming Shadow Chancellor in 1992. But before all that, there was another General Election in 1987. This Election, held on June 11 1987, was a slight improvement for Labour, but they still failed to make a significant impact on Tory constituencies of the Home Counties and elsewhere. But things seemed to be moving in the correct direction for Brown, who romped home once again in Dunfermline, and as good news as any for the Labour Party was the failure of the new Social Democrat-Liberal Alliance to grab any substantial ground from Labour. In the meantime, perceptive commentators noted the apparent friendship between

Tony Blair and Gordon Brown, and felt that the party was moving forward.

The Leader Neil Kinnock had had a good election in 1987, but crucially had not won. This meant that there were murmurings about his leadership, but Brown was wise enough to distance himself from any incipient rebellion. Tony Benn did stand against him at one point, but the party entered the Election in April 1992 with Kinnock still the leader. By this time, Mrs Thatcher had gone, ousted by a conspiracy which proved that the Labour Party was not the only one capable of blood-letting. Mrs Thatcher's replacement was a man called John Major, a capable and competent man but clearly the compromise choice of the Conservatives and a man somewhat lacking in charisma, apart from when it came to the real love of his life, which was cricket!

The 1992 election was the General Election that Labour ought to have won. Apart from anything else, the British Electorate historically tends to say to its parties that they have had enough of one of them and that it is now time for the other lot. But there were other less nebulous considerations. The economy was not doing too well and the Conservatives were still reeling following their leadership contests. Brown himself, predictably, had no trouble in Dunfermline, and indeed Scotland was hugely pro-Labour, but in England the Conservatives once again turned up trumps with a comfortable majority into which Labour had made inroads, but not enough to win.

Once again, Labour turned in on itself, but this time came up with a better formula. Neil Kinnock, arguably the best Leader of the Opposition the country has ever seen, resigned for another job, and was replaced by a Scotsman, the excellent John Smith, a man who combined Christianity with Socialism (perhaps not unlike Brown himself). How good Smith would have been, no-one can say, for he was only given two years as Leader of the Opposition before he died suddenly of a heart attack in May 1994.

For Brown, Smith's election to the Leadership created the opportunity that he had craved for some time, namely that of Shadow Chancellor, a job that he entered into with vigour and did creditably from 1992 until 1994. But Smith's sudden death, although a major blow to the Party and to Brown himself, did suddenly present Brown with the opportunity to go all the way and become Leader of the Labour Party. His main obstacle was the man with whom he had become identified as a friend and associate, Tony Blair, the Shadow Home Secretary and a couple of years younger than Brown. The other candidates, John Prescott and Margaret Beckett were looked upon as lightweights, and could easily be countered but the two Bs, Blair and Brown, were regarded as the main challengers for the Labour throne.

Perhaps surprisingly to his friends and admirers, Brown decided not to stand. The Press wondered why, and very soon came up with the story of a pact between the two men concocted famously over dinner at the Granita restaurant in Islington, London, whereby Brown would back Blair for the job in return for Brown being given the Chancellor of the Exchequer job both in Opposition and in Government, and also for Blair stepping down as Prime Minister at a given time to allow Brown to have the job.

To what extent this story is true we do not know, but there have been a few books and even television dramas of this event. It certainly fits the pattern of subsequent happenings, for Blair did indeed defeat Prescott and Becket in the leadership contest of July 1994, and, surprise, surprise, Brown did indeed stay on as Shadow Chancellor of the Exchequer, a job which he relished and impressed everyone with his knowledge and ability, winning even, on occasion, reluctant praise from unlikely sources like *The Daily Telegraph* or *The Daily Mail.*

By this time the Tories who had been in power since 1979 were really beginning to struggle. John Major was a competent Prime Minister, but by no means an inspiring one. He was frequently the target of plots and conspiracies, on one occasion being caught by a TV microphone using the word "bastards" to describe some of his rivals, and more importantly, stories of scandals, financial and sexual, dogged the performance of the Government. The Government were hardly alone in all this, of course, for the Royal Family was equally dogged with scandal as this was the time when Diana, Princess of Wales, was publicly paying back a few old scores over her husband and his mother. Against this, the team of Blair and Brown were young and looked enthusiastic about taking over.

It often seemed that the Tory Press were so concerned about this team that they tried everything to break it up, but both men were wise enough to realise that a "falling out" would not do either of them any good. Brown, in particular, given his knowledge of Labour history, twigged that what had led to the downfall of so many Labour governments and Labour leaders in the past was their inability to get on with each other. Perhaps his Church of Scotland background as well had taught him how the gentle art of mild hypocrisy is often so much better than full frontal attacks on someone whose services you may well need in the future.

And so the pair of them "got on". This did not necessarily preclude a certain amount of tension behind the scenes, and it was occasionally claimed that John Prescott, a man who might himself have had pretentions to the leadership had he not, on one occasion, attacked a man who threw an egg at him, intervened to settle matters down, his role being likened to "a marriage guidance counsellor".

Blair was of course the front man (sometimes called "Bambi" because of his sparking eyes and young, fresh appearance) but behind him was the solid Brown, who was always very careful to stress to the Establishment that he was no real threat, and in particular went out of his way repeatedly to say that he was not going to raise income tax. This was of course the point that had terrified and antagonised the city when previous Labour Governments were in power. To hard-line Socialists or "Old Labour" as they were increasingly dubbed, this seemed like a betrayal, but it was a sign of the new pragmatism. After all, a Labour Government is no use to anyone if it can't get itself elected, a lesson that Harold Wilson had learned in 1964, and one which the Blair-Brown axis appreciated now in 1997.

Crucially, as far as Scotland was concerned, the Labour Manifesto contained a promise to hold a Referendum on a devolved Scottish Parliament. This idea had failed miserably, as we have seen, in 1979, but things had changed, for Scotland had for many years suffered from an unelected Tory Government. As it happened, when the referendum was held in September 1997, the support was overwhelming.

The General Election itself had been held some time before the referendum on May 1 1997, and the word "landslide" didn't quite cover a description of how comprehensively Labour won, even better than 1945 and the biggest hammering for the Conservatives since 1906. A large part of this came through the solid and realistic economic promises made by Gordon Brown. There was to be a national minimum wage, for example, cuts in NHS waiting times, cuts in class sizes and a windfall tax of the privatised utilities – this last one a none too subtle nod to the Old Labour veterans, most of whom were still upset about income tax not being raised.

But mainly, under Gordon Brown, clearly a wizard in economics, there was to be a promise of continued growth. All of this in stark contrast to the prolonged economic crises of the Conservatives including the day called "Black Wednesday" in September 1992 when everything collapsed to such an extent that the Government was forced to withdraw sterling from the European exchange rate.

This day did little to help those in the Conservative Party who were pro-Europe, and the word "Eurosceptic" became current to describe those who wished to leave the "Common Market" (as it was still called) and they were of course the forerunner of UKIP. But Labour, for the first time for over 20 years, were more or less united on Europe, and in addition had quietly eschewed the policy of unilateral nuclear disarmament on the grounds that, however desirable from a moral point of view, this idea was an electoral liability.

The main reason for Labour's triumph was of course the fact that the Tories had been in for so long, and that the British electorate needed, as it did from time to time historically, a change. That was of course the accepted wisdom, but there was more to it than that. Labour for the first time since the days of Harold Wilson in the 1960s presented a slick, credible and attractive pairing in Tony Blair and Gordon Brown. Tony was still young enough to look like the sort of young man you would want your daughter to marry, whereas Gordon combined the aspects of being sociable, intelligent and tough, imparting words of wisdom in his refined but still recognisable Scottish accent. This was often put down to the excellent public relations and co-ordination of Blair's spin doctors, notably Alistair Campbell.

While not neglecting his own constituency, Brown appeared frequently on television, backing up Blair and being an excellent foil to him. The Conservatives and some of the Press did their best to foster rumours of discord and jealousy between the two of them, but had a fairly clear dearth of facts to back it up, as Labour romped home in triumph. On the morning after the election, John Major resigned immediately and then went off to the Oval to watch the cricket!

418 seats faced 165 in the new House of Commons, but there was even more than that, as the Tories were all but obliterated in Scotland – and they have continued to remain a negligible trifle in the eyes of Scottish voters. Having been out of office for 18 years, there was a distinct lack of experience of high office in Labour circles, but that did not matter, for there was a distinct presence of idealism, determination and sheer talent. This reminded Parliamentary correspondents of the Labour class of 1964, the difference of course being that the majority in 1964 was paper thin whereas 1997 had such an overwhelming majority that commentators openly said that the real opposition was likely to come from the massed ranks of Labour backbenchers rather

than the pitiful rump of Conservative MPs who were the official opposition.

So thus it was that the Minister's son from Kirkcaldy became Chancellor of the Exchequer and took up residence in 11 Downing Street. He was, as yet, a bachelor and there was no lady there – at least none that the press and the media could find for the delectation of the prurient – and his tenure of the Chancellorship would go on unchallenged for well over 10 years. He would of course marry Sarah Macaulay in 2000, but that was in the future as the bright dawn arrived in 1997.

There can be little doubt that Brown's decade as Chancellor was an unqualified success. There were those of the Old Left (including perhaps your writer) who felt that he could well have increased income tax to find more money to build more schools, hospitals and roads, but the general feeling in the country (even among Tory voters) was that progress was being made, and that prosperity was increasing. Certainly what cannot be denied is that he managed to put a brake on the two scourges of previous governments, namely inflation and unemployment. And all this at a time where he was able to increase public spending.

Most of his changes to fiscal policies were above the heads of most of his voters, but it was he who took the important decision not to join the European single currency in 1997 on the grounds that five important conditions had not been met. Economists may well argue whether he was right or wrong, but certainly there had been no great movement in the country to join the single currency, particularly in view of the all too obvious indications of what happens when it all goes wrong as it has done in countries like Greece and Spain.

Those who hunt for idealism in politics would have cause to be happy in Brown's support for the Jubilee 2000 campaign to write off the debts of Third World countries. This is a complex issue, to put it mildly, but it meant that poor countries were never able to rid themselves of the burden of debt because rich countries, with their grasping financiers and capitalists, were always prepared to lend more and more money at exorbitant rates, normally using euphemisms like "Overseas Aid". Thus the developing countries, however well intentioned (and they were by no means all idealistic, because they had their fair share of vicious dictators) were never able to make any real progress because, of course, loans were always tied to "conditions". It was, and is, like being in permanent thraldom to a loan shark or a pay-day lender.

Brown was bright enough to realise that this state of affairs did not really work in the interests of the rich countries either. Apart from the humanitarian concerns that poverty tends to lead to more wars than necessary (in the same way that poor families in Kirkcaldy and elsewhere tend to have more problems of violence and criminality), Brown realised that having a strong economic base in a developing country like Mozambique, for example, could pay dividends for a rich country like Britain, in that more countries could use their enhanced economic base to trade with Britain and buy British goods. It was classic Keynesian economics with possibly a bit of Adam Smith thrown in, and Brown can certainly claim a certain amount of credit for the reduction of such debt. The problem however remains a huge one, and is far from being solved, but Jubilee 2000 and Gordon Brown can claim to have pointed in the right direction.

In the meantime, the Government, Brown included, had a major propaganda success in April 1998 when the Good Friday agreement seemed to have solved the age-old problem of Northern Ireland. Sceptics demurred, but the agreement has to a large extent survived, and an issue which had caused the country all sorts of problems in the 1920s and then again from 1969 onwards, seeming on occasion to be about to turn into a cataclysm, was hushed. Sectarianism was quietly given up (or better still, laughed at and ridiculed), violence was renounced, age-old enemies sat down together to talk about improving education and building roads rather than the Pope and the Orangemen, words were swallowed, and generally civilization returned as the province collectively grew up. Brown had enough money to plough into economic development of Ulster and happily did so. Northern Ireland has not been a big issue in the 21st century. Indeed, as with apartheid in South Africa, it was a success, and a pointer that progress is possible.

Scotland after 1999 had its own Parliament, held originally in the Church of Scotland Assembly Rooms until such time as the new Parliament building could be built. Although there was a great deal of moaning about the delays and the cost of the new building, everyone was eventually impressed by it, and the establishment of a devolved Scottish Assembly actually happened. After so many years of wrangling, bickering and the real danger of the issue being made to disappear because of sheer frustration and boredom, it was a clear indication that things, in Scotland, were vibrant and booming. It was also a clear indication that this Government at least could be relied upon to keep its word and deliver on promises.

It was hardly a total surprise when Blair and Brown decided to call another General Election earlier than they needed to in June 2001. The economy, thanks to Brown's firm handling and pursuit of wise policies, had seldom been better and was in stark contrast to the chaos that had seemed to exist on several occasions in the 1990s when the Conservatives had been in power. Labour had also been remarkably free of silly internal spats, had dropped the policies, like nuclear disarmament, which were electoral losers, and the pact of Blair and Brown, at least on the surface, remained solid. On a quiet day, a newspaper would now and again try to come up with a story of a rift, but all that they could prove was differences of opinion when Scotland played England at football or rugby!

The 2001 General Election has been called, in retrospect, the "quiet election" and the results were remarkably similar to four years previously in 1997. The Conservatives gained a handful of seats, but Labour still retained an overwhelming and impregnable majority in the House of Commons. Brown himself, it goes almost without saying, had no problems whatsoever in his own constituency, nor did Tony Blair have the slightest hesitation about re-appointing him to the Chancellorship. There was no need to change what was obviously a winning team.

Brown with Sarah and the children

By this time Brown was married, a happy marriage but one not without its tragedy when in winter 2001/02 a baby girl was born prematurely and died a few days later. No-one who has not been through this sort of trauma can ever begin to imagine what it can do to parents, but it is to Brown's credit that he kept working as well as he could, and never allowed himself to be excessively deflected from his course.

But the world changed "more than somewhat" on September 11 2001 with the attacks on the Twin Towers of New York, the Pentagon and the less successful one on the White House. Blair and Brown deserve a great deal of credit, initially at least, for their efforts to take the heat out of the situation and generally to calm down President George W Bush – a retaliatory nuclear strike would not have been entirely out of the question, given the hysteria of the times – but it was Blair and Brown's long term reaction to the crisis which cause the biggest (and possibly the only) blot on Labour's copybook.

Not unnaturally, the Americans looked for some kind of revenge, and as often is the case with angry American politicians, the word "freedom" was heard a lot. It was however difficult to pinpoint exactly who had committed these outrages. Osama Bin Laden was claimed to be the organiser but he was in hiding somewhere in the caves of Afghanistan, it was said, and no country was the obvious protector of the terrorists. Yet there was this desire to strike back in the war against terror, a war in which by its very nature there was not likely to be any D Day or VE Day or anything vaguely like that. But there had certainly been a Pearl Harbour.

But there was still some unfinished business with the Dictator of Iraq, Saddam Hussain. In 1990 Saddam had invaded Kuwait with obvious desire to seize the oilfields, and the United Nations, spear headed by the United States, had duly turfed him out of Kuwait. This had all been legal and proper with even an ultimatum of January 14 1991 being delivered, before military action had been taken. Naturally the world had defeated Iraq in what became known as the First Gulf War, but Saddam had not been removed from Baghdad.

Suddenly President George W Bush, the son of the President who had removed Saddam from Kuwait, saw an opportunity for USA to show the world once again who was boss. He either became himself totally convinced about Iraq having "weapons of mass destruction" or it suited him to say so, but by early 2003, the USA began to plan for an invasion of Iraq. Worse still, he managed to convince Britain to join him.

Just how he managed to do that, we do not know. Blair, we can only assume, was totally deceived by the specious arguments of Bush, or perhaps he fancied a little of the glory for himself. But for whatever reason, to the horror of most Labour supporters, Blair allied himself uncompromisingly with the Americans, talking about Iraq's "weapons of mass destruction", when we all knew that there were quite a lot of such monstrosities lying in Faslane!

Brown, on the other hand, a less gullible man than Tony Blair, was a different matter. He now faced a major dilemma. He had been brought up in the 1960s when a previous Labour Prime Minister, Harold Wilson, had refused to be bullied by American Presidents like Lyndon B Johnston and Richard M Nixon (both of whom kept talking about "freedom" as well!) into fighting a war in Vietnam against the Communists who, we were assured by the Americans, were hell bent on destroying the world. Australia (to its cost) and a few other countries had naively joined this evil and bloody war, dancing lamentably to the tune of the Americans, but Great Britain had said no.

Brown must have been aware of this precedent – indeed he would have had every cause to be grateful to Harold Wilson, because he was a young man in the late 1960s and would have been very much involved, if not having to join the Army and fight himself, then certainly seeing many of his friends perish in South East Asia – but nevertheless, he, like most of the rest of the Labour Government (but emphatically not like the rest of the Labour Party and the Labour movement) went along with his leader and supported the war.

Yet, one can sympathise with Brown as well. He must have known in his heart of hearts that going to war was the wrong decision, yet given the doctrine of collective responsibility, he would have had to resign if he had openly disagreed. He might then have become a rallying point for the anti-war brigade, a few others might have resigned as well on conscience reasons, and the Government might even have fallen. Certainly the Labour Party would have been fundamentally split.

There was also his personal position to consider. He still aspired to be Prime Minister. He believed that he could do the job well, and that his time was yet to come. A resignation at this critical point would probably have jeopardised his position irretrievably. He would have had his conscience, his self-respect and an almost heroic status in the entire Labour movement, but he would have stayed on the back benches for a very long time and might not have come off them until his moment had well passed. He might have become like Michael Foot – the "keeper of the party's conscience", a much loved and respected character – but bereft of any power.

But there was also the even earlier precedent of Ramsay MacDonald in 1914. He declared himself against the Great War at the very start, was compelled to resign from the leadership of the Labour Party as early as August 5 1914 (the day after war began), yet that did not prevent him coming back and being Labour's first Prime Minister! Brown might have been able to do that, especially if it became apparent, as in Ramsay MacDonald's case, that he was right enough in the first place.

There are times when one has to choose between idealism and expediency. One can well imagine that Brown still has the horrors about this moment, but he certainly put a brave face on it and gave the media not the slightest opportunity to talk about any split. As it happened, the military action was very effective and very fast – the United States and Great Britain against Iraq was like Real Madrid playing against a Sunday Pub team from the Beveridge Park – and the war was over in a matter of weeks, but nevertheless, lives were lost and the occupation went on for several years without anyone ever finding a single weapon of mass destruction.

One might well decide to ask whether, if there had been no oil in the area, there would have been any fuss (there were countless other genocidal conflicts in Africa at the same time which struggled even to get a mention in the British Press), but the fact remains that the implications of this war and invasion of Iraq continue to this day, and we would really like to have heard what Brown said in private about this war. Indeed, it would be fascinating to hear his candid opinions now. He is far too intelligent a man to be deceived by the simplistic assumptions of George W Bush. Perhaps things might have been a little simpler if he had been Prime Minister. As it was, Tony Blair made the decision but Brown cannot be entirely exempt from blame. He did go along with it.

What saved the Government was of course the success of the military operation. It would have been a different story if there had been a huge amount of casualties. As it was, to most people the affair began to slip from public prominence, and the Government continued to go from strength to strength with the economy as strong as it had ever been. For this Brown deserves a great deal of credit, and it was with a great deal of confidence that Blair decided to go to the country in May 2005 to ask for a renewal of his mandate.

For Brown, this meant a return home. The boundaries for the Parliamentary constituencies had been redrawn, and Brown now found himself representing Kirkcaldy rather than Dunfermline. In practical terms, this meant very little difference for Brown, whose 24,000 votes were rather more than the other eight candidates put together! In the country, generally, however the results were rather sobering for Labour. They still had a majority of about 60, but they had lost a great deal of seats, something that reflected perhaps a certain dissatisfaction with, not the economy, but with the spin and the half-truths of Tony Blair concerning the war in Iraq.

Labour were aware that the war was their Achilles heel as far as popularity were concerned, and tried to evade the issue as often as possible, concentrating on the economy with slogans like "Britain's working. Don't let the Tories wreck it again". They also made sure that the hero of the hour, Gordon Brown, was often seen at Tony Blair's side, something that also helped to scotch any stories, still much hinted at in the press, that there was some kind of rift between the two of them. The relationship was given a certain frisson with Blair's statement in October 2004 that he would serve a full third term (assuming that he won the 2005 Election) but that he would not seek a fourth term. This seemed to indicate that Brown's time was fast approaching. Certainly there was no other obvious successor.

Blair may well have tired of being Prime Minister, a job with awesome responsibilities. He may even have had a guilty conscience about Iraq, and his subsequent career following his resignation from the Premiership in 2007 would tend to indicate that his conscience has bothered him to such an extent that he has spent the rest of his time, under the guise of being some "international do-gooder" (as someone has claimed), trying to justify the actions of 2003, a task which in fact is becoming more and more difficult with every passing year.

There was no real leadership election. The word "coronation" was heard frequently, and on June 27 2007, the leadership of the Labour Party and the job of Prime Minister of Great Britain passed seamlessly to Gordon Brown, the son of the one-time minister of St Brycedale Kirk, Kirkcaldy. It was clearly one of the greatest moments in the town's history, but was little celebrated, although TV News companies did pay the occasional, token visit to interview a few people on the now sadly almost derelict High Street.

The mood was one of quiet pride rather than exuberant enthusiasm. Such is the nature of British politics that it does not (thank heaven!) lend itself to personality cults, and Brown himself was not the sort of man who would do anything to encourage that. Quiet efficiency was the way in which he had earned the crown through his work at rebuilding the economy when he was Chancellor of the Exchequer, and no-one really expected the governance of the country to change in any significant or dramatic way when he was Prime Minister.

He thus joins the ranks of Prime Ministers like James Callaghan, Sir Alec Douglas-Hume and Neville Chamberlain who became Prime Minister without having fought a General Election to do so. He was the first truly Scottish Prime Minister since Ramsay MacDonald – others like Sir Alec Douglas-Hume and Tony Blair had Scottish connections, but were hardly Scottish – and in England at least, people wondered what his attitude was to the Scottish Parliament (which had now been in existence for almost a decade) and possible Scottish independence might be. But Gordon was, and remained a committed unionist.

Much was made of the fact that his father had been a "Minister" of the Church of Scotland. Not everyone in the Anglican, Episcopalian or Roman Catholic communities had any clear idea of what a "Minister" was, and some of the English press felt compelled to tell everyone in detail what exactly Gordon's father had done to earn a living. The question was also frequently asked what sort of effect being a "son of the manse" might have on the new Prime Minister. They might also have asked what sort of effect the experimental fast-track education that he enjoyed might have affected him. And of course, questions, as always, were asked about his wife and family. His wife would on one occasion confound everyone by introducing her husband to the Labour Party Conference!

There is a common, albeit unjustified, perception in England that Scotsmen are "dour". This word would frequently be used to describe Gordon Brown, the next word often being "Presbyterian". This stereotype (it is a wonder that the perpetrators of this phrase were not accused of racism!) is grossly unfair and untrue of this calm, efficient man who apparently can show emotion when Raith Rovers or the Scotland rugby team are playing, although it would have to be noted that of the four medieval humours, the "phlegmatic" one is what would spring to mind, rather than "choleric", "sanguine" or "melancholic". The Labour spin doctors clearly picked up on this mood, for they coined and used the slogan "Nothing Flash – Just Gordon", clearly designed to reassure older voters, "Flash Gordon" having been a radio hero of the 1950s and earlier, the prototype of Buzz Lightyear and other subsequent ones.

The policies of his Government were basically to be more of the same as we had seen under Blair. There would be nothing daft or controversial. More land was to be released for housing, more money to be spent on schools and health, international development, a nod or two in the direction of the "Green" lobby with research on an "eco-house" etc. It was good traditional Labour, "Fabian gradualism" sort of stuff.

Whenever the political press gets bored, it is the fashion to talk about a "snap" General Election. The change of Prime Minister having failed to generate sufficient excitement, clichés like "seeking a mandate" "giving the country a chance to ratify the change" and "reinforcement" began to be heard. Fortunately, Gordon treated such ideas with contempt. He had a healthy Parliamentary majority of about 60, the last General Election had been little over two years ago, and he might have been accused of playing at politics for a little fun. Had he won the General Election, it would have made little real difference, and had he lost, he would have become an international and historical figure of ridicule as the "Prime Minister that nobody wanted". Wisely, he ignored such siren calls and moved on, choosing as his successor as Chancellor, Alistair Darling.

It was ironic that the man who had built up his reputation as an economic wizard, and used his fame and glory to reach the top job, would find that his major problem was an economic one. We can go back 50 years to find a parallel in Anthony Eden who became Prime Minister in 1955 because of what he had achieved in foreign affairs, only to fall from grace because of a foreign miscalculation and misadventure at Suez in 1956. The difference was that Eden's Premiership was brought about entirely by his own folly; Brown's eventual defeat in 2010 was caused by events over which neither he nor anyone else seemed to have any control.

"Global recession" and "trade slump" by 2008 had replaced "snap General Election" as the buzz words in the Press and media. What "global recession" actually means, we cannot really tell, but it would have to be admitted that in comparison with other seismic worldwide economic disturbances in the past like 1929-1931 for example, this one was very much a storm in a teacup, at least as far as Great Britain was concerned. It was far more serious in countries like Spain and Greece, where weak Governments were bullied by Angela Merkel and others into making expenditure cuts.

But the media latched on to it, and how! The BBC News would begin some days with alarmist banner headlines about the price of houses going down! Now, in so far as it affected anyone at all, this would have appeared to many people as being GOOD news, but it was shown as a clear sign that there was not enough money going around, and even worse, the Financial Times was having clear problems about its Index!

Ho, hum! Most of us could be pardoned for not getting too bothered about such lofty considerations, although there was a marginal increase in unemployment. But at a Government level, the "economic crisis" meant that Brown's socialism had to be less vigorous than, one suspects, he would have liked it to be. Nevertheless, laudably, he stuck with the policies which he had employed as Chancellor – those of steady expansion and growth.

He had always been a great believer in "international co-operation" to deal with any economic problem. More keenly than most, he realised to what extent Governments and their economies depended on everyone else, and no effort was ever spared as he went round the world frequently to talk to other Governments.

Given his background as well, it was gratifying to notice that he did not avoid going to Third World countries.

Throughout 2008 and 2009, the question began to be asked when the next General Election would be held with all sorts of political pundits making a fool of themselves by confidently predicting spring 2009, then autumn 2009 before Brown plumped for the obvious time of May 2010, some five years after the last one. It was in fact "the least well-kept secret of our time".

Brown promised more of the same to Great Britain – having been in power now for 13 years, he could hardly have embarked on anything more radical without the question being begged "Why didn't you do it before?" – but found that he had several things to battle against, not least his image of the grumpy old Scotsman, much fostered and encouraged by the London Press. In addition, there was one unfortunate incident where he was heard on a microphone talking about a "bigoted woman" after he had just taken some stick from her about Eastern Europeans and immigration. The interesting and revealing thing about this incident however was that Brown's stand against xenophobia was not praised, but used by the media as a stick to beat him, proving that "political correctness" is a phrase only used when it suits the individuals!

This was the first election in which television had a debate between all three leaders of the major political parties. They were much watched by the population but became tedious when it gradually began to be obvious that there was nothing really new in the debating, merely the trotting out of clichés and the party line on any given issue. It was "generally" agreed, however, (by whom, we are not quite sure!) that Brown performed less well than his slicker opponents David Cameron and Nick Clegg.

To what extent this affected the result of the election no-one was really sure.

And what was the result of the election? As one commentator put it the morning after "The country has spoken, but no-one is sure what it has said". It was in fact the nightmare of everyone, apart from the political commentators and psychologists who clearly relished the whole business. But Labour had clearly lost, ending up with 258 seats as distinct from the Conservatives with 307 and the Liberals with 57 and a wide spectrum of "others". Another political commentator with a clear love of cricket stated "The Umpire has raised his finger. Mr Brown is out and should go".

But he didn't go immediately. There was still a theoretical chance that Brown could be Prime Minister of a fantasy "rainbow coalition" of Labour, Liberal, Scottish Nationalist, Welsh Nationalist, Green Party, Irish MPs and others, but sadly the numbers did not quite add up, and in any case the Liberals were likely to insist on a leader other than Gordon Brown. A dignified resignation was in order, and he advised the Queen to ask David Cameron to form a new government, as Cameron's negotiations with the Liberals seemed to be bearing fruit. The Liberals then gave credence to the old adage once expressed by Kerry Packer, the Australian millionaire who ruined cricket, that "there is a bit of the whore in all of us" and joined a Coalition with the Conservatives, a Party with which they had seemed to have little in common over the past 200 years!

So on May 11 2010, Gordon Brown withdrew from the scene. He was still of course MP for Kirkcaldy, a constituency he had won with considerable ease in the Election. This did emphatically not mean that he was finished as a major public figure. There was still one more theatre in which he would play a major role.

The Scottish Nationalists had won the Scottish Election of 2011 and had a clear majority over everyone else. A referendum on Scottish independence was set for September 18 2014. This scenario put Labour (and Brown) in a dilemma. It might have seemed sensible for them to ally themselves with the Scottish National Party, clearly a left wing and progressive party well led by people like Alex Salmond and Nicola Sturgeon. But such was the nature of politics – that had been bitter at a local level – that this was not possible and Labour, to the distress of very many of its natural followers, decided to ally themselves with the Unionist cause, failing to see the benefits for Labour in an independent Scotland.

For a long time in summer 2014, it seemed that the Unionist cause was going to win, but towards the end of the summer, it began to appear that the "YES" vote was doing well. At this point Gordon Brown, who had been keeping a low profile so far, intervened on the side of "NO". He appeared several times at venues like Kirkcaldy Old Kirk and on TV, and it was probably true to say that his influence was decisive in that it tipped the balance as far as the wavering Labour vote was concerned. Had he appeared on the "YES" side as many of his followers would have wanted him to do, the vote might have been totally different, for he was still a very influential politician in Scotland.

It was probably going too far to imply, as some have done, that David Cameron suggested that he should do this, but it was still a little disappointing to quite a few Labour followers that Brown found himself on the same side as the British Establishment, the Conservatives and bodies like the Royal Bank of Scotland rather than on the same side of the aspirations of the Scottish working class. And of course, Labour paid the price in the catastrophic General Election failure of May 2015 which included a massive swing to the SNP in Kirkcaldy. Brown was at least partly to blame for that, yet he was also the man who embodied Labour in its successful years as well.

To the end, Gordon Brown remains a very complex figure.

James H Logan

James H Logan is a surprisingly unsung hero of Raith
Rovers and indeed of Kirkcaldy. Yet his contribution
was immense. He was unfortunate in that, both as a
player and a Manager, he never won anything
significant, although he came close, playing in Raith
Rovers' solitary appearance in a Scottish Cup final in
1913, and managing a team that came both third, and
then fourth in the old Scottish First Division and which
made Raith Rovers a household word throughout
Scotland. In addition, he was a war hero, being
hospitalised and sent home after the horrendous first day
of the Battle of the Somme in 1916, recovering and then
being commissioned as an officer near the end of the
war.

Logan joined Raith Rovers in May 1912. He was
born in Dunbar in 1885 and had played for St Bernard's
in Edinburgh before moving to England to play, none
too successfully, with both Bradford teams, City and
Park Avenue, and then Chesterfield. He was aged 27
when he joined Raith Rovers, probably suffering a little
from homesickness and keen to make some sort of
impact on Scottish football before retirement. He was
tall, commanding, good in the air and reasonable on the

ground. He had not however attracted the attention of any big Scottish or English team, and probably appreciated the chance to go part-time with Raith Rovers.

Raith Rovers had been in the First Division for 2 years now, and had finished fourth bottom in both cases. The occasional good result – they had twice beaten the strong and successful Falkirk in 1911/12 and drawn with Celtic at Celtic Park - had to be balanced against a generally mediocre record with away form being particularly poor. Nor had the Scottish Cup brought any cheer, so new talent was needed. Seven new players were signed in the summer of 1912, among them James Logan a tall, large striding half back.

Football was still a new and exciting sport in Scotland in the days before the Great War. Raith Rovers had been founded in 1883, and had been admitted to the Second Division of the Scottish League in time for the 1902/03 season. Their progress had been undistinguished and fitful until, in 1908, they won the Second Division. But, although there was as yet no automatic promotion, two good seasons in 1909 and 1910, when they finished second in both cases was enough to get them elected to the First Division in 1910/11, aided by a little skilful lobbying and "knocking on doors" as the local press delicately puts it.

The local press sometimes gives the impression of being a little in awe of the power of this comparatively young game, and the almost demonic effect it had on young men. But there could be little doubt that it had its attraction, and Church opinion, while still not overly happy about the excesses of the sport, possibly reckoned that if they were playing football, the youth of Kirkcaldy (often described as "shiftless" or "feckless") were not visiting public houses or falling to the attractions of desirable but deleterious young ladies. Older men too enjoyed watching this game, and crowds of several thousand had been known to attend matches at Stark's Park.

The main attraction lay, of course, in that this was a sport in which Scotland were at least the match of, and often better than England. At the massive new stadium opened in Glasgow in 1903 called Hampden Park, Scotland had famously in 1910 defeated England mainly through the agency of the great Jimmy Quinn of Celtic, and this had boosted all Scotland. There had been bad days as well – the Ibrox Disaster of 1902 in which 26 people had been killed at the Scotland v England match, and the Hampden Riot of 1909 when the new stadium had been ripped apart by the fans of Celtic and Rangers, not in a sectarian riot against each other (that would happen in 1980!), but because they felt that they had been cheated of extra time in the Scottish Cup final replay of that year!

Kirkcaldy like everywhere else looked on in amazement at all this. This game seemed to be more important than anything else! The Prime Minister, Mr Asquith, not unknown in Kirkcaldy because of his friendship to the McIntosh family of furniture manufacturers, had to yield in public esteem to people like the mighty Jimmy Quinn, the miner boy from Croy, and even when King Edward VII died in 1910 and folk were heard saying that "the great man" was dead, many people wondered whether it was the King they were talking about, or the famous Peter McWilliam of

Newcastle United, Scottish born of course, who was indeed called "Peter The Great".

Raith's elevation to the First Division in 1910 brought the big teams to Stark's Park, and many a mother would worry about the very real possibility of her son being crushed in the massive crowds, sometimes now, when a "big" team appeared, 10,000 or more, seen tramping along Pratt Street to the "fitba". Shops and pubs also did well when a team from Glasgow or Edinburgh arrived, for they brought many supporters. Football was a huge, massive, burgeoning industry in the days when James Logan made his subdued entrance to the Kirkcaldy sporting scene.

The make-up of the team in 1912/13 being totally different from the previous two none-too-successful seasons, the team took a long time to settle, and if anything, League form was worse than previously and the team finished third bottom. For Logan, this was a difficult time. He was described as a half back, and played in all three half back positions, (and occasionally at centre forward) before settling at centre half. The season however was the most talked-about that Raith Rovers had had up to then, and is worth going into in some detail.

The Fifeshire Advertiser and *The Kirkcaldy Times* are not without their criticisms of both Logan and the team in general. In the opening game, for example, at Pittodrie against Aberdeen, the team were well beaten and lucky to get off with a 0-2 defeat and wing halves McLay and Logan are roundly criticised for "failing to place the ball properly to forwards". The following week, however, although the team lost 0-1 to Falkirk in their first home game, *The Kirkcaldy Times* is compelled to concede that "there is a slight improvement in the play of Logan... yet he has a tendency to roam and this gives the opposing wing full scope".

But gradually he settled, and when moved to centre half, an improvement was noticed not only in Logan himself, but in the team in general. A creditable 1-1 draw at Motherwell was followed by a spectacular 5-0 thumping of Queen's Park, and then came the occasion when James H Logan "won his spurs" and made the town and Scottish football in general pay attention to him.

This was on October 19 1912 when the mighty Celtic came to town. The arrival of Celtic, still referred to by the local press as "the Irishmen" even though most of their 11 players had been born in Scotland, was a great event in 1912. They were the Scottish Cup holders, and from 1905-1910 had amazed all Scotland by winning six League championships in a row. They had a huge support, a great stadium and could reasonably claim at that time in history to be the best team in the world. Their arrival was much looked forward to, and from early morning the railway station was a busy place as their supporters poured into town.

This day however they were without their two "mesmeric tacticians" in Patsy Gallacher and Jimmy McMenemy, but they had two Fife men with strong Kirkcaldy connections in their team in Peter Johnstone and John Brown. They also had of course the man who dominated all footballing conversation, the great Jimmy Quinn, the champion goal scorer, the "boy from Croy", the "bison" (because of his massive shoulders) and the man whose goals for Celtic and Scotland were talked about wherever football was played. Yet he was famously "just like an ordinary man" when he came off the train that day and walked with his team mates along the road to the park, being friendly to his own supporters and to those of Raith Rovers as well, who reverentially cleared a path for him to walk along. It was to be Logan's job that day to stop this mighty man.

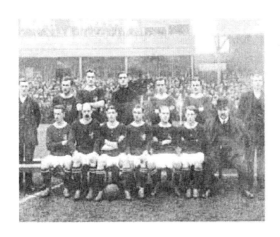

Raith Rovers before the Scottish Cup final of 1913.
Logan is third from the left in the back row

Quinn however was now in his thirties "not the Quinn of old" and had been badly affected by injuries of late, but he was still Jimmy Quinn. Logan however focussed on the task, playing him hard but fairly, on one occasion using his strength to bundle Quinn to the ground, but more often simply getting to the ball that little bit faster than the ageing Quinn, and not being afraid to boot the ball up field and keep the ball away from danger. *The Fife Free Press* says that Logan "overshadowed Quinn" and that Logan "did the bottling all right, and this had the desired effect". Quinn did not score that day, (Celtic's goal came from a Joe Dodds penalty kick) and Rovers, to the delight of their fans, won 2-1.

Action from the 1913 Scottish Cup final against Falkirk at Celtic Park

Like all truly great men, Quinn was humble and dignified in defeat, and made a point of shaking the hand of the man who had got the better of him that day. It was Logan's greatest moment so far, and a great day in the history of Raith Rovers. It would have been nice to report that that fine form was maintained, but the following week Raith Rovers went down 0-2 to Partick Thistle, and inconsistency returned. Logan was out injured in a 3-5 defeat by Hamilton Academical (described amazingly as a "disappointing game" by *The Kirkcaldy Times)* and then Logan found himself deployed all over the half back line on his return, and on two occasions at centre forward!

Centre forward and centre half were not all that different from each other in 1912, for many teams played the attacking centre half game, and *The Kirkcaldy Times* has this to say about him a propos of a 2-2 draw against Motherwell "that Logan is not a centre (forward) is admitted, but he was not a failure". But the following week a 0-2 defeat to Hearts saw the end of that experiment, and we find Logan playing at left half in a creditable 2-2 draw when Rangers came to town on December 7.

As the year of 1912 came to an end it was hard to detect any great pattern to Raith Rovers. But then again this was hardly surprising, for they had no Manager! Peter Hodge had been sacked in November after being compelled to censure his trainer for an article written in a newspaper about training methods. The team was being run by the Directors. One suspects that Logan, still new to the club, used this as a learning experience for management in that it told him how NOT to do it, but it must have been very unsettling, and the surprise was not that Rovers were infuriatingly inconsistent, but that they managed to achieve anything at all!

Good wins over Clyde and against Hibs (at Easter Road) had to be balanced by a dreadful drubbing at the hands of Hamilton Academical and a depressing 0-0 draw when Aberdeen came to town early in the New Year. Similarly, there was no clear indication of where Logan was to be played. He was clearly a good player, very versatile and a handy man to have in emergencies and when someone was injured, but he had yet to command any one place for himself. A strong Manager would have helped at this point, and Logan would have stored this up for the future, realising that strength and consistency in running a club was important.

But it was the Scottish Cup which really had the town in a ferment in the spring of 1913. The 5-0 defeat of Broxburn was hardly surprising, but eyebrows were raised on March 1 1913 with an impressive defeat of Hibs in a replay at Easter Road. It was generally agreed that Rovers were lucky to earn a replay at Stark's Park with goals from the two Freds, Gibson and Martin, Martin having recently joined the club from Sunderland. Indeed, the common perception was that Hibs were "at it" – a surprisingly common accusation, sometimes hinted at obliquely in newspapers, other times stated more bluntly - and that a 2-2 draw meant a replay and another big crowd. They had, it was asserted, allowed Rovers back into the game.

The first game at Stark's Park on February 22 1913 was a huge occasion for the town and the club. The weather was excellent for the time of year, and a record crowd of "well in excess of 10,000" appeared with serious complaints being made about the club not having enough turnstiles open in Pratt Street particularly just before kick-off when a train arrived disgorging a "huge amount of Edinburgh Irishmen". Pickpocketing, that famous crime of Victorian London, had clearly made its way north and the police were deluged with complaints about wallets being removed from hip pockets and the local press feeling compelled to give advice about keeping money safe in big crowds by "secreting it elsewhere about your person".

If Hibs were indeed "at it", i.e. deliberately allowing Raith Rovers to score twice, they would have huge regrets the following week at Easter Road. This was another of Logan's great performance as a "gritty exhibition of combined play" saw Rovers through. Harry Graham's goal was the only goal of the game, and

Logan, back at centre half and who had been off the field for a spell with an injury, returned in the later stages and co-ordinated the defence as they defended desperately to save the day to the delight of the estimated 4,000 travelling Kirkcaldy fans in the 23,000 crowd.

Further good news came the following week when Raith beat St Mirren 2-1 at Stark's Park. Rangers had gone down to Falkirk in the previous round and now with the news that Celtic, Scottish Cup winners for the last two years, had gone out to Hearts on the same day that Rovers beat St Mirren, people in Kirkcaldy began to believe that the Scottish Cup could be won by their team who made up for lack of outstanding talent and big names with determination, doggedness and a little luck.

The St Mirren game's attendance was a little down on the Hibs one, but it was another fine day and the club had taken the precautions of having "Ambulance volunteers" in attendance and arranging for the 4th Company of the local Boys Brigade under Lieutenant Pearson to entertain the crowd before the game and at half time. They did this with their music and a display of club swinging. Rovers lost an early goal, but Gibson and Cranston pulled them back into the game, and with Logan once again superb at centre half, Rovers saw off a desperate second half surge by the Buddies, and reached the semi-final for the first time in their history.

If excitement in Kirkcaldy had been high before, it now reached fever pitch, for the semi-final against Clyde was to be played at Tynecastle. So three "football specials" were hired to take supporters across the river, and Kirkcaldy was well represented, although *The Kirkcaldy Times* had sadly to relate that "not a few were in that condition when the match started that they had some difficulty in distinguishing between the teams".

But there was no lack of vocal encouragement from the fans, some of whom had departed as early as 9.00 am that morning, and who had enjoyed hearing the Craigmillar and Duddingston Band playing "all the ragtime favourites" before the game started. The game was a disappointing one - a 1-1 draw, Gourlay scoring for Raith Rovers but then some hesitation from goalkeeper McLeod allowed Reid of Clyde to equalize late in the game.

The semi-final replay was again at Tynecastle the following week. Surprisingly to our modern eyes, the England v Scotland International was played that same day at Stamford Bridge. Disappointingly, Scotland lost, but Kirkcaldy was none too bothered about that for Fred Martin had scored the goal that put the Rovers into the Scottish Cup final to be played the following week, April 12 1913 at Celtic Park.

Rovers' opponents were Falkirk, and it was nice, although annoying, to see the national Press patronising two "smaller" clubs for reaching the Final. A glance at *The Kirkcaldy Times* and *The Fife Free Press* of the week leading up to the final appears to reveal an apparent lack of local interest in the game, other than on the football page. Typical of 1913, the front page was all adverts and the Editorial attempts to display a high patrician disregard for this vulgar game of football.

The reality of course was different. The football page told us that two special trains were to leave Dysart, one at 12.20 and another half an hour later to arrive at Parkhead at 2.30 and 3.05 respectively in time for the 3.30 kick off. On the Monday night before the big game, Rovers had played a poor game against Partick Thistle before a poor crowd (in spite of it being a local holiday) of 2,000 and lost 0-2. The reporter comments acridly and probably accurately that "they were not exerting themselves in view of the final on Saturday".

Glasgow awoke on the morning of April 12 to an unseasonal, although by no means unprecedented fall of snow. Celtic's manager Willie Maley was early on the scene at Celtic Park directing operations and the pitch was "swept and garnished" to ensure the playing of the game, albeit on a wet surface. The trains, special and ordinary, rolled in from Kirkcaldy and Falkirk, and quite a few Glaswegians turned up as well, impressed, no doubt, by *The Scottish Referee*'s description of Raith Rovers "having set ablaze the noble Forth that laves the linoleum centre of Scotland". All in all, the attendance was 45,000 giving receipts of £992 and £279 from the stands.

The team which ran out of the old pavilion at Celtic Park were;

Falkirk: Stewart, Orrock and Donaldson; McDonald, Logan and McMillan; McNaught, Gibbons, Robertson, Croal and Terris.

Raith Rovers: McLeod, Morrison and Cumming; J.Gibson, Logan and Anderson; Cranston, Graham, Martin, Gourlay and F.Gibson.

Both centre halves were called Logan. Both teams would normally wear blue, but Falkirk appeared in all white "suggestive of the weather we had been suffering from" according to *The Fife Free Press*, but the sun had now appeared, and the snow which had been piled up at the side of the park, was now rapidly melting, as both sets of fans settled down to watch the first ever Scottish Cup Final appearance of either side, and one which would stay in the memory of everyone for a very long time.

Left half Harry Anderson was prominent in the early stages of the game which, according to the reporter of *The Fife Free Press*, was fast and open with chances at both ends, until in the 22nd minute Falkirk went ahead. "Croal's shot was held by the custodian but thrown out on to Robertson's head ere McLeod recovered" - which seems to say that Robertson was on hand to head home a rebound after McLeod had saved from Croal. This meant that Rovers were 0-1 down at half time, although the reporter felt that their play deserved a draw.

But in the second half, Rovers' fate was sealed when, after only five minutes play, right winger McNaught after some "peculiar play" (peculiarly good play, one assumes) crossed into the middle and "centre half Logan, going forward to their aid, he shot through quite out of McLeod's reach and our spirits went down - not the liquid kind, dear reader" as the reporter quaintly puts it. This account is ungrammatical, confusing and contains an attempt to be funny as he tries to convince the strong temperance lobby that the reporter did not indulge in alcoholic refreshment. It looks like it was Falkirk's Logan who scored rather than an own goal from James Logan of Raith Rovers. It mattered not, for Raith were 0-2 down.

At this point Raith's Logan rallied his stricken troops, cajoling, shouting and trying to inspire a fight back. Indeed, there was a revival (and it was as well that our reporter stayed sober enough to enjoy it!) but the Falkirk defence held out for a 2-0 victory which the chivalrous *Fife Free Press* concedes was deserved, although it thinks that 1-0 would have been fairer for Rovers.

A Cup Final defeat is always painful, but in 1913 decorum and self-control remained paramount. As was the custom those days, the Cup was presented off the park, in this case the Balcony Hall of the old Celtic Park pavilion by Mr. Robertson of the S.F.A. Mr. Liddell of Falkirk called for three cheers for the gallant losers, and Mr. D.A. Whyte, the chairman of Raith Rovers graciously replied. It seems to have been a thoroughly dignified occasion, totally unlike the scenes of agony and ecstasy which fill our TV screens nowadays whenever somebody wins a Cup.

So Rovers and their fans trooped home, defeated but not disgraced. It was not the first time of course (nor would it be the last) that Logan had experienced the power of the game to kick someone in the teeth. Back home in Kirkcaldy, *The Fife Free Press* was able to boast that the result was "phoned through" and displayed in their window in Kirk Wynd less than two minutes after the full and half time whistles went! Not only that, but Mackie's the Ironmonger in the High Street and McLeod the Saddler in Dysart were informed by *The Fife Free Press* and they too were able to tell the waiting public.

It had been a good first season for Logan. The Scottish Cup run had been exhilarating but this could not disguise the fact that League form had been poor (the team finished third bottom) and that a new Manager was needed. One was appointed in John Richardson from the junior side Petershill in Glasgow. How would the Rovers do in the season that was to come?

Sadly, the answer has to be: a lot less well. The League position improved certainly, but hopes of a Scottish Cup run were dashed in February as the team were on the wrong end of a 4-1 beating by Third Lanark at Cathkin Park, after a good 2-0 win over Hearts at Stark's Park in the previous round. The Hearts game in fact attracted an enormous crowd of about 25,000 (it was said) and everyone left singing the praises of Raith's half back line of Logan, Porter and Anderson. Rovers then disappointed their many travelling fans by collapsing woefully to Third Lanark, but there was a crumb of comfort at least for left half Harry Anderson who became Raith's first ever Scotland Internationalist when he turned out for Scotland against Wales the following week.

Logan had now settled in Kirkcaldy in David Street, clearly revelling in his role with this clearly ambitious little club. No-one of course could have predicted what summer 1914 would have brought to the world, and Logan was as amazed as everyone when the 1914/15 season opened with the country at war. By the turn of the year, it had become obvious that the war was going to be a long one, and Logan, possibly affected by public opinion, decided to enlist.

Logan thus joined up in early December, and clearly a man of leadership ability, became a Corporal in January 1915, a Sergeant in May, a Sergeant-Major in June and a Lieutenant sometime after that. There were of course tragic and sinister reasons for this rapid promotion in that so many able men were being killed in the awful year of 1915, particularly in the autumn at the Battle of Loos, that officers were needed in a hurry.

Logan is on the extreme right of this World War I
photograph

The excellent book "McCrae's Batallion" by Jack
Alexander tells us that Logan in company with six other
Raith Rovers players – George McLay, Willie Porter,
Willie Lavery, Jock Rattray, Jimmy Scott and Jimmy
Todd – appeared in Edinburgh on Tuesday December 1
1914 to join what became known as McCrae's Battalion,
the 16th Royal Scots which consisted to a large extent of
professional football players. McLay, Todd and Scott did
not return, Scott disappearing at the Battle of the
Somme, while Willie Lavery played a less respectable
part in the war, going AWOL from the Royal Scots in
September 1916 and being arrested when he turned out
for Raith Rovers in a 1-2 defeat at the hands of Morton!
The Redcaps (Military Police) graciously and sportingly
allowed him to finish the game before arresting him!

Logan survived the war, but he had his brush with death on the infamous day of Saturday July 1 1916 when so many men perished in the first wave of the Battle of the Somme. By then a Lieutenant, he was found dazed and distressed by stretcher bearers when nightfall eventually brought a halt to the slaughter on the darkest day of the British army. He was diagnosed as suffering from shellshock and deafness and was sent home for treatment in London. From there it was decided that he would recover better at home, and so to the immense relief of his wife and himself, one would imagine, he found himself back in Kirkcaldy by July 6.

He was of course treated as a hero, which indeed he was, but was able to tell little of what had happened to him on that awful day at the Somme. He was on firmer ground remembering the football he had played, notably his role in the Scotland team which had played England in the Military International at Goodison Park on May 13 1916. It was a narrow and unlucky 3-4 defeat, and this match was the closest that Logan ever came to a Scotland cap.

He duly recovered, although it took time and there is seldom a 100% cure from shellshock, and returned to the war. By the time that the war ended, he was a Captain. Although he was clearly a good soldier, he yearned for peace and longed to get back to what he really loved, football. Now in his mid-30s, he may well have suspected that his best years were behind him as a player, thinking he might have a future as a trainer or a coach. Raith Rovers went one better than that, and at the start of the 1919/20 season appointed him as Manager when Peter Hodge left that post for Leicester City.

Logan was still technically in the Army at the time. It took longer for officers to be demobbed, - and Logan was happy enough to stay on - and in any case, even though the Treaty of Versailles was officially signed in June 1919 bringing the Great War officially to an end, there was still military action going on in various parts of the globe – in the Middle East, Russia, Turkey and closer to home, Ireland. But Logan's soldiering days were over, as indeed was his playing career and he soon was able to devote all his attention to giving Kirkcaldy fans the best Raith Rovers team there has ever been. It was a brief few years in the midst of decades of under-achievement, but it was a glorious time and all the more welcome because the times of the 1920s were so miserable for everyone.

Things were still generally rather chaotic for both Raith Rovers and for Scottish football in general in season 1919/1920, and one could not really judge Logan by his first season. Yet the fans turned up in great numbers and expected a great deal more than they actually got. It was an odd time in Kirkcaldy. There were swaggering ex-soldiers, miserable widows, many wounded both physically and in the way that was far more common than anyone realized, mentally, as the scars of shellshock and trauma, not always visible at first sight, took a long time to heal and in many cases, never did.

Things were also chaotic on the labour front. In addition to the lack of jobs available for all the returning soldiers, the Unions now began to play up as well, demanding (not without cause) to know where the fruits of victory were, and why Prime Minister David Lloyd George had talked about a "country fit for heroes to live in" when there were so many obvious signs of poverty, appalling houses and zero health facilities to stop the many illnesses that kept sweeping the land causing unnecessary deaths and misery.

Kirkcaldy would of course make its own legitimate protest against such things on March 4 1921 when it shocked Scotland by voting for a Labour candidate, called Tom Kennedy, at a by-election, and by this time, there were clear signs that things were beginning to improve at Stark's Park. Logan had, for example, assembled a mighty half-back line of Raeburn, Morris and Collier, and as was always the case in the 1920s, the half back line was the mainstay of the team.

Logan had made loads of contacts in his war years, and two of these men Jimmy Raeburn and David Morris were tip-offs from the junior ranks – Raeburn from Tranent and Morris from Newtongrange Star – whereas Collier was a local boy. But good teams take a long time to bed in, and although season 1920/21 was better than the previous one, the team was still a long way away from where they would have liked to be. Yet a few straws in the wind were seen towards the end of that season, particularly on April 9. While most attention was being paid to the Scotland v England International at Hampden Park, Raith Rovers beat Celtic 2-0 at Stark's Park.

It was by no means Celtic's best side, but it was a significant victory nonetheless, and Rovers' hero was a man called John Duncan, nicknamed "Tokey", presumably because of his ability to "toe-poke" the ball in from close distance.

"Oh Charlie Shaw, he never saw

Where Tokey Duncan pit the baw"

He pit the baw richt in the net

An' Charlie Shaw sat doon and gret"

This was the song born that day – Charlie Shaw being Celtic's legendary goalkeeper – and although Rangers supporters stole it and made Alan Morton do the scoring, the song originated in Kirkcaldy. It is no coincidence that it goes to the tune of "The Red Flag", a song that was heard often in those turbulent times of the early 1920s,

Duncan was a local boy who had joined the club from Lochgelly in 1918, so he was not really a Logan signing, but Logan saw the talent there and gave him every encouragement even to the extent of bringing his brother Tommy to the club as well. The brothers Duncan formed a mighty right-wing, and although the club lost unluckily to Rangers in the last League game of the season, there was hope that things might be on the mend for the Kirkcaldy side. No-one knew, however, just how good things were going to be, as Brown, Inglis and Moyes; Raeburn, Morris and Collier; T Duncan J Duncan, Jennings, Bauld and Archibald began to assemble themselves as Raith Rovers greatest ever team.

Season 1921/22 is often regarded as Raith Rovers best ever season. Yet it was disappointing as well, for, although the team finished third in the Scottish League, they were a distant 16 points behind winners Celtic, and received a major blow when they exited the Scottish Cup anonymously to Clyde at Shawfield one wet Wednesday afternoon, after they had failed to beat the Glasgow men at Stark's Park the previous Saturday.

But the team were consistently impressive winning plaudits and admiration from the national press and from men like Willie Maley, the manager of Celtic. Will Collier, the left half, became Raith Rovers second

Internationalist when he was invited to play for Scotland against Wales at Wrexham on February 4. Logan was of course delighted at the success of this young man, but Collier could, for a number of reasons, count himself very unlucky that this was his first and last game for Scotland.

He was genuinely depressed at having gone out of the Scottish Cup at Clyde a couple of days before the Scotland party travelled to Wales on February 3. It was also true that the weather conditions were dreadful. The referee, Mr Ward of England, might well have put the game off had he not been afraid of some disorder from the large travelling support of "Caledonians". Scotland playing with a ball looking like a "Xmas pudding covered in white sauce" went down 1-2, and Collier was one of those blamed for the defeat.

Raith Rovers won comfortably at Clydebank that day after Logan had not minced his words in what he thought of their performance on Wednesday afternoon, and from then on, no Rovers team was accused of being half-hearted, finishing their programme with a 1-0 win over Hamilton Accies at Stark's Park. For a provincial team like Raith Rovers, finishing third was a great feat.

Logan was clearly on the crest of a wave, and the fact that he was at that point working for an ambitious Board of Directors was seen when the team went to Denmark in the summer. Foreign travel was in vogue in the 1920s, and although Raith were not quite so adventurous as Third Lanark who went all the way to South America, their Danish tour of 1922 was followed a year later with a trip to the Canary Islands, suffering what might, with a touch of exaggeration, be called a shipwreck on the way there. What happened was the ship ran aground through the incompetence of the captain, and everyone was rescued with a degree of ease, but it must nevertheless have been a scary moment for Logan and his men.

A further example of the ambition of the club at this point in their history is seen in their commitment to build a new stand. It was much needed, the previous one having been burned in a fire towards the end of the Great War, and of course it still remains today – a curious L shaped construction which is one of the landmarks of Scottish football. It could never stretch the length of the park because of the shape of Pratt Street. It was worked on through most of the summer and autumn of 1922, and eventually was officially opened by Viscount Novar before the start of the game against Celtic on December 30 1922.

This of course had to be paid for, and Logan would have been distressed (although he possibly, at this stage, saw the reason for it and the thinking behind it), when the two Duncans were sold to Leicester City in July 1922. The loss of John Duncan, in particular, was a blow, for "Tokey" had been a prolific scorer for the club, and he would eventually win a Scottish cap against Wales in October 1925, scoring the first goal in Scotland's 3-0 victory.

His departure might have cost the club dear, had it not been for the fact that they had a Manager, at the peak of his powers with driving ambition, who immediately set about rebuilding the club's forward line, so that in a couple of years the Duncans had more or less been forgotten about, and Rovers had a new hero to cheer about.

This was a man called Alec James. Logan probably had nothing directly to do with the bringing of James to

Kirkcaldy – this was always attributed to Mr. Morrison, one of the Directors – but the moment that Logan saw him, he recognized that there was something special in this youngster. Yet there was also something unprepossessing about this boy. He was small and rather scrawny – even by the appalling standards of the 1920s he would have been looked upon as a weakling – he suffered from rheumatism (a surprisingly common complaint among young men of that time but put down to damp houses with inadequate heating and ventilation) and he wore baggy pants which almost reached to his knees!

But he could play. Sometimes *The Fife Free Press* criticizes him for over doing the trickery and the fancy football, but more often they (and the supporters) were in raptures at his play. The fact that he was so small meant that all the matronly ladies fell in love with him, and in any case everyone, now for the past 10 years indoctrinated by the concept of "gallant little Belgium" getting the better of the bullying Kaiser, enjoyed the sight of a small man making a fool of huge, brutal defenders.

From his debut at Celtic Park in September 1922, it was clear that Rovers had something special here. James ("Jimmy" to the supporters) was played in both inside positions and was soon a hero with the fans. Occasionally prone to selfishness and trouble making, and not always the easiest of men to get on with in the eyes of his team mates, James needed firm handling. Logan was exactly the man to deal with him, frequently taking him to one side, telling him how good he was but also warning him that the team was the thing. Playing for what was perceived as a poor team would not help his individual career. Raith Rovers therefore must never be allowed to become a poor team.

Not that Raith could in any way be described as an under-performing outfit in season 1922/23. They ended up ninth, some six places down on 1921/22, but considering the size of the town and the support, they did remarkably well. On December 30 when the new stand was opened Celtic won easily, but the Glasgow men were a great deal less impressive when Rovers went to Parkhead on Scottish Cup business in late February, and contemporary accounts indicated that Rovers were worth a draw. Then on March 10 1923 came one of their best ever performances when Brown; Inglis and Moyes; Raeburn, Morris and Collier; Bell, Miller, Jennings, James and Archibald beat Rangers 2-0.

By this time, Logan had nurtured another great Rovers player and brought him to International recognition. This was centre half David Morris, a man who could "head a ball further than most could kick it" in the opinion of one who saw him. Not only was he a great player, he was also a great leader. Logan saw Morris as a man in his own mould and he did all he could to encourage him. Morris made his Scotland debut on March 3 1923 in Belfast – not the easiest of places to visit in the 1920s in the wake of the ongoing Irish troubles – and played brilliantly as Scotland beat Ireland 1-0. For reasons lost in the arcane minds of the Scottish selectors he was not chosen for the other two Scotland Internationals that season – losing his place to Celtic's Willie Cringan (a fine player as well, it must be said), but his moment of real Scottish glory was yet to come.

Summer 1923 was of course the year of the trip to the Canary Islands and the shipwreck, but the following season was another great season. They finished fourth behind Rangers, Airdrie and Celtic. The football played by the team was consistently good, and included two successive weeks in March when Rangers and Celtic were beaten 1-0, and was characterized by an alleged bizarre attempt (possibly owing more to journalistic fantasy than reality) by Millwall (of all teams) to buy the whole Rovers forwards line of Bell, Miller, Jennings, James and Archibald for no less than £50,000!

A moment's pause will immediately cause the reader to realize that this was indeed fantasy. In 1923, £50,000 was a gigantic amount and it is hard to see how a 3rd Division team from the poorer, dockland area of London could in the hard times of the early 1920s afford anything like such an amount. But Logan was clever enough not to deny it. It showed these five excellent players in a good light and it showed Logan himself in an even better light, for he it was who had fashioned and moulded them into the "£50,000 forward line". In truth, with the possible exception of James, none of these players was worth anything like £10,000 each, but it was a handy myth to keep going.

The supporters of Raith Rovers needed something to cheer them in the 1920s. These were grim times. The war wounded were admitted free and particular attention given to the war blinded in the shape of a commentator who would tell them what was happening, but so many people simply struggled to get the one shilling necessary for admission. Coal miners were still comparatively well treated in terms of wages – this would of course be the cause of the General Strike in 1926 – but the linoleum industry was struggling to get back on its feet, not helped of course by the virtual total destruction of the German market. Peace had certainly not brought the much promised "land fit for heroes to live in".

Logan's great team of the early 1920s. Logan is standing on the extreme right

Thank heavens then that the working classes still had football! Kirkcaldy revelled in the great team that Logan was producing, but the 1923/24 season was not without its moments of controversy and in one of them, in particular, a question must be asked of James Logan.

The prodigious Alec James, like many talented Scottish players throughout the ages, seemed to have embarked on a wayward path towards self-destruction, sometimes earning the wrath of the local press for his selfishness and wasting of the ball, and continuing showing off and playing to the gallery. This could be coped with because his good points still out-weighed his bad ones, but when in early November he was sent off in two successive weeks and would eventually be suspended for 14 days, it was apparent that there was a serious problem here.

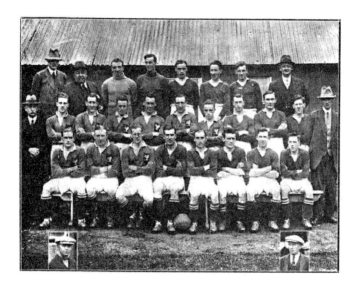

Raith Rovers in 1924. Logan is at the back on the extreme left. Alec James is in the front row on the extreme right

The first sending off was at Love Street in what was acknowledged to be a really tough game with James "not the only offender". That phrase, however, admits that the sending off was probably justified in the rough house, even though it was easy for the referee to send off the little man, who probably did not help his cause by arguing the toss.

The following week's sending off was at home to Falkirk. This was a funny one because James was apparently sent off for arguing after Raith Rovers had converted a penalty (!) but did not go. The referee had not noticed that he had not gone until he was involved in another incident, being "in grips" with an opposition player. He definitely went this time. Whatever had happened, it was clear that Logan had a problem to deal with in this player.

The pressure must have been on Logan to drop James, to transfer him anonymously to some minor team or to keep him out of football altogether, for he was becoming a liability to the club. But to his credit, Logan persevered with him, seeing a great deal of talent there in the same way that Jock Stein went the extra mile, time and time again, for Jimmy Johnstone. Had Logan not supported James at this crucial and vulnerable time of his life, there might have been no Wembley Wizard and no Arsenal legend.

That was to Logan's credit, but February 23 1924 was the day which probably guaranteed Logan's departure a couple of years later, and the departure of some of his great players a great deal earlier than that. The club were still doing well, and having easily defeated Broxburn and then (gloriously, in a replay) Dundee in earlier rounds of the Scottish Cup, they now seemed to have an easy passage into the quarter final when they were drawn against St Bernard's at Stark's Park.

St Bernard's (now defunct) were a team who played in Stockbridge, Edinburgh. They had won the Scottish Cup in 1895 (Logan himself had played for them a few years later) but had fallen on hard times and were now in the Second Division. It looked that Rovers were odds on to win, and those who liked a flutter (illegal, but nevertheless widespread, in 1924) would have been inclined to back on the Rovers.

A cigarette card of Dave Morris, arguably Logan's best ever player

But Will Collier's father knew differently. Will himself was out of the team with a bad injury at this time, but was still close enough to the action to tell his father what was going on. Collier senior went about his place of work in the linoleum factory, telling everyone to bet on a draw. Raith Rovers Directors had, apparently, refused to pay the players a bonus to beat a Second Division team, so the players had, allegedly, decided to draw the game, putting a large amount of money (discreetly through various anonymous sources) on that result with local (and illegal) bookmakers, then win the game in the Stockbridge replay on the Wednesday. It would be their way of getting a "bonus".

No-one will ever know what exactly happened at Stark's Park that day of February 23 1924. The facts are that Raith pressed and pressed, couldn't (or didn't) score with several chances put over the bar, then late in the game St Bernard's (who presumably were either not involved in the deal or refused to co-operate) scored a late goal after an uncharacteristic Dave Morris mistake, and Raith's frantic attempts to equalize came to nothing. The Second Division team, who had seemed to be in irreversible decline from their great days of last century, had pulled off one of the shocks of this and several other seasons.

The full time whistle came with Stark's Park in "shellshock", according to the local press. The mixture of boos and stony silence told its own story, for now everyone began to believe all the stories that had been circulating the town for the past few days, and there was even a certain feeling of a team getting its just deserts, and that they deserved all that they got. They had tried to cheat the system, ignoring the interests of their supporters, and had failed. Nemesis had come in a big way.

Fortunately, no prosecution ever took place – it could never, of course, be proved, although the local press hotched with innuendo and speculation – and the club moved on, although their reputation was severely impaired, but the whole nasty business leaves several questions to be asked of Manager James Logan. The best interpretation was that there was no scam and that everything was as it seemed on the surface. Logan's talented side simply had a bad day. Not many people thought that way at the time, but it might have of course been true ("bad days" were by no means impossible even in a good season like 1923/24) Certainly St Bernard's had a good day and it may be that Logan is guilty of no more than underestimating the opposition. Rangers at Berwick in 1967, Celtic at Clyde in 2006 and Aberdeen at Stenhousemuir in 1995 are guilty of the same thing.

But if there was something shady going on, we must ask whether Logan was involved. Judging by the rest of his career and his general integrity and reputation, this seems unlikely. What is more feasible is that Logan was genuinely unaware of what was going on. In which case he stands accused of naivety, but not corruption. Or he may have been aware of the conspiracy – everyone in Kirkcaldy on the Friday before the game seems to have heard a few whispers – and he was either unable or unwilling to take a stand and stop it. He may have decided to act like an ostrich and put his head in the sand and hope it all went away. It was certainly a nasty, unpleasant business, and it would be a long time, well over 30 years, before Raith Rovers really recovered from this devastating blow.

The irony was that 1924 was the year in which Raith Rovers could have won the Scottish Cup. Things had changed since the war – there was now a Labour Government in power, for example, and in football, as in everything else, there was a new order. Since 1920, Kilmarnock, Partick Thistle and Morton had already won the Scottish Cup. In 1924, Celtic were already out, and on that same day of the Raith catastrophe, Rangers went down to Hibs. The Scottish Cup final would that year be won by Airdrie beating Hibs 2-0, and both of these teams were definitely within the compass of Raith Rovers. Dave Morris, the centre half who made the fatal error, was certainly forgiven as far as Scotland were concerned for he found himself at centre half for Scotland in their first ever visit to the mighty stadium called Wembley on April 12 1924. He played well, too, in the creditable 1-1 draw.

But summer 1924 saw the beginning of the end of the great side. Those who criticized players for greed, pointing to the distressing events of February 23, have a point. But holding up the Directors as some sort of moral guardians will not wash either. With scant respect for the feelings of their loyal supporters, the Directors began a massive programme of asset stripping. It would not have been so bad if there had been any huge financial necessity. What happened seemed to supporters, to the local Press and to Logan himself as little other than pocket lining by those who professed love for the club and its supporters, but whose real motives were a great deal more suspect than that. In later times, attitudes have hardly changed.

By the start of the 1924/25 season, Collier, Inglis and Archibald were away. Hardly surprisingly, two things happened that season – one was that the performances of the team declined, and so too did the attendances. To an extent, one can blame tough economic times, but that is only half the story, and then the supporters and Logan were delivered another kick in the teeth with the selling of Tom Jennings to Leeds United in March 1925. The crowd turned nasty as well with frequent cries of "St Bernard's" – a reference to last year's dodgy and as yet unexplained events – heard from the sullen and unhappy terraces. The supporters had been shown a taste of the good life. It had now been taken away from them.

How Logan felt during all this is hard to say. Possibly a bit of him thought that one had to be realistic about being the Manager of a small team – the supporters of Airdrieonians were about to see a similar piece of asset-stripping throughout the 1920s – but it was galling all the same to have been on the brink of some major Scottish triumph and then to see it all being taken away from him.

But season 1924/25 still had its good points. There was still "Jimmy" – Alex James, an endless source of trickery and craft. Much loved by the fans, James probably could be guaranteed to add a few hundred to the gate every week. The sheer attraction of the little man with the curious baggy pants taking on the brutal defenders which seemed to abound in every team in the 1920s had of course a subliminal attraction. As well as "gallant little Belgium" fans subconsciously saw Charlie Chaplin against the bully – a common motif in the 1920s cinema, and possibly, closer to home, the workers against the capitalists. Logan realized all this, and did all he could to encourage James. He was not always the easiest of men to handle, but Logan was always prepared to go the extra mile for his talented talisman as the local press went into overdrive with words like "gem" and "jewel", being quite prepared to quote Robert Burns with

"Why did go make the gem so small, and why so huge the granite?

Because he hoped mankind would set the greater value on it!"

But 1925 was also the apogee of another of Logan's star men, Dave Morris. Scotland won the Home International Championship that year beating Wales 3-1 in the heavy rain at Tynecastle, Ireland 3-0 in Belfast and then, gloriously, England 2-0 at Hampden on April 4 – and Dave Morris of Raith Rovers was the captain! Logan was, of course, only indirectly involved in all this, but he must have taken a great deal of pride as he watched his protegee skipper great men like Willie McStay, Hughie Gallacher, Tommy Cairns and Alan Morton to what was, and arguably remains, Scotland's greatest ever year. What a shame there was as yet no World Cup, to prove what everyone already knew – namely that Scotland were the best team in the world!

All this of course did not solve the problems of Raith Rovers who were now beginning to struggle without their star players who had already gone, and the new season opened with colossal and seemingly never-ending speculation about the sale of more players. It was in fact Preston North End who stepped in for Logan's two star men – Alec James in September 1925 and Dave Morris three months later just before Christmas in December. Logan was devastated.

To an extent, one can sympathise with the usual clichés turned out by selling clubs about needing to sell to survive – but only to an extent. Football fans are interested in seeing a successful team, and are less enthusiastic about Directors lining their pockets. In recent years, of course, we in Scotland have seen some spectacular bankruptcies and big teams going into administration – in many cases because of profligacy in the transfer market and we should always be aware of the need to balance the books. Some wise transfers may indeed be necessary from time to time, but in 1925, when football was in a boom and when everyone on town talked incessantly about the fortunes of their favourite club, was not the time when players HAD to be sold – or at least they did not have to be sold with such obvious enthusiasm and relish!

Logan of course was wise enough to understand the economics of the game, but he was also bright enough to see what was going on here. How it hurt when the team went downhill with the speed of an express train, going from 4th in 1924 to relegation in 1926! How it hurt when the boos and the abuse from the dwindling support began to be directed at him, the man who had been a local celebrity for the past 14 years as a player before the war, war hero in 1916 and manager of the best team that the town had seen in the early 1920s!

He announced his resignation in the middle of the General Strike of 1926 at the end of the desperately unhappy 1925/26 season. *The Fifeshire Advertiser*, unable because of the strike to produce a full newspaper but nevertheless able to issue a typewritten news sheet to denounce AJ Cook, the miners and the TUC, hints at the reason for Logan's departure when it said that "many of the Rover's (sic) players who were involved in the past season's transfer rush were spotted by him". Logan did not take kindly to the dismantling of his team. Football meant more to him than money did.

He seems to have decided to give football a rest for a spell and we next hear of him becoming "mine host" of the Airlie Arms Hotel in Kirriemuir, where he would regale the locals with stories of the fine players that he had developed, no doubt rail against those who sold them and occasionally turn up at Station Park, Forfar or Dens Park, Dundee to watch a game. He also no doubt kept an eye on the talent that he had been forced to let go to England, but with one exception, it could fairly be said that all these players enjoyed their best days at Stark's Park, rather than England. Collier and Morris in particular lapsed into anonymity in England.

The exception was of course Alec James who earned immortality by being a Wembley Wizard in the great 5-1 victory of 1928, then winning Cups and Leagues with

Arsenal, his best years coinciding with those of Arsenal's legendary manager Herbert Chapman. Logan would have been proud of all that, but in 1930 he returned to Kirkcaldy. At one point he ran a tobacconist's shop on the High Street – a lucrative trade in the days when everyone smoked – and then in December 1930, at what would have to be described as a low point of the fortunes of Raith Rovers who were now in the Second Division, James Logan was re-appointed Manager.

This decision, an uncharacteristically wise one from the Board, engendered a certain amount of enthusiasm in the town, and hopes were expressed that the talismanic Logan might resurrect the moribund Rovers and bring them back to where they belonged – the First Division. A return to the halcyon days of 1922 and 1924 seemed to beckon.

But things were against Logan. The team was poor, the town was suffering more than most towns from the horrendous economic depression, and although interest in football remained high (as always), gates were poor in spite of laudable attempts by clubs to introduce an "unemployed gate" to allow more impoverished supporters to watch the game.

Lacking players of any real talent – "honest journeyman" was a good description of most of them, Raith Rovers nevertheless made a decent effort to get promotion in 1931, but lost out to Third Lanark and Dundee United. 1932 also saw the team do well in the Second Division but a late season collapse (which included heavy defeats at Dumbarton and East Stirlingshire, and a pitiful home defeat to an incredulous Forfar) did nothing to dispel the commonly held belief that the Directors lacked ambition and that they didn't want promotion and the extra expense that it would entail.

Such allegations (they would surface again in 1981) are damaging and difficult to disprove, but the result led to low morale and lower attendances. Logan, reluctant to give in and constantly at odds with the Directors over major issues like transfers, soldiered on through mediocrity in season 1932/33 before resigning in September 1933, stating that he wished to concentrate on his shop in the High Street but also seeing fit to deliver a broadside at his former employers. No customer entered his shop without being aware of the strength of the opinions of the kindly but dignified Mr. Logan, sometimes still referred to as "the Manager" because of his football record or "the Captain" because of his military career.

The rest of his life passed without any reference to Raith Rovers. Football remained in his blood – he was manager of Wrexham for a few years before the Second World War – and he died in Edinburgh in 1961. The local press mentions his passing, but does not make a big issue of it. This is a shame, because it would be hard to find anyone in the 130 and more years of Raith Rovers who made more of a contribution. A great player, a war hero, and inspiring Manager who would have done a great deal more if those who were running the club had shared his ambition.

Michael Nairn
1804-1858

The name Nairn is more or less synonymous with Kirkcaldy. The "queer like smell" so immortalised in the poem of the boy on the train is of course that of linoleum and it is indeed a very distinctive one, noticeable still on occasion in the 21st century, well over 150 years after the first time that the (not entirely unpleasant odour) reached the nostrils of the Kirkcaldy population for the first time.

The story of Michael Nairn (not to be confused with his son Michael Barker Nairn) is an epic Victorian one of enterprise and capitalism (but with a benevolent and philanthropic face, if we can believe all we are told!) involving hard work, risk taking, innovating and at the end of the day producing something that has left its mark on future ages.

Being born in 1804 and dying in 1858 compels Nairn to have lived in interesting times, irrespective of what he himself did with his life. His boyhood coincided with the Napoleonic wars. That war did not necessarily impact on a child's life in the way that the two massive wars of the 20th century did on the children of their age, but an 11 year old cannot fail to have been enthused, for example, when the news reached Kirkcaldy of the Battle of Waterloo. It is also an uncomfortable fact, not always acknowledged, that wars do bring with them a certain amount of prosperity. There is often a period of readjustment when the peacetime market for certain goods collapses, but very soon there is a demand for the necessities of war, notably weapons and uniforms. Kirkcaldy's weavers would soon find themselves, for example, making material for the "sodgers".

Conversely, sadly, peace brings its economic problems. The euphoria of Waterloo in 1815 and the defeat of "Boney" (as Napoleon Bonaparte was called) did not last long. A slump in trade inevitably followed, and the Government had to resort to repressive measures to keep the eager, but rebellious, populace down. As happened 100 years later in the 1920s, those who had fought and made sacrifices during the war felt entitled to some of the fruits of victory, and when such fruits were not forthcoming, trouble was likely.

It was the era of the "Gag Acts" and the Peterloo massacre. Everyone thought that George Stephenson was mad when he claimed to have invented the "gridiron", the metal box that moved without horses and which caused such distress to peasants and horses with its noise and steam. It would be 20 years before it reached Kirkcaldy, but Nairn would soon spot and exploit its potential.

Parliament would be reformed, slavery would be abolished, and the Poor Law would be amended, but they would still talk about the "hungry thirties" as the Chartists and the Anti-Corn Law League protested about the excesses of poverty during Nairn's early working life as Michael, with all his frugality and prudence, lived a life that was generally financially secure (although there was no guarantee that this standard of living would last) but by no means opulent.

When Michael was in his infancy, the Parish Church, by now in some danger of falling apart, was rebuilt into what is more or less the same building as the Old Kirk is today. Nairn did not seem to have been directly involved, but like everyone else in the town, he would have been shocked to the core by the collapse of the gallery in June 1828, involving as it did so many deaths in the panic that ensued. Clearly faulty design or workmanship was to blame, and it was a long time before people felt happy about returning to Church.

The Kirk tower remained from medieval times, with no clear record of when it was built (something which in itself indicates a certain antiquity) but the Church itself was only twenty years old. Religious affairs played a huge part in everyone's life in the 1830s, and 1843 saw the Church fall out with itself. The business of the Queen being allowed to appoint ministers, a clearly outdated idea, led to the Free Church establishing itself throughout Scotland as ministers, including Dr John Alexander of Kirkcaldy Parish Church, walking out with some of their congregations to found a Church which would be "free" of Royal interference. In time, and long after Michael's death, Kirkcaldy Free Church would build a fine new building for itself, later called St Brycedale and now St Bryce Church, a great deal of the money for the erection of this building coming from the profits of Nairn's linoleum industry.

The young Queen Victoria came to the throne in 1837. Only 19, she was nevertheless a clear and obvious improvement on her two crazy uncles who had held the throne before her – the profligate wastrel George IV, deservedly pilloried and ridiculed in the modern TV series "Blackadder" and then the quixotic and unpredictable William IV, called, not without cause, "silly billy". The young Queen married a German and the pair became immensely popular with all classes, introducing things like a postal service, Christmas trees and Christmas cards, while Charles Dickens began to write immensely popular and certainly entertaining but sometimes bitingly satirical novels about orphanages, paupers and debtors' prisons.

Robert Peel, the man who founded a police force to counter lawlessness in London, became Prime Minister in the early 1840s. His reform of the Corn Laws, much resisted by the reactionaries in his own party, was a brave effort to reduce the price of food for the starving, but it came too late to avert the appalling effects of the Irish potato famine of 1846, something for which the Irish have never forgiven Great Britain to this day. The starving Irish would appear to have had the support of the two richest institutions of the day, namely the British

Empire and the Roman Catholic Church. It has to be said that neither of the two of them lifted a finger to help the Irish, who were forced to flee to Canada, the USA, Australia, England and Scotland, with not a few arriving in Kirkcaldy, mainly in the Pathhead area which, like Lochee in Dundee, became known as "little Tip" (i.e. Tipperary). Nairn would be able to employ some of them.

Another cause of the swelling of population had of course been the Highland Clearances, something that had been going on since the Jacobite Rebellion of the previous century, when the landlords (for whom little forgiveness is possible, any more than one can look with compassion on their Irish counterparts) simply cleared the peasants off the land to make way for cattle and sheep. They did so, of course, with the whole hearted support of the Church, who no doubt told everyone that it was the "will of God", and that in any case suffering was good for you! The Church thus, as in later years, showed its dismal propensity to side uncompromisingly with the rich against the poor!

Soon after Nairn established himself in the early 1850s, Britain, after a long period of peace found herself at war in the Crimea, along with their erstwhile foes the French and against the nation that many thought were the real enemy all the time, the Russians. While this war was portrayed as "heroic" and "patriotic", and certainly yielded many legends and heroes in the shape of Florence Nightingale, the charge of the Light Brigade and a garment called a "balaclava", the reality was that this was an ill-thought-out and foolish piece of imperialistic glory hunting, for which the Queen was quite right to observe that "we are not amused" in the context of the dreadful amount of casualties. That particular quote is often wrongly assigned to the Queen in the context of disapproval of some sexual behaviour, but she and Albert said it about something that was far more serious!

A year before Nairn died in 1858, we had the Indian Mutiny, the causes of which were diverse, but it was basically a protest by Indians (so often described in the British press as "backward" and "ungrateful") at the rape of their land by the British. The Indians did not necessarily see the building of railways as progress, even though it did make it easier for the British to transport their goods, and they had been awaiting impatiently for any improvement in their living conditions that the British occupation could bring them. The violence on both sides and the repression and the reprisals afterwards were appalling. The notion of "pax Britannica" took a rather severe knock, for peace and tranquillity were certainly not evident here!

Thus quite a great deal was going on during Nairn's lifetime, but even all these events detailed above were secondary to the massive Industrial Revolution which, basically, lasted all the 19th century, as more and more people came to live in large cities, some of whom like Glasgow and Manchester grew phenomenally – and Kirkcaldy took part in this growth - and large factories fairly rapidly replaced the cottage industries which had existed before.

The down side of all this has been well documented. Child labour, child mortality, poverty, starvation, gin drinking, filth, workhouses and degradation have all been well detailed by first hand sources like Charles Dickens and others. It is hard to equate this with any idea of "progress", but the Victorians are not entirely wrong to claim a credit side to their life. A start was made, at least, to consider the welfare of the poor, to educate children (Scotland had of course always been better than England in this respect because of the emphasis that the Church put on parish schooling) and for a few enlightened employers to put into practice their plans for making profits for themselves certainly (and that was always the priority) but in so doing to give their employees a decent standard of living and a little self-respect and pride in their work. Robert Owen was the best known of this category but a reasonable claim can be made to include Michael Nairn among those who professed "enlightened self-interest".

It is important to realise however and to stress that, as far as the Nairn family were concerned, this was no "rags to riches" story. The Nairn family were emphatically not poor. They were comfortable, middle class (if such a term means anything in the early 19th century) and already well known in the town when Michael was born in 1804. Nor is it particularly true at the other end of Michael's life, that wealth had taken over the household. He died in comfortable surroundings, certainly, but the family had not yet reached the colossal wealth of Croesus that his son would reach by the time that he died in 1915. All the time of his life, Michael Nairn remained considerably better off than the rest of the Kirkcaldy population, but he was never one of the mega-rich.

Michael Nairn was the third son of John Nairn and Isobel Barker. Little is known for certain of his father. The family tradition was weaving, but John himself is reported as having been, at several times, a grocer and then a shoemaker, but he was rich enough and important enough in Kirkcaldy to have been made in 1786 a "burgess", a member of the self-perpetuating oligarchy of those whose faces fitted the picture, as it were, and who basically ran the town, filling all the duties of magistrates and councillors. Being an "elder" of the Kirk was often a concomitant position.

Not a great deal is known of the childhood of Michael Nairn, but it is hard to imagine that he would not have been deeply affected by the sea, as Adam Smith had been eighty years earlier. The Forth of course was a very busy place in the Napoleonic War, not necessarily with a huge traffic in war ships but more in trade with places like Russia, Denmark and Holland, as steam ships brought raw materials for Kirkcaldy's weavers and spinners to make into linen and canvas. It was indeed weaving that Michael became interested in, and there is a tradition that he went to Dundee to learn the craft. He was clearly a success, for by 1825 there is a mention of him as a "manufacturer" in Linktown of Abbotshall.

He did not have the same misfortune as another manufacturer called David Landale who in 1826 took part in Scotland's last duel, in which he killed a banker called George Morgan. Morgan had been spreading rumours in his bank about Landale being in debt and unable to pay his way; Landale challenged him to a duel and shot him. Naturally Nairn would have been aware of all this; in fact, he may even have been at Cardenbarns on the fatal morning of August 2 1826 when Morgan was shot dead. If so, he would he would have realised that violence is no answer to anything, but that hard work and endeavour was.

But it was 1828, a year known for an even darker event in Kirkcaldy, which saw things really begin to happen as far as the establishment of the Nairn dynasty was concerned. June 1828, as we have observed, saw the saddest day of Kirkcaldy Parish Church when the gallery on the north side of the Church collapsed causing multiple deaths and injuries. It was caused by the appearance of the famous preacher Edward Irving, the son in law of the minister Mr Martin, entering the Church as a guest preacher. As everyone in the gallery leaned forward, a crack was heard and a total of 28 people were killed.

But that same year also saw Michael Nairn, now a burgess, like his father before him, open a factory in what is now Coal Wynd for the purpose of weaving canvas. This factory, of which traces of the building remain, was quite large and possibly provided employment for about 20 or 30 people. It was a bold venture for a 24 year old man to enter into, and he moved house in order to do so. He moved from Linktown into Kirkcaldy itself, bought a house near the Port Brae end of the High Street (or Main Street as it was then known) and his factory was situated on the eminence above his house.

His intention would have been, one imagines, to sell canvas as sails for the sailing ships that started and ended their journeys in Kirkcaldy, although the heyday of sailing ships was passing in favour of steam ships which were of course more reliable and faster. But Nairn worked unstintingly at his trade, putting in long hours and always being prepared to travel throughout Britain to research his market, and to build up a network of contacts. It was through this hard work and travel that he began to realise that canvas was being used more and more as backing material for the floor cloth industry that had been developing slowly for some time.

This gave him an idea. If he was successfully selling canvas as floor cloth backing, why did not try to make his own floor cloth? He was aware that floor cloth was hardly a new idea, but he was also aware that it was still considered a luxury, miles away from the pocket of even the emergent and growing middle classes, let alone the working classes. If someone could perfect floor cloth at an economic price for more people, this idea would surely be a winner. It would of course all depend on quality and fine balance between outlaying enough money to guarantee that it would be good, paying his workers enough to ensure loyalty and "ownership" and pride in the product, yet keeping prices sufficiently low to ensure that enough families would be able to buy it.

SCOTTISH FLOOR CLOTH
MANUFACTORY,
KIRKALDY.

MICHAEL NAIRN,
FLOOR CLOTH MANUFACTURER.

THE ONLY MANUFACTURER OF THE ABOVE DESCRIPTION IN SCOTLAND.

The whole of the Fabric Manufactured on the Premises, from
Half-a-Yard to Eight Yards wide, WITHOUT SEAM.

Another factor that Nairn was aware of was that, although there were several factories of floor cloth in England, there were none as yet in Scotland. In fact, the furthest north was Newcastle, and Nairn realised that the economy of Scotland was now expanding at a phenomenal rate, particularly in the Central Belt between Edinburgh and Glasgow where there was a well-used and successful canal, and that the market was there, if he could grasp the opportunity.

Yet another factor was the railway. Railways had proliferated throughout Great Britain in the 1830s. There had been some initial resistance and indeed fear of these noisy and dirty monstrosities, but people soon saw their value as goods and passengers could now be transported across the country at a phenomenal rate, far faster than the stage coach or even the steam ship, let alone the old sailing boats. But the progress had been patchy, and Fife had until the late 1840s been virtually excluded from the rapid expansion of the railways, whereas there was already a vibrant railway in other parts of Scotland, like between Forfar and Arbroath, for example.

The Civic Society unveils a plaque to Michael Nairn on the site of his "folly"

Nairn on his travels had seen the benefits of rail travel. He was probably, in the 1840s, one of the few Langtonians who had ever travelled in a train, and he realised that if the railway were to come to Kirkcaldy (and there was every sign that it was not too far way, for Dundee and Edinburgh were not yet adequately connected and there was a need for this), he would have a great advantage in getting his product transported and sold. His judgement was vindicated when the railway did indeed come to Kirkcaldy.

Nevertheless, it was a big step to take. The canvas factory would have to be incorporated in the new business, but even so, a vast amount of capital would be required, and there would be no great guarantee of getting it back, at least in the short term. But he researched his market, built up a huge network of contacts, and in 1847, work began on his new factory.

The site was in Pathhead, near Nether Street and a few hundred yards to the west of Ravenscraig Castle. It was to be four storeys high from the land side, and higher from the sea side because of the slope, and it would be the largest building in Kirkcaldy, dominating the landscape and visible from sea. Even when it was being built between the years of 1847 and 1849, the building was the main talking point of the town. Some people, even his friends, were wondering whether Michael had taken leave of his senses and certainly wondered where the money was coming from. One suspects that Michael himself in his moments of weakness may have entertained similar doubts. But it was certainly providing loads of people with a job, and that had to be a good thing. Yet as his canvas factory in Coal Wynd was still in existence and even doing well, people began to look at the building and to call it "Nairn's Folly".

Nairn's Folly

The building of "follies" was something that Victorians did a great deal of. They were usually constructed by eccentric, excessively rich landlords, often with the laudable aim of providing employment for some of the people who lived on their estate, and were usually silly looking buildings, often left unfinished, as on Calton Hill in Edinburgh, for example. One can think of the Dunmore Pineapple (pineapples being looked upon as a particular symbol of effete opulence) near Falkirk, or McCaig's Tower in Oban. They were strange and bizarre, of no real economic value and of little practical use, even though they did add to the character of the area by their quirky nature. This is why they were called "follies".

But this one was different. It certainly looked, to an untrained eye, foolish to build such a thing. And it lacked any architectural beauty. In fact, quite a few complained that it detracted from the still imposing

Ravenscraig Castle nearby. It was indeed rather ugly, although no more so than other buildings of the Industrial Revolution like the Dundee jute mills or the Manchester cotton factories. It was not in any case the norm for Victorian planners to consider the architectural amenity of a building. The important thing was to get it built.

One must be careful when talking about "Nairn's folly" because the phrase has been used to describe other buildings in town, notably the strange shaped wall which meanders in and out at the bottom of the Ravenscraig Park. This indeed looks like a "folly" in the Victorian sense of the word, and it was built by the Nairn family when they owned the Ravenscraig Park, then known as Three Trees Park. Michael's descendants in the 1920s and 1930s did not like the way that miners from Dysart were able to use the Nairn family's private estate for the purposes of drinking alcohol and fornication. So a strange shaped wall, still in evidence today was erected. There was of course, in the 1920s and 1930s, an element of class war politics about this, but it must be stressed that this particular "Nairn's folly" was indeed foolish and counter-productive, because determined miners could climb over the wall for their nefarious purposes

Indeed, jokes circulated of the young man and woman who found the wall a barrier to their courtship as she asked him how on earth she was going to be able to climb the wall. He looked downwards and said she could use "that" as a foothold. She said that that would be all very well for getting over, but how on earth were they going to get back? The wall justifiably earned local ridicule in the 1930s, but it was not the original "Nairn's folly" which turned out to be no folly at all, but rather an astute piece of Victorian capitalist thinking.

Crucially the building was visible from both the new railway line and the sea so that potential customers could see it with its pompous and portentous name "Scottish Floor Cloth Manufactory" emblazoned on both sides of the building in large white letters. The choice of title was a good and shrewd one. It appealed to Scottish patriotism on the one hand and implied that this was the only place in Scotland where this new material called Floor Cloth was made – as indeed was the case. People would ask questions about what floor cloth was, and begin to think that it was a good idea because "ma wee laudie stood on a nail coming oot o the flairbaird the other day" etc. And that was if they were lucky enough to have floorboards at all! So many houses were just "floored" by earth.

As well as the visual advertising element, the factory was also close to both methods of transport. The sea and the harbour were adjacent, and Nairn knew that not only was it ten minutes' drive in a horse and cart from Kirkcaldy Station, it was even closer to the smaller projected station at Sinclairtown. The railway could thus connect him with Dundee in the north, and crucially Burntisland, and therefore Edinburgh and Glasgow in the south. It would of course be some fifty years and more before the Forth Railway Bridge was completed, but goods could be ferried to Edinburgh from Burntisland, and thence by train to England or by train or even canal to Glasgow.

The cost of this was to be £4,000 – a phenomenal amount in the middle of the 19th century – and clearly he had to borrow money to pay for it. He knew that even if it were to be successful, it would be some time before he was able to pay that sort of money back, but his credit was good. He was also fortunate in that he had a good woman beside him, his wife Catherine Ingram, a beautiful and charming lady some 11 years his junior, with whom he discussed financial matters and who backed him to the hilt, even if she herself knew that household economies would be, at least in the short term, essential.

He had married Catherine Ingram in the Kirkcaldy Parish Church on December 15 1834, the marriage conducted by the Rev John Martin. Michael is described as a Manufacturer and the son of James Nairn a Resident in Kirkcaldy, while Catherine is described as the daughter of the late Alex Ingram, a Bleacher. She was to be a great support to him all their married life, but in 1834 she was just a charming young girl, not yet 20. Five weeks previously, Michael's sister, Isabella, had married in the same church one Charles Melville, the "Parochial Schoolmaster" of the town.

As with many families in the Victorian age, unhappiness and tragedy was never far away. Michael and Catherine had 8 children, 5 of whom made it to adulthood but tragically three of them didn't. There was Alexander, for example, the second eldest who was born in 1836 and died in 1837, and then the double tragedy of early 1852 when two boys James born 1845 and Peter born 1847 both died of one of the many fevers that swept through towns in the mid-19th century, sparing neither rich nor poor. The Kirkcaldy Old Kirk Burial Records tell us that the two boys were buried on the same day, March 5 1852, and both in the same coffin.

The frequency of child deaths did not in any way make them easier to cope with, and this must have been a devastating blow to the family, but there are of course two ways of dealing with the situation. One can choose to mope and invite that most deleterious of emotions, self-pity, to take over (Queen Victoria herself, spectacularly, chose that course for at least 10 years after her husband Prince Albert died in 1861) or one can take it on the chin, mourn for a spell – but then fight back! The latter course Nairn clearly adopted. His two boys died just as his business was beginning to make headway, and it seems that Michael Nairn decided that he would immerse himself in his business, possibly even to the detriment of his own health, for it was his way of coping with unspeakable grief. Apart from anything else, he owed it to his wife and his surviving children to guarantee their financial well-being.

This of course is another factor that we, almost two centuries later, tend to forget. There was no economic safety net, if a business failed. Bankruptcies and factory closures were common, and Victorian society showed little mercy to the victims. "The higher they climb, the harder they fall" was often the answer to a business which collapsed, and the only recourse for an impoverished family was to get into debt, the inadequate and patronising parish relief or the "poor house" (usually called the workhouse in England and much lampooned by men like Charles Dickens). Michael Nairn had no option but to work hard at his business.

The Fifeshire Advertiser (which appeared once a fortnight in 1849) of Saturday 2 June 1849 is very impressed with the factory now that it is completed. "We had the privilege the other day of paying a visit to the gigantic building lately erected in Pathhead by Mr Nairne (sic) for the manufacture of floor cloth…" It tells us that the building was 136 feet by 87 feet, and was of some 70 feet in height with 145 windows and numerous skylights. Bizarrely, some red-pine Russian trees (adapted for the purpose) were used as pillars. The journalist records "the up-stair floors on which the workmen stand while engaged in stamping the patterns etc. are supported by 25 wooden pillars, each 50 feet in height and the finest specimens of foreign trees we ever saw, and are of themselves quite a sight. They are redwood pines and grown by the Emperor of Russia". (Not personally, one assumes!)

Clearly in some danger of running away with himself, the awestruck writer then changes track and records that although the factory has now been in business for six months, not a single piece of floor cloth has found its way out of the factory. But he did see some 200 pieces, delicately wrought, hanging out to dry, and they had already attracted the attention and admiration of merchants like Mr Whytock of Edinburgh. In fact, they would be bought and exported to buyers in Edinburgh and Glasgow very soon, in the time between the visit of *The Fifeshire Advertiser* and its publication on Saturday 2 June, for there is a small postscript to this effect, adding that the customers were delighted with "the excellence of manufacture and the cheapness of the price".

The Fifeshire Advertiser is keen to play the Scottish patriotic card in all this, and states that all Scotland should be proud of this building, for there was no other in Scotland and apart from London, there were only another two floor cloth factories, one in Birmingham and one in Liverpool, and both of these were smaller and made of wood, whereas "the structure of Mr Nairne (sic) was of the strongest and most substantial masonry"

In this respect, the journalist makes an important, if subtle, point, for not all factories of the Industrial Revolution, which were sprouting at a phenomenal rate in the 1840s, were in any way well built, nor were they subject to any rigorous testing by building inspectors. "Industrial accidents" of factories falling down on their workers were frequent, but once again we see evidence of the "caring" side of Michael Nairn who possibly was not quite as altruistic as to think primarily of his workers before profit, but nevertheless reckoned that any profit to be made from this venture would only come if the safety of his workers could be guaranteed. The welfare of those who made his floor cloth was important, and he was very conscious of the fact that he would have to retain the support of people in Kirkcaldy. In this he has something in common with his fellow Langtonian of a century previously – Adam Smith – who was a capitalist, certainly, but one enlightened enough to see that the welfare of workers was crucial to the wellbeing of a business.

The writer goes on to add that "the cost, trouble and anxiety of mind which the erection of this massive concern, and the bringing of it to a successful conclusion, seeing that it has all been done by the energy and enterprise of a single individual, must indeed have been very great". This is of course true. "Nairn's Folly" was a huge gamble, and it might well have ended in tears – something that was of course very true in 1849, for the enterprise was still in its infancy, but *The Fifeshire Advertiser* wishes him well and remains optimistic about Nairn's eventual success.

"From the saving of the freight alone of sending up the cloth in its green state to London and afterwards returning it manufactured, Mr Nairne (sic) will always have a great advantage over his southern competitors…that he may meet with all the success that his indomitable spirit merits, and length of days to enjoy it, is our ardent wish."

It is clear from this that Nairn had more than a little local encouragement in his project. It is not clear from what *The Fifeshire Advertiser* says how many people Nairn employed at this point, but it would seem that his work force would be not inconsiderable. It would seem that the key quality required from Nairn and his family in the early years would be patience. He would certainly not become an instant millionaire, for such was the stress on quality, that a long time would be required to have everything prepared in first rate order. Nairn himself estimated that not a huge amount, certainly no more than £6,000 could be "got up" in one year, and that pre-supposed that everything that was made could find a buyer.

When one bears in mind that Nairn apparently borrowed £4,000 to start the building of the factory, and that wages and the overheads still had to be paid even though the factory was as yet not producing the goods, it can be reckoned that it would be many years before Nairn's business enterprise would start yielding profits. Nairn himself died less than ten years later – possible hints of ill health may be detected in *The Fifeshire Advertiser*'s wish for his longevity when in 1849 he was only 45 – and it is hard to believe that he would have died a wealthy man. It would be his family, who also, of course, in their own way, worked hard in the development of the business who would have reaped the financial benefits. It was an excellent example of the Victorian adage, current at the time that "large oaks from little acorns grow".

Augustus Muir in his "Nairns of Kirkcaldy" is keen to stress that Nairn, at this tricky time, was very keen not to skimp on quality. It was as if he had decided that it was to be either bankruptcy or success for the new concern. There were to be no half measures, and even when the factory was still being built, Nairn continued his travels round the British Isles looking for the best quality raw materials that he could find.

The process of making floor cloth was complicated and, for a layman, difficult to comprehend with pumice stone, ochre, paint, dye, linseed oil and all sorts of other things required for the making of the material. But Nairn was prepared to settle only for the best, and the story is told of how some printers came from London but were dismissed and how he stated categorically that he did not want any more from that quarter unless he was satisfied that such printers were "of sober and steady habits" – that quote giving a clear indication and hint of why the London men were sent home!

The decision was made to close down the canvas factory in Coal Wynd. The looms were sold, and every worker was offered a job in the new concern. Robert Bell from Glasgow is mentioned as being his supplier of printing blocks, but Nairn was determined that not a single yard of his floor cloth would leave his factory until it had been "thoroughly seasoned". Eventually in summer 1849, as we have seen, with the factory now complete, the first supply of floor cloth left the gates of the Scottish Floor Cloth Manufactory, still known to the Kirkcaldy populace as "Nairn's Folly".

The floor cloth had just been rolling out of the factory when an opportunity presented itself for Nairn to advertise his wares. This was the Great Exhibition of London, or to give it its proper title, the Great Exhibition of the Works of Industries of All Nations. It was the brainchild of Albert, the Prince Consort, the popular German husband of Queen Victoria. It was a very novel way of attracting visitors to London, to the big glass house built in Hyde Park and called the "Crystal Palace". It would later be moved to Sydenham and give its name to the football field that would house FA Cup finals and International football games, and of course give birth to the football team still in existence called Crystal Palace, although Selhurst Park is now their normal residence.

The Great Exhibition was, of course, British propaganda. Britain was, as everyone knew, far more advanced in the industrial sense than any of its rivals, France, Prussia, Russia or even its wayward colony, the United States of America who insisted on continuing to speak English and to talk affectionately about the "old country", but who had nevertheless declared its independence three quarters of a century ago. This exhibition would show Britain to its best advantage, and would encourage, in summer 1851, a "feel good" factor. Britain was now developing at a phenomenal rate the railways, the symbol of its greatness, and railways too would feature largely in the Exhibition.

Nairn saw this as a tremendous opportunity. He had always been ambitious, and now he saw that with the advent of the railway (now up and running in Kirkcaldy and attracting a great deal of attention to the extent that everything now stopped when a train was heard approaching so that children could see the icon of the new age), Great Britain, at least, if not the whole world, was now within his grasp and where better to show off his new material than in the huge city that was, without a shadow of a doubt, the capital of the world?

He had of course been to London before, but this time he was going to take a great deal of his merchandise and one or two of his workers so that orders could be taken and so that the visitors to the Great Exhibition could see how his floor cloth was made. For people in

Kirkcaldy to go to London in 1851 was like going to another planet today, and those lucky workers who were asked to go with him would have an experience they would never forget. They would speak about their experiences at length for the rest of their days.

In the competitive section of the Great Exhibition, Nairn did not win – the prize for the best floor cloth going to a well-established Bristol firm called John Hare and Company. This did not come as any great surprise, but it was no great disappointment either, for Nairn looked upon his London adventure (the Great Exhibition lasted from May to October 1851) as a learning experience. The fact that a few people were critical of his product in a few technical journals was no great problem for his customers – the ones that he had in mind, namely middle class householders and even a few of the better paid artisans – would not have read the criticisms, but he took them on board nevertheless and worked out ways in which things might be improved. In any case, he knew well that there was no such thing as bad publicity. The fact that the name was mentioned at all was a great thing.

He also made even more contacts at the Great Exhibition. Naturally a sociable man , he managed to talk to his competitors – whom he was at pains to stress were not really his enemies, for they were all in the same business – about the future of the industry and find out a few of their secrets under the guise of comparing ideas. He had had the fortune to meet the great railway designer and engineer Isambard Kingdom Brunel, and travelled on Brunel's great masterpiece the Great Western Railway (sometimes called God's Wonderful Railway) to Bristol several times to visit the firm of John Hare and Company. They had, of course, won the prize but were gracious enough to welcome the earnest Scotsman and to give him every encouragement in his still young business.

All this travel was, of course, necessary but it would cause him stress and would in time have an effect on his health. It also pre-supposed that his factory could continue to work in his absence. In this he was lucky in that he had a supportive wife, who, in spite of family commitments with her young children (and most unusually for her time), took it upon herself to visit the factory now and again to see that all was in order. He also reaped the benefit of having been careful with the workers that he chose and treated well so that he could rely on them not to "play while the cat was away". His chief clerk was a very efficient man called Robert Johnstone who kept things ticking over in his absence at the "Folly" which was now, it was claimed, employing close to 100 people.

A feature of the Nairn concern throughout the years has been the lack of labour problems at a time when they abounded elsewhere. Michael Nairn was no ivory tower distant figure. Nor was he the stereotypical grasping Victorian capitalist. He came to realise early on that the occasional word with one of his workers concerning the health of the man's wife for example or an expression of sympathy in the case of child bereavement – something that happened with appalling frequency in the 1850s and would continue to do so for another 50 years, and of course, it was something that he could identify with – worked wonders in the man's attitude to his work. On the other hand, he had little sympathy for those who were "not of sober habits".

In the meantime, Nairn's family were growing up. The infant mortality already alluded to, had a devastating effect on Nairn's eight children, of whom only five survived childhood, but those who survived would in due time carry on the tradition, notably Robert and Michael. At his time however they were still young. But their moment would come.

He also kept on involving himself in worthwhile local causes – at the Church, for example, and as a Manager (we would call it a Director) of the Savings Bank, and he also worked hard on the Board of the Subscription Library, a new and modern idea to encourage more people to read books without any exorbitant expense. Everyone who joined was meant to pay a subscription to entitle them to an unlimited amount of books, but subscriptions could be waived in the case of the indigent. It was something that Nairn, a man far ahead of his time, thought should be encouraged. Being public-spirited, of course, had its benefits as far as business was concerned.

One particular, and to our modern eyes surprising, problem about Nairn's floor cloth (and highlighted by the critics at the Great Exhibition) was that the end product was neither flat nor smooth. There were raised mounds and dots on the cloth. There were some advantages in this in that it helped to prevent people slipping, but the consensus of opinion was that flat floor cloth would be better. Apart from anything else, it would allow for a better pattern to be reproduced on the cloth. Using the advice of Robert Bell from Glasgow, he devised a solution to the problem, described in great technical detail in the book *Nairns of Kirkcaldy* by Augustus Muir.

"The boxwood surface of the block was sawn into tiny squares; these numbered eighty-one to the square inch, with the saw cutting into the wood one-quarter of an inch deep; then all the squares were chipped out by the wood-cutter except those needed for the particular colour allocated to the block. Thus the solid colouring was still imprinted in collections of tiny dots, or rather squares, but these were smoothed out in a final process. After the surface had been printed in all the colours demanded by a particular design, yet another block was applied. Its surface was divided by a thin saw, into a large number of very fine parallel lines, which had the effect of merging the tiny squares of pigment into one another and of blending colours where blending was called for, leaving the completed surface with a richness of finish that was infinitely finer than the work turned out by floor cloth makers before the middle of the (19th) century"

That is by no means an easy read and was possibly a little too technical for the layman to understand, but it did the job and allowed a further development. This time he picked the brains of a designer called Owen Jones, a man whom he had met at the Great Exhibition and who had already written two books on design, one called, eccentrically, *The Grammar of Ornament*. Using some of this man's ideas, but also some of his own, he experimented and by the middle of the 1850s, his floor cloth was beginning to attract attention.

War clouds loomed in 1853 in Crimea. It was by no means the most glorious chapter in the history of the British Empire, but it did have several beneficial effects, not least in that it at last united in a common cause these old enemies Britain and France against the distant, mysterious and sinister power in the East called Russia. The war did not really affect Nairn directly – had he still had his canvas factory, it might have – for floor cloth was hardly a priority for the military establishment, but it did have the indirect effect of creating more wealth (wars often do) and releasing more money for more and more people to think about house improvements, including floor cloth.

It is odd that a man who had done so much to and for the town finds his death almost eschewed by contemporary sources. He died on January 18 1858, and *The Fifeshire Advertiser* fails to mention his death at all, other than in the death notices where he is described tersely as a floor cloth manufacturer without any indication that he employed so many people and was a major reason for the prosperity of the town. He was buried in a humble grave in the Parish Church graveyard, along with his three children who had died young, and his resting place is now marked with a plaque erected by the Kirkcaldy Civic Society.

Admittedly there were other things going on in the world to occupy the attention and the news space of *The Fifeshire Advertiser*. The Indian Mutiny was still in full flow, there had been an assassination attempt on Napoleon III, the Emperor of France and there was a Royal Wedding in London. This was Princess Victoria to a German Prince on January 25 1858, a union which would a year later yield the man who would become the Kaiser! In spite of all these stories, it is still hard to explain how the death of such a man in the town of Kirkcaldy was minimised. Seldom was there a better example of a "prophet is without honour in his own town".

One must not however exclude the possibility that we are looking at all this from through later eyes. It was of course the younger Michael Nairn, commonly known as Michael Barker Nairn to distinguish him from his father, who developed the firm and made it such a well-known and world famous concern. By the time of Michael Barker Nairn's death in the middle of the First World War, the Nairns were very wealthy indeed, but Michal Nairn himself on his death in 1858 was not necessarily as yet all that well known outside Kirkcaldy. There is also a hint or two that he was not always very popular. Nevertheless, it remains strange that there is not large grave stone in the Old Kirk graveyard for such an influential man.

Sometime after the death and burial of Michael Nairn in 1858, there seems to have been a "falling out" with the Parish Kirk and a transfer of allegiance by the family to the new Free Kirk which met in Tolbooth Street. They built a new Church which was opened in 1881 and is now known as St Brycedale Church or (more spuriously) St Bryce Kirk after a disastrous attempt by the Church of Scotland to unite them in 2000. The erection of this building in 1881 caused a huge stir in the town. It seemed to have been built with a huge spire with no other intention than to dwarf the squat medieval Parish Church tower. A walk in the Ravenscraig Park and a glance along at the skyline of Kirkcaldy will bear this out.

There was of course no secret about where the money had come from. Indeed, it was even justified and explained away in terms of something being given back to the town of Kirkcaldy. It was after all the people of Kirkcaldy who had worked in the factories of the Nairn family, although, less romantically, it may also have been funded by Michael Barker Nairn out of some spite at a perceived injustice done, either to himself or to his father, the original Michael Nairn. Perhaps it was felt that Michael Nairn senior had not been sufficiently recognised by the Parish Church, but the fact that he is buried in the Old Kirk graveyard in 1858 would tend to make us think that the "falling out" happened at a later stage. We shall never really know the truth, but the ill feeling and rivalry between the two Churches has not evaporated even in the 21st Century when very few people go to Church!

As for the rest of Michael Nairn's family, his daughter Isabella Nairn died tragically young at the age of 31 at Mentone (now Menton) in France, although her usual residence is given as The Priory, on 12 March 1882. She had been born on 19 October 1850 in the early years of The Folly. She never married, and, one presumes, had been in poor health and was staying on the French Riviera in an attempt to recover her health.

Robert Nairn, the eldest son of Michael Nairn, was born in 1835 and died at the age of 51 on 6 June 1886 at The Priory. *The Fife Free Press,* although also full of details of the fall of the Gladstone government at that time, pays full tribute to the death of Robert Nairn. His death was somewhat unexpected although he had been in indifferent health for a while. He had recently gone to the USA, but took ill when in New York and came home with his brother Michael Barker Nairn earlier than he had anticipated.

He had of course been involved in the firm, but was of a "retiring nature" and far from the dynamic, ruthless capitalist that his brother had become. He took no active part in public matters, but always took a "kindly interest" in the affairs of the town. He was held in high esteem by his workers for his "singular excellence and amiability of character". He had recently bought a site at the foot of Kirk Wynd to be used by the National Savings Bank, and had also bought some property at the bottom of Carlisle Road described rather strangely by the Rev Stalker of St Brycedale Church in the following terms "… he very recently secured for the congregation the power of protecting this structure (i.e. the Church building) from the creation of any building on the other side of the road which would injure the amenity of its situation".

Indeed, he seemed to spend most of his wealth (as his brother did) on St Brycedale Church, of which he was a Deacon. He was "a generous subscriber to its various funds, the present handsome edifice included". The Deacons Court paid him a handsome tribute "The Court hereby place on record their sense of loss sustained by the congregation through the death of Mr Robert Nairn. Mr Nairn was well versed in the history of the Free Church, and was a warm admirer of these great men whom God raised up at the Disruption to vindicate the principles for which She (i.e. the Church, one presumes,) had to contend. In the building of St Brycedale Church he took a lively interest and contributed largely to the success of this undertaking. As a citizen he cherished a deep affection for the place of his abode; in the social circle he had many friends; and he was enabled to maintain a blameless character and to cherish an unaffected and growing piety. The Court are, however, aware that it was in the charities and kindnesses of home that he chiefly shone, and they desire to convey to his family the expression of their sincere sympathy with them in their bereavement…"

Michael Nairn's widow Catherine lived until her 77th year when she died in her residence The Priory in Victoria Road on Sunday May 3 1891. Her death is recorded with due respect in *The Fife Free Press* thus "Mrs Nairn, widow of Mr Michael Nairn, the founder of the floorcloth industry in Kirkcaldy, died at her residence The Priory on Sunday evening. Mrs Nairn's loss will be felt throughout the district where she took a keen interest in all cases of distress and poverty". She was buried a few days later, not in the Old Kirk graveyard beside her husband funnily enough – an indication perhaps of the intensity of the feud between the Nairns and the Old Kirk after the death of Michael - but at the top of the western section of the Bennochy cemetery in a large, impressive, table-shaped tomb, which is still evident today.

Michael Nairn's daughter Euphemia died only a few days short of her 83rd birthday on November 23 1921 at The Priory. She was described as "kindly and lady-like" and much tribute was paid to her for her charitable works and her attendance and devotion to St Brycedale Church.

The man who carried on the Nairn enterprise was of course Sir Michael Barker Nairn. He has been well detailed in many biographies, and remains an interesting character. He died in 1915, having seen his father's business expand into a worldwide concern. But he was always very proud of his father, the original Michael Nairn.

Rev George Gillespie

A placard in the South Porch of Kirkcaldy Old Kirk reads

GEORGE GILLESPIE 1613 – 1648

In 1612 a second Minister was appointed by the Town Council, a John Gillespie from Alva known as the "thundering preacher". He became the main Minister before he died in 1627. George Gillespie was born in Kirkcaldy, son of John Gillespie, Minister at Kirkcaldy. John's other son, Patrick Gillespie became the second charge Minister here from 1642 – 1648. George Gillespie studied at St Andrews and in 1638 was ordained at Kirkcaldy Presbytery and appointed to St Mary's by the Sea at East Wemyss, being one of the first appointed without a Bishop's blessing. He showed characteristic fearlessness at the Glasgow Assembly that same year and was translated to Edinburgh in 1642, and in 1643 was sent up to the Westminster Assembly, where he took great part in the debates on discipline and dogma. His *Aaron's Rod Blossoming* (1646) is a masterly statement of the high Presbyterian claim for spiritual independence. George joined the Covenanting Army (Lords of the Congregation) and left it in 1640. He was Moderator of the Church of Scotland at a very difficult time.

He died in Kirkcaldy in 1648 and was buried in the Old Parish Churchyard but the grave was later destroyed on the orders of Archbishop Sharp. The adjoining plaque was erected by his grandson George Gillespie, Minister of Strathmiglo in 1746.

More about the "adjoining plaque" later but it is true that remarkably little is known by so many people, even in Kirkcaldy itself, about the Reverend George Gillespie.

Yet his contribution to Kirkcaldy, Scottish and even British society is by no means negligible. There are several reasons for the neglect of this great cleric, the mains reason, of course, being the fact that he lived a long time ago (1613 – 1648) and that he involved himself in religion and politics at a time when both were intertwined, but in circumstances which are difficult for us, some 4 centuries after his birth, to understand and to come to terms with. A by-product of civil and religious strife is of course the "damnatio memoriae" – the pretence almost that the man didn't exist – of political opponents in the years immediately after his death. This happened in ancient Rome and in the Soviet Union where they even tried to pretend for a while that Stalin hadn't existed! In the case of Gillespie, as we shall see, attempts were made by enemies immediately after his death not so much to blacken his memory as to erase it altogether!

Any serious study of this man must necessarily involve a fair knowledge of the background of the early 17th century and a clear understanding of terms like Episcopalians, Covenanters and the Westminster Confession of Faith – concepts which are not necessarily immediately understood, even among those who profess the Presbyterian, reformed religion. The Church of Scotland nevertheless, once a great and influential power in the land although sadly having lost its way in recent decades, owes a great deal to the influence of George Gillespie.

Kirkcaldy people do, of course, have a chance to meet George every Hallowe'en on the annual Ghost Walk. He appears, played by a well-known and talented local actor, to talk to those on the walk, from the door on the South Side of Kirkcaldy Old Kirk. This is appropriate because of course he was what is known as a "son of the Manse" there, and the Church houses his portrait. There is a tombstone, written in Latin and outrageously partisan, about him on the inside of the Church and its position there is for a reason. He was one of those men who were not allowed, literally, by their enemies to rest in peace. But we digress. Better to begin at the beginning.

It is difficult for us to imagine what Kirkcaldy would have been like as George entered the world on the (presumably) very cold day of January 21 1613. Possibly the only feature of the town that we would have recognised would have been the Old Kirk Tower, but given the lack of evidence that we have on when it was built, we cannot even be sure of that. Out of town, the Seafield Tower would have been there on the one side and the Ravenscraig Castle on the other, and along with the Old Kirk Tower it is possible that they were Kirkcaldy's main line of defence, given that any attack was likely to come from the sea. Constant vigilance would have been required, hence the Latin motto for the town of "vigilando munio" – "I defend by staying awake". The other feature of Kirkcaldy life that was definitely in existence in 1613 and has lasted the pace, is the Links Market, known to have pre-dated George's birth by at least a couple of centuries. Again however, the concept "market" was totally different from the twenty-first century one! In any case, we may confidently assume that the Presbyterian religion of the Gillespies would have disapproved of it, as they disapproved of most pleasant things!

The Parish Church of Kirkcaldy, sometimes called the Church of St Brisse, was in the same place as the Old Kirk is now, but was substantially different. The Church itself was rebuilt in the early 19th century, although we have plans of what the Church would have looked like in Gillespie's day. The "manse" (the house of the Minister, for his father was the Minister) in which George was born was presumably within walking distance of the Church, maybe even in Kirk Wynd where the large Victorian building which served as the manse in later years is now, but once more we cannot be sure, particularly as George's father, the Rev. John Gillespie was only the "Second Minister" of the parish. And there is near the Church a street called Glebe Park, situated, presumably on the "glebe" which was the land owned by the Church for the Minister to grow his crops and raise his cattle.

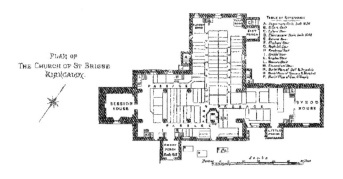

A plan of the Parish Church at the time of George Gillespie

John Gillespie (known in later years as "The Thundering Preacher") had been appointed in 1612, the year before George' birth, from his parish at Alva.

George was John's second son. The firstborn, Patrick, would also have a distinguished career, rising to become Principal of Glasgow University, and at the start of George's life, there seems to have been a sharp difference in the prognostications for his future life as predicted by both his parents. His mother, an unpleasant harsh sounding lady called Lilias Simpson felt, according to a source called Woodrow's Analecta, that George was "somewhat dull and soft-like", and "would have stricken and abused him, and she would have made much of Patrick, his younger brother".

But his father was in no doubt that George was the brighter of the two, saying apparently that "though Patrick may yet have some respect given him in the Church, yet my son George will be the great man in the Church of Scotland". Yet even the Thundering Preacher would perhaps have been surprised to hear his son described in later centuries by Dr WM Campbell in his Records of the Scottish Church History Society as "one of the most remarkable geniuses that Scotland has ever produced".

John Gillespie's appointment to Kirkcaldy seems to have been very political, but before we can discuss this issue, it is perhaps pertinent to look at the wider picture of what was going on in both Scotland and England at that time. Before 1603, relationships between Scotland and England had been violent and bloody. In 1603, the Crowns were united under James VI of Scotland who also became known as James I of England. This has been seen, by later historians as, among other things, an attempt to persuade Scotland and England to get along in peaceful disagreement, if not yet outright harmony and mutual tolerance. It has to be known that for the next 150 years, (until the collapse of the second Jacobite rebellion in 1745) such a peace attempt was a total and miserable failure, but it was at least an attempt by the sincere and well meaning, if occasionally tactless and inept, "Jamie the Saxth". And if anything it prevented Scotland and England fighting each other, even though it failed to prevent conflict in other spheres.

James VI and I was accused of ignoring Scotland and Scottish interests in his attempt to consolidate his fragile Union. In particular, he wanted the Scottish Church to be Episcopalian rather than Presbyterian. Such terms need explanation. Episcopalian means rule by Bishop, a Bishop being a "jumped up priest" who has been promoted to look after a given area of the country. The joke is frequently told of the suburb of Glasgow called Bishopbriggs. "Do you know Bishop Briggs?" "Aye, I remember him when he was just a priest!" Presbyterian, on the other hand, means rule by Minister and a session of lay people, called elders. It is hard nowadays for us to imagine how such a disagreement about how a Church should be governed, should cause such angst, but in the time of the Gillespie it was a major issue.

It is interesting, in passing to note what the words meant in Greek. The word episkopos becomes in Christian terminology a Bishop, but was originally an overseer or examiner, whereas presbyteros means an older, and therefore a wiser and more experienced man. Presbyterianism has over the centuries become a by-word for grim, repressive, doctrinaire and bigoted religion, but that is perhaps a stereotype rather than the actuality.

All this, of course, has to be seen with the Reformation in the background. The Reformation had been in existence for a century, having started in

Germany with Martin Luther a hundred years previously and Scotland, thanks to people like John Knox, had embraced Protestantism more quickly than most countries. But there was also what history calls the Counter Reformation when folk like the Jesuits tried to win people back to Rome. The whole business was bloody and violent, and one often has to question what the peace loving, gentle carpenter's son from Nazareth would have made of it all.

Religion was of course the big issue of the day. 1605 saw the Gunpowder Plot of Guy Fawkes much celebrated today every November 5, and 1611 saw the publication of what history now calls the "King James" edition of the Bible, recognised as the best translation of the Bible and virtually unchallenged until the 1950s when the New English Bible appeared. But the "devil" was around as well, at least in Kirkcaldy, for in 1616 the Kirk Session was compelled to ordain that "all convicted of witchcraft should make public repentance" and in 1619 Isobel Hervie and in 1621 Alison Dick were accused of witchcraft, Alison Dick being imprisoned in the tower.

James VI and I very much took the "English" or Episcopalian side of the argument between Episcopalianism and Presbyterianism. He was reputed to have said "No Bishop, No King" and tried in 1610 to impose the episcopacy in Scotland. It was only a partial success, however, for Scottish "thrawnness" is nowhere more obvious than in religious matters and when in 1612, Kirkcaldy decided to appoint a second Minister, one John Gillespie, the impression than one gets is that this was an attempt to find someone with Presbyterian tendencies to counteract the sad Episcopalian collaboration of the "first charge" Minister, the ageing

David Spens. John Gillespie may also have been the Schoolmaster – in some cases, this is almost what "Second Charge" or "Second Minister" actually means.

Prior to the Education Act of 1872, it was, of course, the Church which ran education. John Knox, cold, austere, unlovable bigot though he may have been, was very keen that every Parish should have a school so that people would not be dependent on venal, corrupt and themselves barely literate Priests for the reading and understanding of the Bible. The Parish School is reported to have been situated on Hill Street, more or less under the aegis and protection, in every sense, of the Parish Kirk.

There were no major wars going on at the time when George was born in 1613, and Kirkcaldy, although not exactly thriving, seemed to be holding its own in the economic sense. The town earned its living, one way or other from the sea with its comparatively safe place in the bay on the Forth, and as to what went on in the town we can but guess, although we know that there was a certain amount of weaving and trading with Holland. Coal mining was also practised even at this distant stage of the town's existence. The design of some of the houses in the High Street areas with their narrow roofs and small windows shows a certain amount of Dutch influence. The Church was well placed on an eminence above the primitive harbour and the commercial centre, if we can call it that, of the town.

George was 7 in 1620 when his father John, already having earned the nickname of "The Thundering Preacher" was "called before the Commission for disregarding the Articles of Perth". Frustratingly little is known about this incident – it appears in Lachlan McBean's The Kirkcaldy Burgh Records of 1908 – but it is a fair bet that it was something to do with his unashamed Presbyterian tendencies. But he does not seem to have suffered any great punishment for it – indeed 5 years later in 1625 he became the "First Charge" Minister when David Spens was compelled to demit his charge on account of his "gryt age and infirmitie". Gillespie senior would not have earned his nickname for nothing, and we can assume that his preaching was full-blooded, vitriolic and even, perhaps, entertaining.

The Church would have been full every Sunday with only illness accepted as an excuse for not attending. Indeed, there would have been little else to do on a Sunday, and the Church was also the local meeting place where everyone came, socialised and caught up with gossip before, after and possibly even during the Church service which could sometimes last a long time. As well as the Education Department of the town, the Church too would have been the Social Work Department of the town, dispensing "monies" to those in need. It would have, doubtless, been done in a patronising, condescending sort of a way, but it was indeed a laudable attempt to prevent hunger and starvation. On the other hand, Kirk Session minutes are full of debates about the necessity to drive out of town "worthless beggars and vagrants".

Spens died in 1626, and John Gillespie himself not much later in 1627 with no evidence available as to what he died of. By this time George would have been at school, and fairly soon after that he would have gone, at an age which is fairly young by modern standards, to the University of St Andrews. Some sources claim that he went as to St Andrews when he was as young as 12, and that he graduated in 1629 when he was only 16. This seems a little on the young side, but certainly Donald Beaton described him as "an exceptional brilliant student."

We know that he attended the University as a "presbytery bursar". The Session of Kirkcaldy, we find, decided to give him 20 merks "as much money for his entertainment (sic) as Dysart does". By 1627, when George would have been at University, his mother was a widow and certainly could not have supported her son at University, without help. The Church was always good at supporting its own, and young George may well have been a major beneficiary here out of respect for his father's memory. There may also have been a political motive here, with the Presbyterian cause keen to breed as many of their own persuasion as it could, and it would have been assumed that the son of so mighty a father would have been a Presbyterian.

The move from home to University is a daunting one at the best of times, but the 20 mile move from Kirkcaldy to St Andrews in the early 17th century must have felt like moving to a new world, well away from mother, family and home town to a different environment with no easy facilities to return home or even to communicate with one's family. It may even be that his father died while the young George was in the middle of his University course, but the young man was determined, in the family tradition, to become a Minister of the Church of Scotland, even though at the time the Church was not entirely what he would have liked in terms of political orientation. Not until 1638 was dispensation granted from the need of Episcopalian appointment, this being a great triumph for Gillespie and his like.

If we can believe what we are told, Gillespie graduated as a Minister from the University of St Andrews in 1629 when he was only 16, although the likelihood is that it would have been a few years later. We have no detailed knowledge of what he studied, but he would have been well grounded in Latin and Greek literature and in Hebrew and early Christian theology. He might even have been lucky enough to have had a look at the new Bible, now 20 years old, since its publication from Hampton Court. King James died in 1625 and had been replaced by his son King Charles 1, but this made little real difference, at least at this point in time, to the governance of the strange country called Britain which amused foreigners by having two parliaments but only one monarch!

What students did to amuse themselves in St Andrews at that time, we can but guess; particularly if, as seems likely in George's case, his University career coincided with puberty. Fleshpots were few – that is not to say that they did not exist or couldn't be found if one looked hard enough in the small fishing town – but alehouses were a little more frequent, and it is hard to imagine that a young man, however saintly or young, did not at least wonder what the wild side of life was all about. Indeed, he might well have sampled it using up some at least of the 20 merks voted him by the Kirkcaldy Session! Somehow, we would think more of him if he had!

What we do know of his time at the University of St Andrews however would indicate that he was a great debater, and that it was at St Andrews that he learned how to make his point and win his case. This issue that obsessed him was of course the same issue that would obsess him for the rest of his life, namely the relationship between Church and State, and the necessity for there to be no Royal interference, either directly or more subtly through a Bishop, in the way that the Church conducted its business.

Having graduated, George immediately faced a major and immediate impediment to his becoming a Minister. Anyone appointment to preach in the Church of Scotland had to be confirmed by a Bishop, something that was of course anathema to his family tradition and his own personal commitment. So his "calling" was put on hold. But he was far too good a man to be unemployed, and he found himself appointed to the post of personal chaplain to Sir John Gordon of Lochinvar, later appointed Viscount of Kenmure and then Lord Lochinvar by Charles I. This seems to be a sinecure of a job, and it is tempting to imagine George spending long summer days at Kenmure Castle in the South-West of Scotland, going for long walks, studying and preparing for Sunday's sermon while dozens of flunkeys attended to his every need. Once again we would perhaps think more of him if he indulged in a little imbibing or whoring.

There may well be elements of truth in this idyllic picture – who knows? - but this was also the time of his life (he would only have been 20 in 1633) when he was at his most active on the political scene, fighting, in writings and arguments, the Presbyterian cause against the perceived Episcopalian and godless reprobates. His employer and patron, Sir John Gordon may well have been a strong supporter of the Stuart monarchy, but Gillespie was anything but. He had already seen the bad effect of royal interference (particularly if it came from someone who was as convinced in the Divine Right of Kings as Charles I undeniably was) and Gillespie wished the monarch to disestablish itself from any religious involvement at all. Half the problem with Bishops was that they saw themselves as appointed by God, and therefore they could not be wrong, and Kings and Queens were under the same misapprehension. Presbyterians, on the other hand, believed that we were all, in theory at least, equal under God.

It is interesting to pause and speculate on what a thorny issue this continued to be in later centuries in Scotland, and was only really resolved when the Free Kirk seceded in 1843 on the grounds of royal patronage. It is ironic that Gillespie who fought against royal patronage was so associated with the Old Kirk, for by the 19th century, it was the Old or Parish Kirk which stayed with the idea of Queen Victoria appointing Ministers, while the rebels left for Tolbooth Street, and eventually became St Brycedale Church, calling themselves "Free" because they were not dependent on royal patronage!

George was enough of a Calvinist to believe in the value of education, so that every man should be able to read his own Bible and would not be dependent on a priest or some self-styled "Man of God". The Scottish Calvinism of John Knox meant that education was extremely important, and although Scottish education fell a great deal short of the ideal of education for all and a Bible for every house – in fact that remained an airy-fairy, never-never land until the early 20th century, and even then, it was far from universal – nevertheless, education was important, and part of Gillespie's duties at Kenmure Castle would have involved working as a teacher to the peasants and their children on the estate.

It was when he was at Kenmure that the young Gillespie met the distinguished scholar and man of letters called Samuel Rutherford, then the Minister at Anwoth in Kirkcudbrightshire. Rutherford was some 13 years older than George, but he saw some value in the young Kirkcaldy man and the two of them became firm friends, their friendship all the stronger because of their common commitment to the cause of Presbyterianism. They would both play a huge part for the rest of their lives in espousing and developing the cause. DP Thomson in his "Born in Kirkcaldy" book published in 1952 states categorically that "If the older man (Rutherford) mined the ore, it was the Kirkcaldy lad who forged the bullets".

Be that as it may, Gordon died in 1634 and it seems that at about the same time, Gillespie moved post and worked for John Kennedy, the 6th Earl of Cassilis. Cassilis (pronounced Cassels) is obscure and difficult to pinpoint with any kind of accuracy, but seems to have been in South Ayrshire and thus in the same geographical region as his previous place of employment. Little is known of his actual work here, although it seems likely that it was while he was here that he wrote his first major work, a vicious and dogmatic attack on what was going on in the Church of Scotland with the lengthy but informative title of "A Dispute Against the English Popish Ceremonies Obtruded Upon the Church of Scotland".

This work was part of a series of works which included less well known ones like "Dialogue Between a Civilian and a Divine", "A Piece Against Toleration (sic)" and another one with the even less likely title of "Wholesale Severity Reconciled with Christian Liberty". It was the "Dispute Against the English Popish Ceremonies Obtruded Upon the Church of Scotland" which caused all the problems. It was first published anonymously in Leiden in Holland, but soon became the medieval equivalent of a "best seller" and was described by a partisan follower as having been written in "trenchant style" and "he divides his work into four arguments so as to completely demolish the position of his antagonists".

The obtruding of Popish practices was a lively issue. In July 1637 rioting ensued in Edinburgh after a lady in St Giles Church called Jenny Geddes had taken exception to what she called "Mass" being spoken at her "lug" (ear) by the Minister who was also accused of causing her severe colic pains in her stomach. So upset was she that she threw a stool at the "villain", thus inciting the rest of the congregation to protest against Popery and to cause general mayhem in the streets of Edinburgh.

This story need not necessarily be strictly true – indeed there is no proof that Jenny Geddes even existed – but it does give some sort of indication of how people felt at the time about "Popish" practices being slipped clandestinely into Scottish worship. Certainly Gillespie was well to the fore in any movement against Episcopalianism and Catholicism, occasionally even obfuscating the clear and obvious differences between the two. He was keen to stress how strong the connections were between "England" and "Rome" as far as religious practice was concerned, pointing out and repeating that Henry VIII had been give the title "Defender of the Faith" (Fidei Defensor) by Pope Leo X in 1521, and conveniently ignoring all the other enmity that there had been between the two of them and their successors over the past 100 years and more!

Such was the effect of Gillespie's treatise on "English Popish Ceremonies Obtruding upon the Church of Scotland" that the Privy Council, alarmed by such rabble rousing, ordered that all copies of this document should be seized and burnt. It was proclaimed as an "obnoxious publication" and "stirred the hearts and affections of the subjects from their due obedience and allegiance". As is often the way with censorship, the opposite effect was achieved, and people made more of an effort to lay hands on this document which had so upset the censors. It was indeed difficult for the Privy Council to implement this ridiculous order, and there were two reasons for this.

One was that the printing press meant that copies could be reproduced more or less at will as long as there was paper. The treatise was soon readily available in Edinburgh. William Caxton is often hailed as one of the reasons for the success of the Reformation, and he certainly played his part here. And the other was the sheer curiosity of the population. They wanted to know more, even those who would have had no real interest if there hadn't been such a fuss! One recalls a similar case in the early 1960s when a previously obscure work of DH Lawrence called Lady Chatterley's Lover reached dizzy heights of popularity when someone silly tried to get it banned. It was for markedly different reasons – but it was the same phenomenon of counter-productivity when censorship is employed! Suddenly Lady Chatterley's sexual relations with her gamekeeper (disappointingly tame and none too graphically explained other than the odd Anglo-Saxon word) cause all sorts of ructions in British society. Similarly with Gillespie's "Popish Practices".

Gillespie suddenly became known, and even notorious in some circles. But he did also have the ability to be charming, courteous and kind, characteristics which were of great value to any aspiring politician of any age. The fact that his two patrons, Gordon and Kennedy, were also well known, helped his popularity as well, and all the time the Presbyterians were beginning to gain ground within the Church of Scotland, and the writings of young Gillespie (still in his early 20s) were beginning to have an effect on people's thinking. By 1638, such had been the influence of Gillespie, Rutherford and others that the National Covenant of Scotland was signed in Greyfriars Church in Edinburgh, and then five years later in 1643 the Solemn League and Covenant, both documents laying the foundations for the Covenanting movement which would play such a large part in Scottish history over the rest of the century, and introducing the word "covenanter" to the English language.

Both these documents were political rather than religious and although couched in vague and ambiguous language sometimes, the general message is clear that the King and the Crown cannot interfere in religion on the grounds that only Jesus Christ can be the head of the Church. They spell out the case for Presbyterianism rather than any other kind of Church government, be it Episcopalian or Papal.

For whatever reason, but possibly influenced by such trends, in 1638 the Scottish Church had a swing back to Presbyterianism and was thus able to dispense with the necessity of Episcopalian patronage in the appointment of its clergy. Thus George Gillespie was now at the age of 25 able to begin the career that he always wanted – that of a parish Minister and preacher of the Word of God. In practice however, he would have little time to do the job of a conscientious cleric, for he was by now heavily involved in politics, something that interested him a great deal more than occasionally sterile discussions of theology.

He was also now able to return to his beloved Fife where he found a post not too far away from his home town of Kirkcaldy. This was in Wemyss. Fife now has Coaltown of Wemyss, East Wemyss and West Wemyss; there is in Kirkcaldy a building (at one point the headquarters of Fife Education Department) called Wemyssfield, and of course, the Wemyss Coal Company even today retains the hatred bestowed upon it by its workers for the excesses perpetrated at the time of the General Strike and other times of labour dispute. A more honourable place in history can be attributed to First Sea Lord Admiral Rosslyn Wester Wemyss who was actually one of the team who negotiated the armistice in the forest of Compiegne in November 1918, and in 1925 unveiled the War Memorial in the gardens of what is now Kirkcaldy Galleries.

However that may be, it was Wemyss to which Gillespie returned in Fife in April 1638. The "Presbyterie Booke of Kirkcaldie" tells us that George was asked to preach on one text – 2 Thessalonians 2.13 "If we suffer, we shall also reign with him: if we deny him, he also will deny us. If we believe not, yet he abideth faithful. He cannot deny himself". This was a text which "the brethren" had been asked by the Moderator to "praescryve" for him, and he duly did so on January 18 1638. This was to "try" George for the post at Wemyss. The "Presbyterie Booke" then records

Kirkcaldie Januarii 18 1638, whilk day Mr George Gillespie preached upon the text praescryvit to him viz. 2 Thessalonians 2. 13 wherein he gave the brethren full contentment so that thai wir content to signifie their approbation of him be thair testimonial whilk they appoyntit the Clerk to writt to him and to subscryve in their names and to writ back answer to the Moderator.

A couple of months later the same tome announces

Kirktowne of Wemyss April 26 1638, whilk day Mr Robert Douglas, Minister of Kirkcaldie preached upon the 1st Epistle of Peter 2.3.4. whereafter the consent of the parochiners being required and Master Georg Gillespie demandit of certaine questions proponed to him be the moderator and his oath of alegance to the Kings majestie being taine, the said Mr Georg was admittit and ordained Minister of the Kirk of Wemyss be imposition of hands with prayer to God and singing of psalms and resaved by the elders and parochiners who both promised mutuall duties to others.

It is interesting to read that George here took an oath of allegiance to the "Kings majestie". We cannot be entirely sure what this means, If the "King" is Jesus Christ, then of course there is no problem but if it means King Charles I, it would seem out of character for Gillespie to take such an oath. Perhaps he felt however that it would be an idea to pay some homage to the King simply to get Archbishop Bischope of St Andrews on his side – at least for the time being. However that may be, he was now a Minister and we read also on a more mundane and practical note that "Maii 31 1638, whilk day the Moderator and Mr Mungo Law declairit that they went to the Weyms and designit Mr George Gillespie his gleib and manss"

Yet however much Gillespie loved his native Fife and the people there, he cannot but have been aware that Fife was a backwater, and that the real power in Scotland lay in Edinburgh, Stirling and Perth, and increasingly in that small but growing town in the west of Scotland on the banks of the Clyde called Glasgow. It was in Glasgow in that year at an Assembly of the Church of Scotland (not, apparently, what we now call the General Assembly) that Gillespie further made an impact on Scottish religious politics by preaching a sermon against the interference by the King on Church matters. The very fact that one of the Commissioners, the Duke of Argyll, saw fit to distance himself from this "outburst" saying that Gillespie had "encroached too nearly on the royal prerogative" was further good publicity for him.

Once again, Gillespie touched on a burning issue. In both England and Scotland, the joint King Charles 1 had managed to upset both his Parliaments by his constant interfering and attempting to impose doctrine (mainly of the Roman Catholic variety) on both Churches. Such a foolhardy and obstinately determined policy would of course lead to his military defeat and eventual execution in 1649. For the moment however, Gillespie, having tasted blood as it were, bent himself to the cause using his vast intellectual powers and his rhetorical expertise. Not for nothing had his father been called "the thundering preacher". He had inherited his father's oratorical ability, and in the mid-17th century, it was a mighty gift to have.

An indication of how important a man he had become comes in 1639 when the Scottish Covenanting Army marched south under Alexander Leslie, and Leslie himself asked for Gillespie to be the Chaplain. Leslie, otherwise known as the First Earl of Leven, had served with distinction in the army of the Swedish King Gustavus Adolphus in the Thirty Years War, and very soon after having secured Edinburgh Castle for the Covenanting cause, defeated the English Royalists at the

Battle of Newburn before capturing Newcastle and compelling King Charles 1 to negotiate.

However, in 1640 when Gillespie was asked again, he this time seems to have refused on the grounds of ill health. "Julii 9 1640, whilk day my Lord of Elcho (*otherwise known as the Earl of Wemyss*) desyred that he myt have one of their number to goe with him to preache to his regiment, whereupon the brethren condescendit and grantit that Mr Georg Gillespie sould go with him...and ane thousand merks were their voluntar contribution for further defraying the publick charges of the Countrie" But George had to say No "Mr Georg Gillespie declaired his inabilitie to follow the regiment in respect of his health. The Presbyterie ansers they cannot urge him..."

Whether this illness was a diplomatic one to get him out of going with the Army we cannot tell. It would be nice to think that he had a conscientious Christian revulsion against military life and unnecessary bloodshed, but in any case, he recovered soon afterwards and was chosen as one of the Scottish Commissioners along with Thomas Henderson, Robert Blair and Robert Baillie to "negotiate peace with Charles I". What this actually means we are not sure, but it certainly shows that he was now considered to be one of the more influential clerics in the land. He was also pursued by various congregations in Scotland to become their Minister with a Church in Aberdeen in particular attempting to take him away from Wemyss. He resisted such blandishments for a spell but in 1642, he did move to Edinburgh accepting a call to become Minister of the High Kirk of Edinburgh, possibly at Greyfriars.

This clearly brought him much closer to the centre of power than he would have been if he had stayed in

Wemyss. But it would be wrong to depict him as being nothing other than a politician. He was also very active on the writing front, producing at this time all sorts of tracts, normally well backed up by theological references from Old and New Testament sources about the desirability of detaching the King from any participation in Church Government. The old Presbyterian chestnut that there could only be one head of the Church and that was Jesus Christ was the constant tenor of his arguments. It is scarcely an issue which would arouse much passion today, but in that age, it was a live one.

He also travelled several times to London as a representative of the Church of Scotland. This must have been no easy task, for the 1640s were of course the years of the English Civil War in which the Roundheads or the Parliamentarians eventually defeated the Cavaliers or the Supporters of the King. Scotland of course had its own version of this conflict, and although the issues were slightly different in Scotland as compared to England, Gillespie was undeniably on the side of the Parliamentarians, and had, of course, very close links with the Covenanters.

The Covenanters have been described not without cause as "the Scottish Taliban" and the parallel is valid. Fundamentalist religion, propagated by fanatics and showing no mercy to those who disagreed with them were the characteristics of the Covenanters. George Gillespie could not, in any way, be described as a champion of freedom, in our modern sense of the word, although he and his supporters would have seen themselves as arguing for "freedom" – freedom from Bishops, Kings, or any kind of Anglican or Episcopalian liturgy in Church worship. Emphatically, he would not have been in favour of religious tolerance.

On the surface, it would appear that George would have been a strict, unlovable sort of a man, but that is perhaps looking at him too superficially. Certainly in the Church that Gillespie envisaged there would have been little place for jollity – there would certainly have been no celebration of Christmas for example, because it was unbiblical – but one would have to question how far the Church was able to enforce its strictures on its populace. Judging by what Session records tell us, there seems to have been no lack of men getting drunk or young girls getting pregnant, two areas of life in which the Church has been a significant failure over the centuries!

Possibly George would have deplored such things, but they would not have been his main concern. His main concern would have been whether anyone was practising sorcery or witchcraft – certainly there is a great deal of evidence of the persecution of witches all over Scotland – or, possibly even worse, showing "popish" or "Roman" tendencies!

It was to this end that during the Civil War, the Westminster Confession of Faith was commissioned by the English Parliamentarians and the Scottish Covenanters, the de facto government of Scotland in these turbulent times. It was considered important to codify and to document what the country of Great Britain should believe in. George Gillespie was chosen as one of the Scottish Commissioners, and was appointed to play his part in the writing of this weighty and significant document. It has been described as the "subordinate standard of the Church of Scotland" i.e. second only to the Bible itself, and it is fair to say that Gillespie's talents played a major part in its conception and construction.

"The Westminster Assembly of Divines" as they were called sat for the first time in 1643, and the Fasti of the Church of Scotland gave Gillespie a good Press, saying that "by his learning, zeal and sound judgement, he gave essential assistance in the preparation of the Directory and of the Confession of Faith".

Many stories are told about his contribution. Dr WM Campbell states that "It was at the Westminster Assembly that Gillespie made his most important contribution to Presbyterian history. Every proposition had to pass before the keenest theological minds of England... In getting the standards shaped to the Scottish liking the dominating factor was the keen debating power of Gillespie. Time and time again, he swung the Assembly round to the Scottish point of view, especially concerning the place of the laity and the Elders in the Reformed Church."

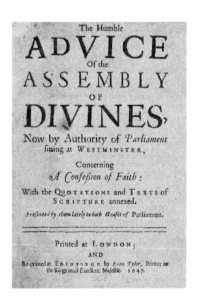

The Humble

ADVICE

Of the

ASSEMBLY

OF

DIVINES,

Now by Authority of *Parliament* sitting at WESTMINSTER,

Concerning

A Confession of Faith :

With the QUOTATIONS and TEXTS of SCRIPTURE annexed.

Presented by them lately to both Houses of Parliament.

Printed at LONDON;
AND
Re-printed at EDINBURGH by *Evan Tyler*, Printer to the Kings most Excellent Majestie. 1647.

On one occasion, he was delayed and arrived late, having just travelled down from Scotland and ridden the last few miles. He arrived when Thomas Goodwin, the great English Puritan was speaking on behalf of Independency, meaning, presumably, that every Church should be self-sufficient and that there should be no General Assembly or anything of that nature. Gillespie, naturally opposed to such views was nevertheless reluctant to come forward to speak for he was still wearing muddy riding boots, but his friend Alexander Henderson insisted and George came forward, still in his muddy attire and spoke extempore for an hour and a half. It was "a triumphant demolition of the Independent's logic".

On another occasion, John Selden the famous English theologian and supporter of Erastianism, whereby the Church was subordinate to the State in matters of discipline, was expatiating eloquently and at length on Matthew XVIII 15-18, as if to prove that this meant that the State was superior to the Church. George sat silently and took notes, while now and again making a few "pithy ejaculations" (sometimes they are called "pious ejaculations" but neither is a phrase that one would be able to use in the 21st century!). He was then prevailed upon by his friends to refute Selden's arguments, one of his friends saying portentously "rise up and defend the right of the Lord Jesus Christ to govern by His own laws the Church which he has purchased by His blood". George then did so, brilliantly and comprehensively winning over the English theologian who was compelled to give his reluctant but sincere credit to the young Scotsman. Then one of George's friends asked to see the notes that George had made during the Englishman's lengthy diatribe. It turned out to be nothing other than three Latin words "Da lucem, Domine" – "Give us light, Lord!"

The Westminster Confession of Faith is an uncompromising defence of Calvinism, affirming the purity of the doctrines of Jesus Christ, advocating strict Sabbatarianism and talking about Predestination as if it were self-evident. It is probably an exaggeration or a perversion of the truth to say that all the narrow, bigoted, small-minded and narrow beliefs of Christianity in Scotland over the next four centuries can trace their origins to this document, (they had, after all, been pretty narrow and intolerant before as well!) but there can be little doubt that the "Wee Frees" and others of intransigent beliefs will find much to console themselves in the Confession of Faith. Similarly, those free thinkers and, in particular, those of the Scottish Enlightenment a hundred years later would have found a great deal to appal them in the narrowness and simplicity of the views expressed.

But that is not the worst of it. The worst of it is surely the way in which it portrays the Pope and the Roman Catholic Church as the anti-Christ. There are frequent attacks on "Popish" practises, and the Westminster Confession of Faith, adopted uncompromisingly by the Church of Scotland in 1646, is a document which will find little acceptance in these (hopefully) more tolerant times of the 21st Century. A good case, sadly, could be made out for saying that the Westminster Confession of Faith is responsible for so much of the religious and sectarian hatred which, until recently, has befouled Scotland. It is probably true to say that anti-Catholicism only became a major issue with the influx of bigoted people from Ulster in the late 19th and early 20th century, but they found fertile ground in

Scotland for their beliefs. "Scotland's shame" is the phrase of the 21st century applied to the intolerance of religious diversity; in this context, it must be said that, in this respect at least, the Confession of Faith is a shameful document.

Gillespie thus stands condemned in the eyes of posterity, but it is important to see him in the context of his times. Ideas and concepts of "peace" and "tolerance" were, frankly, alien to 17th century ears, and we must bear in mind that civil wars were raging all over Britain and indeed all over Europe at the time – in the name of religion, not, assuredly, as the man from Galilee would have wished it, but more to satisfy the needs and aspirations of ambitious and ruthless clerics of all denominations! Bloodshed and violence were much the order of the day when religion and politics became mixed in a dreadful cocktail of bigotry and narrowness. Only a few months after Gillespie's death, we had the unprecedented spectacle of the King, not only being deposed, but being put to death as well by his enemies. Such things may happen today in third world or middle-east countries, but it comes to us with a shock to realise that this was Great Britain less than 400 years ago.

If there is any justification for Gillespie's behaviour, it must surely lie in his determination to keep alive the spirit of the Scottish reformation. He and others like him ensured that Protestantism and the Bible remained alive in Scotland. In this respect at least, he was a success for Calvinism retained its icy grip on Scotland, in theory at least, for the next 300 years. Yet Gillespie would have been happy and proud of all that. He said "Religion and righteousness must flourish or fade away, stand or fall, together. They who are false to God shall never prove faithful to man"

Gillespie returned to Scotland on July 10 1647, and less than a month later was influential in persuading the General Assembly to accept the Westminster Confession of Faith. Flushed with his perceived success, Gillespie resumed his preaching at the High Kirk in Edinburgh. He was now one of the heroes of the day, and in 1648 he was elected Moderator of the General Assembly of the Church of Scotland, at 35 the youngest man who had ever become Moderator. This post, far more prestigious then than it is now, was seen as the thanks rendered by a grateful nation and Church for his services rendered in compiling the Westminster Confession of Faith, but he did not have long to enjoy his popularity and fame.

His hard work and constant travelling back and forth to London (no easy task in the 17th century) had had a bad effect on his health, and by autumn of 1648 he had developed consumption, the disease of the lung known in later days as tuberculosis. Patrick Simpson who lived in Renfrew in 1707 gives a graphic account of Gillespie's last days. He talks first about how George suffered from a great amount of "hoasting (coughing) and sweating" after the "rising (sic) of the Assembly on July 12". He recovered briefly but when these symptoms returned, he went back to his beloved Kirkcaldy, where his brother Patrick was now the Minister, hoping for recovery.

Sadly, this was not to happen. "Ten days before his death, his sweating went away and his hoasting lessened yet his weakness still increased and his flux (diarrhoea) still continued". On December 14 he suffered from heavy sickness and a few days later he was always drowsy and prone "a little to rave" yet until his last half hour he was in full and perfect senses" enjoying a "little refreshment of jelly and a little drink through a reed". It was on December 17 1648 that he passed away, his last words before he lapsed into delirium being "I long for that time. Oh! Happy are they that are there". George Gillespie died at the age of 35, "mourned by the entire nation".

Dr WM Campbell is aware of Gillespie's shortcomings, but nevertheless has this to say about him. "He was a man all through and died fighting. He was upright in all his political conduct; he forsook no cause he sponsored. He gave of the uttermost he had, even to his life, in the cause he served; if he ever spared anyone, least of all did he spare himself. He was a young man in his power, with the pride, the intolerance, the rashness, the courage, the unsparingness, the eagerness of youth. He died with his sword drawn and his armour bright".

This tribute, redolent as it is of military imagery to an extent which our modern thinking perhaps finds offensive, nevertheless does capture the spirit of the man. He was indeed a soldier, and we get the impression that he would not have spared himself in any bloodshed that he deemed necessary for his cause, but the one thing that does shine through about him was his absolute determination to see things through, even at the expense of his own life. Quite a few famous men died young – one thinks of Robert Burns and, of course, Jesus Christ himself – so we do not have the luxury of being able to judge them in their old age. This is a pity in the case of George Gillespie.

It would have been nice to record that Gillespie was a man of vision, and a man ahead of his times in his approach to religious tolerance. Sadly, we cannot say that, but it is important not to judge him too much by modern standards. The 21st century thankfully sees political and religious freedoms which people of the 17th century would have found totally alien, incomprehensible and possibly even offensive. Gillespie was and remains a man of the 17th century. This does not mean that we should dismiss him. We should make an attempt, difficult though it may be, to judge him as a man of his time.

The death of Gillespie in 1648 was by no means the end of his influence over Kirkcaldy and indeed Scotland. He was buried in Kirkcaldy Parish Church graveyard, underneath, it is believed, the South (or sea) Side entrance to the Church. A tombstone was erected in his memory, written in flowery and difficult Latin and in a very partisan style. Indeed, it was so partisan that although it was respected during the "Commonwealth" or the "Republic" when Oliver Cromwell was in command, the Restoration of the Monarchy in 1660 was a different matter altogether. Poor George was not even given the luxury of being able to "rest in peace". Nor did his wife and children ever receive the 1,000 sterling voted to his widow and children by the Committee of Estates of the Church of Scotland. Politics took over, and some people felt that this money was not justifiable, and once The Monarchy was restored in 1660, things took a decisive shift against George Gillespie.

The Restoration, as well as famously relaxing laws on censorship in the theatre and generally presiding over a marked decline in moral and sexual standards, (including allowing horse racing on the sands in Kirkcaldy!) brought back the Episcopacy. Archbishop Sharp who would himself come to a bloody end in 1679 on Magus Muir, is said to have been responsible for giving orders to deface the monument to George Gillespie. This was done by the public hangman at the Mercat Cross, the stone having been carried there for that purpose, although the grave itself is said to have been undisturbed. Such was the respect for the dead or fear of retribution from Gillespie's ghost! The news sheet "Mercurius Caledonicus" of January 19-26 1661 however is jubilant saying that "it was a just indignity of so dangerous a person".

In 1746, Gillespie's grandson, also called George Gillespie and Minister of Strathmiglo restored the stone, and it stands now in the South Porch of the Old Kirk. To what extent the inscription was as originally written in the 1650s and to what extent it was modified in the 1750s we can never be sure, but one might imagine that in the triumphant atmosphere of the 1750s, a little doctoring would have been carried out. The defeat of the Jacobite rebellion in 1746 was of course a great triumph for the Gillespie family who would have sided uncompromisingly with the Hanoverians, the King, the Crown and the Presbyterian form of worship as distinct from the Roman Catholic Young Pretender, who may have eventually become a figure of romance and charm but who in the years immediately after Culloden was demonised by the triumphalist and intolerant Presbyterians.

Whenever it was written, the tombstone (an impressive and difficult piece of Latin) reads

Magister georgius gillespie pastor edinburgensis.

Iuvenilibus annis rituum Anglorum pontificiorum turmam prostravit: gliscente aetate, delegatus cum mandatis in synodo Anglicana, praesulem e Anglia eradicandum, sincerum Dei cultum uniformem promovendum curavit; Erastum Aaronis germinante virga castigavit. In patriam reversus foedifragos Angliam bello lacessentes labefactavit. Synodi Nationalis anno

1648 Edinburgi habitae praeses electus, extremam patriae suae operam cum laude navavit, cumque oculatus testis vidisset malignantium quam praedixerat ruinam, eodem quo foedus trium gentium solemne renovatum fuit die decedens in pace anno aetatis 36 in gaudium Domini intravit. Ingenio profundus, genio mitis, disputatione acutus, eloquio facundus, animo invictus bonos in amorem, malos in invidiam, omnes in sui admirationem rapuit, patriae suae ornamentum, tanto patre digna suboles.

Master George Gillespie
Pastor of Edinburgh

In his youth he destroyed the crowd of priests of the Anglican persuasion; as he grew in years, he was chosen among the delegates at the Anglican Synod and made sure that the prelate from England was removed and that the one true Worship of God was encouraged.

He punished Erastus with the sprouting rod of Aaron. Returning to his country, he defeated the treaty breakers who were provoking England in war. At the General Assembly of 1648 he was elected Moderator and performed with distinction his final work for his country. And when he had seen as an eye witness the ruin of the evil ones which he had predicted, on the same day that the solemn treaty of the three nations was renewed, he died in peace at the age of thirty six. He entered the Joy of the Lord. Of profound intellect, gentle disposition and sharp in debating, a man of eloquence in speech and invincibility in mind; he turned the good to love him, the bad to envy him, everyone to admire him. He was a credit to his Native Land, a worthy offspring of a great father.

AARON'S ROD BLOSSOMING.

THE FIRST BOOK

OF THE JEWISH CHURCH GOVERNMENT.

CHAPTER I.

Rev John Campbell
Minister of Parish Church

John Campbell was born in the lovely Perthshire village of Fortingall on 26 October 1847, the son of Duncan Campbell and Jessie McNaughton. His father was the village schoolmaster, or the "dominie" as he would have been termed. The stereotype of a village dominie in the Victorian era is, of course, one of unremitting, humourless austerity, laced with an ability to wield canes and belts at recalcitrant pupils. To what extent this was true of Campbell's father, we do not know, but certainly certain traits of Campbell's character as they evolved in his time in Kirkcaldy would tend to indicate that he inherited from his father a love of discipline and order, but also a keen desire to find things out and to investigate, allied to an antiquarian interest in old things. The good side of traditional Scottish education, one feels, is not really stressed often enough.

At some point and for whatever reason we do not know, the family moved south and John was educated at the Parish School in Lesmahagow in South Lanarkshire before becoming a student at Glasgow University, where he graduated with MA in 1867 and then, having decided to become a Minister of the Church of Scotland, completed his BD in 1870. He was then licensed by the Presbytery of Lanark.

He was thus a classic case of the "lad o pairts". There is an interesting myth, which has sprung up over the centuries, that "lads o pairts" were from working class backgrounds "poor but honest", who descended en masse to Scottish Universities and amazed Professors with their wide knowledge and ability to fend off adversity like poverty and hunger, eking out an existence in some leaky attic in pursuit of more wisdom. This is of course an idealistic and romantic way of looking at things, but the funny thing is that bits of it were true. Usually in fact a "lad o pairts" would be the son of a rural schoolmaster or a minister. (Only very, very occasionally would it be some boy from a working class urban background), He would, however, thrive on the pursuit of knowledge. There is no reason not to classify the young John Campbell in this category.

Young Campbell was compelled to live in interesting times, as the saying went. Scotland was in the throes of a massive industrial revolution with Glasgow, throughout the 19th century, growing at a phenomenal rate with the accumulation of Highlanders who had come from the Highland Clearances and the Irish fleeing the potato famine of 1846 and its dreadful aftermath. Scotland and the west of Scotland in particular was changing character, and possibly the young, idealistic Campbell felt that the maintenance and propagation of the Christian gospel was all the more necessary in these difficult times.

It would be interesting to know if he ever went through a "subversive" or "rebellious" phase as a student. Certainly his subsequent life would incline us to say "no", for politically he seems to side uncompromisingly with the establishment, but on the other hand he was an intelligent young man, and one would have hoped that he would have been sufficiently idealistic to ask a few questions about the current social order, sympathised with the Chartists or the Anti Corn Law League (both of them, admittedly, well past their prime by the 1860s) or flirted with the Gladstonian liberals or those who advocated further Parliamentary reform, even after the Second Reform Act of 1867. The franchise was still far from universal.

Around about the time that he completed his BD in 1870, war broke out on the continent between France, led by the grandson of the still accursed "Boney" and the new power of Prussia which seemed determined to unify all of Germany, no matter who stood in its way. Denmark had already been given a bloody nose, and now it was the turn of France. It was of course to the credit of Gladstone that he kept Britain out of this conflict (44 years later his successors would tragically fail to do so) and it would have been interesting to know, in view of Campbell's full-blooded and uncompromising support of the Great War in 1914, what he felt about the events of 1870/71? Closer to home, what did he feel about Ireland? And what about that omnipresent political character, William Ewart Gladstone? Some felt that he was threat to the existing social order; others felt that he was a worthy liberal. It was well known that the Queen did not like him.

Whatever he felt about such things, he turned to the Church of Scotland, an organization in the 1870s far removed from what it is now. One must, once more, guard against the stereotypical image of bigotry, guilt and gloom, lit up by ferocious oratory and rabid preaching, which Victorian Churches conjure up, but the Church too reflected the times that it lived in, which were far from happy ones. The Church had of course suffered its own schism in the Disruption of 1843, and struggled to rid itself of the common perception that Churches were for the rich and the blessed, and that for the massive and emerging working class in Scotland, the Kirk was "no for the likes o' us".

It was possibly for such reasons that the Kirk in West Central Scotland, at least, opened itself to the bigoted influences of those who did not like the Catholic Irish. This would lead, of course, to some blood-curdling pronouncements as late as the 1920s and 1930s about the "Irish menace" and the "threat to the Scottish blood" (by no means dissimilar to what was being said about the Jewish race by some folk in Germany at the same time!), but in the 1870s, the Church was in a strange position of being the Establishment, yet at the same time embattled and entrenched against what it saw as modernising influences – not least those who wished to disestablish it. Campbell in his later life would be sadly affected by this, and would side uncompromisingly and usually without any hesitation, with the status quo.

He began as an assistant in St George's In the Fields in Glasgow, then on 18 April 1872 he was ordained to Newhall, also in Glasgow (*The Fifeshire Advertiser* on Campbell's demission in October 1926 says it was Newlands in Rutherglen where he was sent on "mission work"). Wherever it was, he spent three years there before landing what could be described as one of the more important and challenging jobs in the West of Scotland at Airdrie where he was inducted on 15 April

1875. One of Airdrie's distinctions is that it opened the first public library in Scotland in 1853, and by the time that Campbell arrived there in the 1870s, Airdrie and its surrounding area was the epicentre of industry with coalmining, industrial works, foundries and forges in abundance. Tension between the mainly Protestant area of Airdrie and the growing Catholic enclave of the new town of Coatbridge would be apparent as well, and the whole area, while enjoying words like "prosperous" and "thriving" as applied by historians, would also suffer serious problems of deprivation and poverty. It was frequently said that Airdrie and Coatbridge may well have been divided by religion but they were united in drink.

Rev. JOHN CAMPBELL, M.A., D.D.

It may be that Campbell was personally sheltered from the worst effects of the dreadful social conditions, but he can hardly have been unaware of them. How he reacted to them, we cannot be sure, but he soon, within a few years, evinced a desire to move on. On 14 January 1879, he married a lady called Elizabeth Renwick, the daughter of Herbert Renwick of Beattock, and it was possibly under her influence that he decided to move on to what seemed to be an easier, and certainly quieter part of Scotland. By the time he came to Kirkcaldy, the couple had a daughter called Phyllis Carruthers Campbell who was born on 1 November 1880.

His arrival in the town, it would have to be said, caused more than a little stir. He himself emerges with credit, but quite a few others didn't. What seems to have happened is that someone from the Committee entrusted to find a new Minister (the Visiting Committee, as it was known) had "accidentally" heard Campbell speak somewhere and invited him to come to preach twice on 26 December 1880 in "Dysart and Kirkcaldy" (Dysart Old Kirk and then St James in Kirkcaldy) so that more members of the Committee could hear him. Campbell must have preached very well, for they were all impressed (or most of them were), and he preached again on 9 January 1881 in Kirkcaldy Parish Church (as it was then called, although we are more familiar with it as Kirkcaldy Old Kirk). We are told that he based his sermon on Romans 14.7 that "none of us liveth to himself and no man dieth to himself". That was in the morning, whereas in the afternoon session, he moved on to Matthew 27.42 "He saved others; himself He cannot save".

But before he could preach on that Sunday 9 January, John Hunter came into the picture. Hunter was an influential and wealthy member of the congregation who lived in St Brycedale House (which became after his death the Hunter Hospital). He would, in time, give the Hunter Hall to the congregation, as well as have Hunter Street named after him. Frankly, he was very rich and eccentric enough to enjoy the occasional game of politics. He had dissented from the decision, and now, on Saturday 8 January 1881, distributed handbills throughout the town to the effect that, although Mr Campbell deserved a fair hearing, the congregation should have had the opportunity to hear several preachers and that there should have been a leet. But while the congregation could make up their minds about whether to call Campbell or not, Hunter himself preferred a delay on the grounds that there might be better preachers. It was not an outright condemnation of Campbell; rather it was a protest against the Committee who claimed that he (Hunter) was the sole dissenter rather than the rather larger amount (11) that Hunter maintained.

A congregational meeting was thus called for Tuesday 11 January 1881 for the purpose of "calling" Mr Campbell. In spite of the snowy weather which paralysed large parts of Scotland, there was a large turnout with the lower part of the building well filled. *The Fife Free Press* then tells us that under the chairmanship of Rev Spark, the minister of St. James Church, Colonel John McLeod, the Convenor, read out the statement that the Committee, with John Hunter dissenting, wished to call John Campbell.

Normally such things are a formality, but not on this occasion. Seizing on the dissent of John Hunter, two other members of the congregation, a Mr Roger Black and a Mr Laing, a corkcutter, put up strong opposition to the "call" of Mr Campbell. Dr Hardy tried to calm things down by saying that although in the first instance he would have preferred a leet to choose from, having heard Mr Campbell on Sunday, he was quite happy to accept him as Minister.

REV. JOHN CAMPBELL, M.A., D.D.

Black then in a brilliant speech dripping with sarcasm says "a most excellent member of our most excellent committee by the purest accident heard him preach…" This "accident" may or may not have echoed the widely held belief among some members of the congregation that Campbell was related to Colonel MacLeod. Hunter himself denies having said that, but agrees that he had heard the allegation. However, Black goes on to say that this "excellent member" thereupon decided that Campbell was a proper "Gamaliel" (an obscure reference to a rabbi in the New Testament who used his oratorical powers to defend Christians in the Acts of the Apostles) and that Campbell was to be the man for the job.

There was also the matter of a letter which Campbell himself had sent. Campbell apparently stated that he would not accept the job unless he was accepted unanimously by the Committee. Black wondered at what stage this letter was to be read to the congregation, but for whatever reason, this letter was never read out. "Curiouser and curiouser" as Alice in Wonderland would have said. Was Colonel McLeod deliberately suppressing something? And how had Black got to hear about this? Repeatedly Black and Laing asked for the letter to be read out, but repeatedly the Moderator, Mr Spark, refused to do so, saying that the sole purpose of this meeting was to decide whether or not to call John Campbell as minister.

Far more serious allegations were also made in *The Fife Free Press,* however, concerning the roll and those entitled to vote. The feeling of the meeting was clearly far from unanimous, so a vote had to be held. The roll of the Parish Church at this time consisted of 742 members and 23 adherents, and *The Fife Free Press* tells us that "a whole two hours" were taken to call and check the roll. Given the organization of the Church in all ages, the "whole two hours" does not surprise us, but we are then astonished to read that "half of those present, although members, were not on the roll".

Dr Hardy, Mr McKnight, Mr Beveridge and Mr Black having been appointed as markers, the voting eventually took place. Surprisingly, and in contradiction of the Secret Ballot Act of 1872 which now prevailed at Parliamentary elections, each member entitled to vote was called up and declared openly yes or no. Little wonder then that it took two hours! According to *The Fifeshire Advertiser*, the restless congregation were heard to laugh at the "shrill, gruff, emphatic or hesitating tones" of some of the members and much mimicry took place. But it was also claimed that some people voted more than once, that some refrained (sic) or refused to vote, and cries of those who felt that they were being disenfranchised were heard with frequent refrains of "The roll's no' correct" "I'm no' on the roll" and "It's no'richt, that!". There seems however to have been a distinct lack of storming out with loud cries of "I'm no' comin back!" Such behaviour is, of course, by no means uncommon in such circumstances, and there was also a certain enjoyment and relish, one feels, at the sight of the Kirk making a public fool of itself!

In any case, with the night now far advanced (the meeting would eventually break up at 11.30 pm!) the vote was announced "amid extraordinary stillness" that Campbell was elected by 177 votes to 159, a majority of 19, a far from unanimous decision. The result was then greeted with "tremendous hissing and uproar".

Colonel McLeod then tried to speak, but such was the hubbub that he could not be heard, and *The Fife Free Press* tells an interesting story of an old lady called Mrs Geddes (by an odd coincidence bearing the same name as the famous Jenny Geddes who caused such trouble at St Giles a few centuries previously!) shouting about how this was "patronage" and that she wanted to go to the

Queen about it, even though it meant getting up early in the morning to catch a train to do so. This raised a few laughs, but the whole business also raised a few questions about nepotism and corruption. "Patronage" was of course the issue that the Free Kirk had broken away from the Church of Scotland about in 1843, and although royal patronage had now been abolished and churches given the right to appoint their minister, it was clearly still a potent issue in the minds of quite a few people. And the events of the night were clearly proving that the Kirk had little expertise in the business of appointing a minister!

A fine view of Kirkcaldy Old Kirk and its tower

John Hunter then "mounted a seat" and, enjoying and relishing his moment as a soap box orator, told the congregation that he was not the only member of the Committee who had dissented. There were more, he said, but then he claimed (improbably, one feels) that their dissent was ignored because they could not be heard because of the rest of the committee stamping their feet and tapping with their sticks on the wooden floor!

Then McLeod and a man called Pye tried to speak, but they were again shouted down by the now angry congregation who would not even allow the Benediction to be said in quiet, such was their fury. McLeod was described as a "turncoat", a "Tory" (by those of the Liberal persuasion, presumably) and "Norman" – a term which means nothing to 21st century readers.

At 11.30 pm (an astonishingly late time for a Tuesday night, given that people would have to be in their factories and offices very early the following morning) the meeting broke up, and people spilled out into the snowy streets, some of them gathering in "excited groups" to discuss the astonishing events of that night. Some were even unwilling to leave the Church, staying to discuss and argue about the merits or demerits of Hunter, McLeod and Black.

We do not know, of course, what part, if any, Campbell himself played in all this. He would not, of course, have been present that evening, and it may be that he was simply the pawn in a political power struggle of the kind that bedevilled Victorian Churches behind the façade of Christianity, love and serving God. The surprising thing as well is how quickly it all seemed to die down.

The Press who had played their own part in stirring this up, under the guise of trying to calm things down, now tried to keep it going, because it would sell newspapers. It clearly sensed the mood of the congregation who like nothing more, in all ages, than causing trouble and enjoying conflict, even though even a superficial reading of the New Testament might suggest that this was not really what the Good Lord wanted them to do!

The public wish of *The Fifeshire Advertiser* which also stresses that "very few created noise and disorder" (something that seems to be contradicted by their own account!) was that the Kirk should move on. Everyone seems to have agreed, however, a few weeks later that "the fun's over, so let's get on with the rest of our life". By the end of January 1881, Presbytery "sustained the call", and, although *The Fife Free Press* and *The Fifeshire Advertiser* consistently throughout the month of February 1881 both contain a fair smattering of self-righteous letters from indignant and self-exculpating members of the Kirk, Thursday 31 March was set as the date for the induction of the Rev John Campbell to what would prove to be a very lengthy and controversial ministry.

One would have to be sorry for Campbell on the day of 31 March 1881. Hardly likely to be unaware of the shenanigans of early January and already presumably in the throes of moving house and with a five month old baby, he had a Kirk Service at which he was "preached in" at 2.00 pm, then two hours later, he had a Dinner at the Town Hall followed by a Soiree at the Corn Exchange. The Dinner was for men only, limited to 100, but the Soiree was open to ladies who could thus presumably meet Mrs Campbell and the baby!

The Fife Free Press reports verbatim and at length the sermons and speeches at all three events. They give the impression of being somewhat tedious with the Dinner speeches all beginning "Croupiers and Gentlemen", a croupier being a member of the top table in this context, rather than a man at a gambling casino, which is its 20th century meaning. But the Soiree at least was lightened by the occasional song. Miss McGregor, for example, sang "Dinna Cross The Burn" and Mr Philp "You'll Remember Me", numbers well known, presumably to the denizens of the Victorian Music Hall, but less familiar now. Ironically, in view of what had gone before, the final toast was proposed by John Hunter!

Campbell would have been glad to see the end of Sunday April 3 1881 because that meant he was now at last Minister of Kirkcaldy Parish Church. There had been three services that day, and he had taken the middle one in the afternoon, the other two being taken by two friends from the west, the Rev. Robert Shaw Hutton of Newhalls and Rev PC Black of Old Monkland.

Any lingering bad feeling concerning the appointment of Campbell soon dissipated and the Parish settled down to work under Campbell's inspiring leadership. It is important to see the election in its context, for this was the first ever election of a minister in the Parish Church (his predecessor Mark Bryden had been appointed by the "arcana imperii" of patronage) and it is natural that this should bring a certain amount of confusion with people not very certain of how a democratic process should work.

In addition, in Victorian society, any election would bring a great deal of excitement. It was as if the lack of universal franchise was made up for by enthusiasm and even, occasionally hooliganism. Parliamentary elections were always very animated and intense with reports of disturbances, demonstrations and fanaticism of the kind that was subsequently associated with football crowds. So it was hardly surprising that the election should generate such emotions; but once the man was elected, the congregation collectively shrugged their shoulders and got on with it.

Soon, Campbell would win over his congregation because he was affable, courteous, capable of humour, and approachable. Campbell would always claim that his greatest achievement in Kirkcaldy was the building and establishment of St John's Church in Meldrum Road. St John's (now called Bennochy Church) was what was known as a "daughter Church" of the Parish Church and was opened in 1908, more or less in the middle of fields for that part of Kirkcaldy had yet to be built! In fact, the idea of a Church being built there went back a little further than that.

Even before the turn of the century, Campbell and his Kirk Session were becoming concerned about the amount of incomers to the town who were now living "over the railway", possibly about 4,000 of them in number and most of them Presbyterian in religion. Incredibly, as it seems to modern eyes, there was no room for them either in the Parish Church or anywhere else in the town as Abbotshall, Invertiel, St James and Pathhead were all over-subscribed. In any case, a new Church would have to be built because in the strange words of a Parish Church newsletter "Even if we had the fullest power over our pews, people will not go so far for accommodation. We have enough to do to get many to go to Church on any terms. They will not go unless it is on hand"

In 1899, the Caledonian Mills in Prime Gilt Box Street was used for worship by the new Church, which was still not yet looked upon as a Church in its own right, but part of the Parish Church. All the time Campbell was energetic in raising funds for the building of a new Church, negotiating with the landowner,

Oswald of Dunnikier for a site and preparing the way with evangelical zeal for the new Church which seemed to signify to him, the new century and a new beginning in a new part of Kirkcaldy, now ceasing geographically and geometrically to be "the lang toun" and more of a large triangle. The foundation stone was laid in September 1907 and the Church opened in 1908 with the Minister, one Rev Robert Wiseman nominated by the Parish Church – something that does not seem all that far away from "patronage"! It was only later that St John's became a separate entity in its own right, but the Church got off to a good start because Mr Wiseman, as they joked about him, turned out to be indeed a wise man.

Not the least of Campbell's achievements was his literary contributions to the history of the Church and of the Town. In July 1904, he produced a book called *The Church and Parish of Kirkcaldy*, a fairly detailed and still very readable account of the Church in Kirkcaldy from the earliest of times. His reasons for writing this work are detailed, amusingly, in the Preface. In the first place he gave the best of reasons, namely that he wanted to do it. But them he tells us how in 1903 the Church needed a thorough clean and also electric light installed. There was a Sale of Work, and it was also suggested to the Minister that a short history of the Church might help defray expenses. "When everyone else was doing his or her utmost, the Minister could not well refuse."

Thus the minister, in an age when it was not unknown for the clerical profession to be criticised for doing nothing other than revise Greek or Hebrew verbs of a winter afternoon, chose to benefit the Church in two ways. Electric light was duly installed, and his book remains to this day a valuable source of information, written in a readable and engaging style, about the

Church. The illustrations are good, and there is a particularly informative Chapter on the tragic collapse of the gallery in 1828. It is dedicated to a Mrs Walter Heggie and the Ladies of the Congregational Work Party "whose zeal, and enthusiasm and labours have never failed in any emergency" and it is from their "obliged and affectionate Minister" – a dedication, presumably not written tongue in cheek, although a hundred years later such an ascription would lead to that assumption!

What Campbell's feelings were about the great changes going on at the time, particularly after the Liberals swept to power in 1906, we do not know. From his later life, it is difficult to imagine him having been a great social reformer, yet at the same time it is difficult to imagine a man of his talents and education being impervious to the gross poverty and evil that was going on round about him. Enlightened Victorians, and Campbell even after the death of the Queen in 1901 was very definitely a Victorian, would have seen the need for change. Apart from anything else, his profession compelled him to conduct an awful lot of funerals of people who died unnecessarily young.

There is a certain amount of evidence that Campbell, like other Presbyterians, blamed it all on the "demon drink". There can be little doubt that drink, directly and indirectly, was responsible for an awful lot of human misery at that time, but the sad fact is that the Church had very little to say on the necessity to curb the power and wealth making potential and gross profits of the brewing industry. Like the profits made by the slave trade a century earlier, a blind eye was turned to this side of the problem.

Still less was there any great effort made by the Church to recognise the link between drunkenness and the appalling social poverty, the dreadful housing and living conditions of so many of the people, and the shocking poor health which resulted, for example, in so many young men being rejected for service in the Boer War from 1899 until 1902 because they were "unfit". Campbell may well have been happy to denounce (in fiery and frightening language) alcohol from the pulpit, but he, like so many of the Church, failed to see that alcohol abuse was a symptom of the real evil. Perhaps the worthy clerics did indeed recognise this – but it suited them not to, and it was a lot easier to blame it all on Satan, whereas the real Satan owned factories, mines and indeed breweries, leased sub-standard houses to poor families at exorbitant rates - and then sometimes went to Church on a Sunday!

One always wonders what Campbell's feelings about the Suffragette movement were. No doubt he would deplore the excesses of Emmeline Pankhurst and others, which did indeed cross the line into criminality from time to time and even bordered on the insane, (the vandalism of works of art, chaining oneself to railings, putting bombs in pillar boxes, and throwing oneself in front of the King's horse at the Derby) but it is hard to imagine, in the context of his own family that he was totally opposed to votes for women, whether on Biblical grounds or any other grounds!

He had a family of nine, eight of whom were girls, and of the eight girls, five of them became doctors at a time when such things were not only unusual and unprecedented, but even looked upon as more than a little subversive. This was not only because in the course of her duties a woman doctor would from time to time have to look upon or even touch a man's sexual parts, but also because it was firmly believed that women simply did not have the requisite physical strength to cope with the sight of blood and suffering!

But Campbell not only allowed his daughters to become doctors (hardly the actions of the dyed-in-the-wool Victorian reactionary that he is sometimes pictured as being), he presumably, in those days before automatic grants and bursaries, paid for them all! Several of them gained scholarships however, but it would still have been a hefty commitment. Granted, the stipend of the Parish Church would have been a comfortable one, but to send all his children to University shows a commitment to education which is commendable. Thankfully, none of them let him down, for Phyllis (born 1880), Duncan (1882), Jessie (1883), Lizzie (1885), Adeline (1887), Margaret (1889), Annie (1893), Catherine (1898) and Isobel (1906) all did well at St Andrews University with some of them playing hockey and taking part in dramatic activities. Only Phyllis and Jessie married, the others were victims of the dreadful sexual imbalance of the 1920s with so many eligible young men buried under the soil of France.

The boy Duncan, according to the *Fasti Ecclesiae Scoticanae* was decorated with the Order of The Nile for his services as a Mechanical Engineer in the Irrigation Department of the Egyptian Government, and of the girls, the most interesting one was Adeline, because of what she did during the Great War. Having graduated from St Andrews University in 1909, she practised medicine at various hospitals until war broke out. She would have loved to enlist in the British Army, but was not allowed to do so. The Serbian Army however, under considerably more pressure in late 1914, had no such scruples about women, and accepted her services as a doctor.

There she was decorated with the Military Cross of Serbia and the Order and Decoration of St Saba (5th Class) for services to Serbia as a Surgeon in the Scottish Women's Hospital. This commemorated her heroic conduct during a typhoid epidemic at a place called Kragievitz where she served from December 1914 to June 1915. She was them transferred to the British Army, wishing to apply for service in Egypt (where her brother was) but the authorities decided that there was more need for her in Stoke on Trent helping with disabled soldiers. She returned to Scotland in 1923 and died in 1965.

Wounded Serbian soldiers in World War I with female nurses and doctors. The lady on the left may be Adeline Campbell

In some ways, Campbell's best and worst years were between 1914 and 1918. He had a good war, for war had the effect of rallying his hitherto wayward congregation and herding them together, for there now as an obvious and tangible Devil to confront. He was called the Kaiser, and Campbell had no problem at all in identifying the two of them as one, even at the expense of somewhat tenuous theology.

The outbreak of war caught Campbell as much off guard as it did anyone else, but Campbell was not slow in exploiting the possibilities. As early as Sunday August 9 1914, we find Campbell talking about "the present duty" and freely comparing the British Empire to the tribes of Israel who had God on their side, as indeed did Great Britain, even though German pulpits were saying "Gott mit Uns!" at the same time.

Perhaps 21st century eyes and ears are a little disappointed to note that there was no idea of making peace or forgiving the Germans for what they had done. But it is important to see Campbell in his context here, because no minister would dare to preach any anti-war message, for the Church was as much a part of the war as anyone else was, and it has to be said that at this stage of the war, any anti-war feeling as expressed by people like Ramsay MacDonald was stilled by the simple fact that the Germans had invaded Belgium. It was very difficult for anyone to argue against that, and the Kaiser effectively did make himself the Devil by that dastardly and indefensible deed. The sinking of the Lusitania in May 1915 would further confirm this.

Campbell encouraged his flock to enter the war saying things like "We have the strongest navy in the world and soon there will be 800,000 men in the army but confidence lies in the justice of our cause and the protection of the Almighty!" Then without any apparent conscious awareness of the irony of it all, he said "Peace I leave with you: my peace I give unto you" a statement that, a 100 years later, is hard to understand in this context. Presumably, it all hangs of the use of the word "peace" and the difference is between the inner peace and tranquillity which only Christ can give you, and the bogus peace which any deal with the Kaiser would bring, if it involved him being allowed to hold on to Belgium.

In spring 1915, Campbell was awarded the Honorary Degree of Doctor of Divinity from his old University in Glasgow. What he had done to deserve this, we are not sure, but he had now been minister of the Parish Kirk for 34 years, and had impressed everyone by his scholarship and power of preaching. It would be fair also to state that, although he had his enemies among local politicians, nevertheless he was generally well liked by his own congregation for his attentiveness to their needs. He was of course a mighty figure, but there was a compassionate side to him as well. He did not like being disagreed with (ministers are generally bad at that, for they think that are speaking with God's voice!), but there was no arrogance or snobby behaviour about him.

There was of course more to him that just war-mongering. The war also brought out his compassionate side. He was very attentive to visiting war widows, and those who came back from the war with horrific and permanent injuries, and possibly, he occasionally wondered what this war was all about. Yet he supported the war to the hilt. He must of course be seen in his context, for almost every Minister throughout the land would have agreed with him. Rev Todd across the way in St Brycedale's was no different. One suspects that, occasionally, from what we can read between the lines of a sermon, Campbell had a few doubts, but none that he could publicly express. Yet a man so intelligent, so caring and so wise in other respects must now and again have had a few doubts.

As far as the Church itself was concerned, a glance at the Minute Book of the Session reveals a deceptive normality with Communions, Baptisms and Flower Arrangements all well to the fore. Yet now and again, we find something to do with the war – the sending of parcels to serving soldiers, the adoption of a new hymn "Mine Eyes Have Seen the Glory of the Coming of the Lord" when the Americans joined the war in 1917, and a curious business of some members of the Kirk Session wishing to deny "relief" to a Mrs Ketchener whose husband was Austrian, and interned in a British prisoner of war camp! Campbell, in a move that did him credit, overruled the bigots, and Mrs Ketchener, a worthy but now impoverished Kirkcaldy lady was indeed given some financial help.

The war, as we all know, came to an end at 11.00 am on Monday 11 November 1918. Campbell, naturally relieved that the killing had stopped and that the right side had won, was quickly off his mark to arrange a service in the Parish Kirk at 2.30 pm that very afternoon. He managed to invite every other Church of Scotland minister in the town to join him, and spread word through hastily printed hand bills that the service was on. One suspects that he had been preparing for this occasion for some considerable time – indeed the end of the war had been predicted for at least a week – and now that it happened, Campbell, clearly relishing the atmosphere and taking advantage of the opportunity, rose to the occasion.

The Church was packed and contained quite a few people who were far from regular attenders. In fact, some of them had possibly been celebrating and taking advantage of the unilateral decision of quite a few publicans to open that lunch time in defiance of the prevailing licensing laws! The elders were hard put to find a seat for everyone, and a few, we are told, had to stand at the back, but those who were there, saw Campbell in his glory. His inspired preaching always did respond to a packed, attentive audience and there was even a hint of a cheer when he came in and a few sounds that sounded like "Hear! Hear!" when he made a telling point.

His sermon was on the "triumph of righteousness" and his text was "though hand join hand, the wicked shall not go unpunished, but the seed of the righteous shall be delivered". Other ministers in the town were allowed to take prayers or to do readings, but his was the sermon, and indeed his was the enjoyment of what had been for him a great day. It would be nice to think that there might have been a prayer for the defeated Germany and some hope expressed for reconciliation, but in the absence of any direct evidence we must think not. Such concepts of "magnanimity in victory" were alien to the theology of 1918.

Yet it is difficult to imagine such a learned, urbane and gracious person embracing uncompromisingly the mood of triumph that was obtained in late 1918. Apart from anything else, the euphoric mood did not last long, and there were other issues as well like the Spanish flu epidemic which continued to ravage Kirkcaldy, like everywhere else. He would soon have what he thought would have been the pleasant task of visiting members of his congregation who had just returned from the fighting. He saw a few things there that would have shocked him – strong young men now seriously maimed, some suffering from the effects of shellshock with all its unpredictability and sometimes violent disturbances, and sometimes, the reception accorded to him was far from what he had expected as ex-soldiers identified him with the mealy-mouthed utterances of parsons and padres in the front line who talked about "the righteousness of the cause" to someone who had just lost a leg!

Campbell found the post-war world hard to handle. Already aged 71 by Armistice Day in 1918, his roots were far removed from the new pressures that were beginning to pile up on society as he saw it. He was painfully aware that Christianity, although ever-present on the surface, had not had a good war, not least because people asked the not unreasonable question of why God had not stopped it. That question ought of course more properly to have been addressed to the politicians and generals, but established Churches were now beginning to notice a drop in attendances, while the more "freaky" and spiritualist Churches were on the rise, attracting, for example, many gullible war widows who wanted to see their husbands again.

But Campbell feared, more than anything else, the rise of Socialism. He knew that Mother Nature abhorred a vacuum and that something else would take the place of Churches, whether it was the godless barbarism of the Bolsheviks who had been so successful in Russia or the more subtle form of "taking people's money away from them" as advocated by Ramsay MacDonald, that "wolf in sheep's clothing" who had, very uncomfortably for Campbell, been right in 1914 about the war. However much Campbell and other preachers talked about "triumph" and "victory", the fact remained that, had more people listened to Ramsay MacDonald in 1914, millions of young men, now lying beneath the earth in France and elsewhere, would still be alive.

One particular event in Kirkcaldy in 1921 shocked Campbell, and that was the by-election victory of Labour on March 4, characterised in campaigns by a few uncomplimentary references to himself and the "pillars of the Church" who had, of course, done very well out of the war. Campbell was so upset by this, that he announced in advance in *The Fife Free Press* that his next sermon would be "Works of The Devil – Bolshevism"!

In this of course Campbell was like quite a few of the reactionary right in that he perhaps confused in his own mind (or if he didn't, he certainly deliberately obfuscated the issue for the benefit of his audience) the Labour Party and Bolshevism. There was of course a world of difference, other than that Karl Marx was the origin and author of both. Bolshevism was of course an evil dictatorship which had done barbarous things like execute the innocent family of the Czar (the Czar himself was of course far from innocent!) whereas the Labour Party under the bland charisma of the charming Scotsman Ramsay MacDonald merely offered people a fairer society. Indeed, Campbell suspected that quite a few of his own congregation were not without their sympathies for the Labour Party which was gradually replacing the Liberals who were bad enough as "the party of the middle-class conscience."

MacDonald did of course, to Campbell's horror, become Prime Minister in 1924 but did not last long because he had no overall majority, but it was clear that the man would not go away. And Kirkcaldy kept voting for Labour's Tom Kennedy! However, in June 1925,

Campbell had a great day when he was involved in the unveiling of the war memorial near the new Library and Museum. Newsreel photographs show him in the carriage, an august, venerable and dignified but now somewhat aged figure. He played his part in the ceremony, justifiably proud of and yet, inevitably, sad about all those young men from Kirkcaldy, including not a few of his own Church, that no-one would ever see again.

By this time he had also been involved in a literary work called "Kirkcaldy Burgh and Schyre", an amalgam of essays put together by Lachlan McBean, the Editor of *The Fifeshire Advertiser* and published in 1924. Campbell's contribution was "The Coming of Christianity to Fife 397 to 876 AD" , dealing with a little known period of history but mentioning St Ninian, the Culdees and Viking invasions. One feels that Campbell, whose academic discipline was history should perhaps have spent a little more time writing history books, for he was a fine scholar.

It was a shame that Campbell's last year in Kirkcaldy Parish Church was dominated in national consciousness by one event, the General Strike of early May. It originated in the mining industry, of course, affecting Kirkcaldy deeply. It had been coming for a long time, and one must really point the finger at politicians, mine owners and union leaders for their failure to stop it from happening. Indeed, one often gets the impression that men like AJ Cook, the miners' leader on the one hand and Winston Churchill on the other rather enjoyed the whole experience which they had been looking forward to, and indeed fomenting, for some time, while the moderating voice of Christianity failed to make itself heard. (A couple of generations later, Thatcher and

Scargill would clearly relish and enjoy a similar conflict!)

One could argue that it was not so much a strike as a lock-out by the owners who, because of reduced demand for coal, tried to lengthen the hours of miners and reduce their pay, feeling, not without cause, that miners had been paid too much in the Great War, simply because the country needed coal, and that now that there was less need for coal, "trimmings" and "cuttings" would have to be made.

There is little point in denying that the sympathies of Campbell and indeed his Kirk Session would have been entirely on the side of the mine owners, given the Church's dismal and predictable propensity to defend the interests of the rich against the poor. Yet the aged cleric was far too humane and intelligent a man not to admit, at least to himself, that the miners had a case as well. He did have a few miners in his congregation and people of second generation mining backgrounds, and he was by no means impervious to their feelings.

Above all, he feared anarchy and disorder. History books will say that the whole General Strike passed without any real violence and that "it was a gentlemanly, very British way of dealing with a dispute". This is not entirely true, for local newspaper reports in the weeks after the strike contain a fair amount of reports of court cases involving thuggery and intimidation in Cowdenbeath, Methil and Kirkcaldy itself. Campbell's main emotion about all this was sadness. Perhaps if he had been a younger man, he might have tried harder at some sort of conciliation, but he was now 78, with an ailing wife who required a fair amount of his attention.

The General Strike itself lasted barely two weeks in May 1926, and everyone, not least Dr Campbell, breathed a sigh of relief that what had happened in Russia in 1917 was not going to happen here, but the scars remained. The miners themselves stayed out on strike all over the summer (not surprisingly, without success, for less coal was required in summer) until in circumstances of dreadful poverty, deprivation and almost starvation, they were compelled to accept the mine owners' brutal and vindictive terms. Campbell would have been distressed at that, but in any case, by that time he was no longer in Kirkcaldy.

On Sunday October 3 1926, the respected minister preached as normal, paying tribute as well to two ladies of his congregation, a Mrs Hutchison of Braehead for her general munificence, and to Mrs Brown of Abbotshall Road who had provided communion linen, but then on Tuesday October 5, Presbytery heard of his impending demission from office. We are told that he was voted a lump sum of £238 with a £60 annuity *in perpetuitatem*, and great tribute was paid to him, notably by the Rev James Bryden of Markinch who praised his excellent preaching, his genial disposition and said that he and his wife showed the world "what the ideal Scottish manse should be, radiating a fine spiritual influence". He also quoted one of the many Kirkcaldy Provosts that he had worked with who said that "Dr Campbell was not just the Minister of the Parish Kirk; he was the Minister of the whole town" for the past 44 and a half years (which was in truth an incredibly long time), in which he had seen so many things happening in the town. The Fifeshire Advertiser is guilty however of a little rhetorical exaggeration when it claims he had been in Kirkcaldy for 54 years. He had of course been a

Minister for that length of time, but he had only been in Kirkcaldy since 1881, some 45 years ago.

Sunday October 17 1926 was his last day at the Kirkcaldy Parish Kirk. He took the Communion Service in the morning before a congregation given as 400. He was in fine voice, and was listened to with rapt attention. The afternoon and evening services were more or less tributes to what he had done, although at the evening service he was given the honour of preaching the Benediction. The following morning, he and his wife left Kirkcaldy to their new home in Newtonmore – a tactful departure, so that he would not be around when the Church went through all the upheavals of the arrival of a new minster.

The tributes paid to him are reported at length in *The Fife Free Press.* The common theme running through them all was his excellent preaching and genial presence. He was always tactful, discreet and sympathetic with a friendly attitude towards other Christians and people of other Christian denominations, the example being given a bizarre one of how "the late Minister of St Brycedale, over the way, and Dr Campbell, the minister of the parish, stood together at one baptismal font while Dr McMillan of Greenock, baptized their children". Praise was also given for his scholarship with his two books praised highly.

He was almost in his 80th year, and his faculties were not in the slightest impaired apart from his hearing (and that was a minimal problem), and in his 45 and a half years he had had an astonishing total of 13 assistants, one of whom was now the Rev John Kennedy of East Wemyss, one of those who paid him tribute. He was given a reading lamp by his congregation, and Mrs Campbell, whom everyone wished well in her struggle with ill health, was given a gold brooch, a pendant and a chain. In the event, she died only a few months later.

Not much is known of his retirement, but he would have been distressed at what was happening in the world, dominated as it was by the horrors of the depression, and the rise of Hitler. He would hardly have been happy at the arrival to power, for a second time, in the Labour Government of Ramsay MacDonald, even as a minority Government which in the event did not last long before being succeeded by a National Government, but the humane Campbell would have been appalled at the unemployment of 1930 and 1931. He had learned, slowly, from his experiences in Kirkcaldy that unemployment was no remedy for anything. It was a disease.

And as for what was happening in Germany, Campbell might have felt justified in thinking he was right all along in his full-blooded denunciations of the Kaiser and the German people. No-one knew how bad Hitler was going to become, but no-one liked the look of him. The League of Nations seemed to have failed. Campbell would have been sad about that. One would have hoped that he might have wondered if a more humane attitude had been shown at Versailles, this might have meant that there would have been no Hitler.

Rev Dr John Campbell died at Newtonmore on 21 October 1935, just a few days short of his 88th birthday. As befitted a man who had been Minister of the Parish Kirk from 1881 to 1926, *The Fifeshire Advertiser* pays an eloquent tribute to this man who had been a widower for 8 years since his wife died in January 1927. It says that "there was not a philanthropic of benevolent agency which did not have his sympathy and benevolent support", being the governor of the Philp Trust for deserving cases and "manager" (sic) of the Kirkcaldy and District Savings Bank". (By "manager", what *The Fifeshire Advertiser* means presumably is something more akin to what we would call a Director, rather than the man who actually is the day to day running of the bank).

His "preaching was not wanting in the more popular elements, it was especially marked with earnestness of tone, depth of feeling, vigour and freshness of thought and force of expression, but always under the restraint of a severe taste (sic)". His "greatest achievement was the founding of St John's Church", but he was also a great scholar with both his books mentioned as he was an authority on Church history, particularly the local Church, as well as the broader issue of the Celtic Church in Fife.

He was also given great credit for his "broad catholicity of mind" which led to the "occasional exchange of pulpit courtesies – and that at a time when sectarian bitterness and jealousy was keen". This was a tribute to his ecumenical spirit, but how far his "broad catholicity of mind" actually went, we cannot be sure. He certainly tried to build bridges with the Free Kirk (after his retirement in 1929, the Free Kirk and the Church of Scotland were reconciled in any case), but whether he made approaches to the Roman Catholic Church, for example, is far more debatable. This was after all the time when the Church of Scotland repeatedly denounced the Irish as being a "threat to the purity of the Scottish race" and backed education committees who refused to appoint Roman Catholic teachers!

He remained "still interested in Kirkcaldy and delighted to receive visitors". He seldom, if ever in his retirement, returned to the town he had served so well (for fear of cramping the style of his successor) but he kept up friendship with his parishioners and welcomed them when they were passing through Newtonmore on holiday. The newspaper tribute concludes by saying that "five of his daughters are doctors" and that "one daughter was recently appointed Lecturer in Chemistry at Bedford College, London University".

He clearly remained an influential and much loved character in Kirkcaldy, as was natural for someone who was there as Minister for 45 and a half years. This is not necessarily a record, but it is still remarkable especially when one considers the things that happened in that time to the town, the Church and the country in the shape of wars (one major one and several smaller ones like the Boer War) and social reform. He did not agree with everything that happened, nor did everyone agree with him, but for all Kirkcaldy he was a figure of stability and reliability

Children:

Phyllis Carruthers Campbell born November 1 1880

MA St. Ands.

Married Donald Charles McArthur, Queensland March 28 1925

Duncan Macgregor Campbell born February 21 1882

Order of the Nile. Mechanical Engineer, Irrigation Department, Egypt.

Jessie McNaughton Campbell born March 31 1883

MB, ChB St Ands. DPH Edinburgh

Married Alex Maxwell MA Oxon, Home Office in August 1919

Lizzie Mabel Renwick Campbell born May 20 1885

MA, MB, ChB St.Ands

Died Allendale, Northumberland November 3 1939

Adeline Herbert Campbell born June 11 1887

MA, MB, ChB St Ands (Hons).

Red Cross, Military Cross, Order of St Saba of Serbia

Margaret M'Gillewie Campbell born October 26 1889

MA St. Ands

Annie Renwick Campbell born August 20 1893

MB, ChB. St. Ands

Catherine McGregor Campbell born March 29 1898

medical student

Isobel Grace McNaughton Campbell born October 12 1906

(Fasti Ecclesiae Scoticanae 1924)

Robert M Adam

Headmaster

Robert Adam was the Headmaster or Rector of
Kirkcaldy High School between 1948 and 1971. During
that time, the school was widely recognised as being one
of the best in Scotland, certainly one of the best in the
public sector.

Regularly during Adam's tenure would the school feature prominently in the list of Bursary winners at Scotland's four great Universities, and every other school talked about Kirkcaldy High School in hallowed terms, and with a great deal of envy. That this was the case was to a very large extent because of the quality of their leader, RM Adam who was indeed the main man or "the Bod" as he was commonly called by his pupils - but not to his face!

The year 1948 in which he arrived was a significant one. The war was now definitely over – all through 1946 and 1947 there had still been some ex-soldiers trickling back to take up teaching posts, but by 1948, peace was definitely here. Yet, not entirely. Defeated Germany continued to cause problems as the victors, from the West and from the East, like a pair of jackals, ripped her apart. The winners from the East held on to what they had – so determined were they that Germany would never rise again – and for the next 40 years, the world would be subjected to a "Cold War", which fortunately never really heated up, although there were one or two close calls.

Back home, a reforming Labour Government was in power, determined and pledged to make sure that the evil days of the 1920s and 1930 never returned. The National Health Service was born in 1948, and within ten years the country saw the benefit in the elimination and reduction of so many unnecessary and avoidable illnesses. Grim, white-coated nurses and dentists visited schools, stuck needles into children, pulled out teeth, made sure everyone drank a small bottle of milk at school per day, and this generation grew up to be, by and large, healthy – certainly a great deal healthier than previous ones.

It was to this background that Robert Adam began his lengthy and successful headmastership of Kirkcaldy High School. Situated where the Adam Smith college is now, Kirkcaldy High School was in 1948 what might (in 21st century speak) be described as a "failing school". For obvious reasons, the school had been grossly underfunded during the war years, but there was more than that. Previous headmasters had not been as good as one would have expected them to be, and the result was that, although there was still the elite from the prosperous areas of Milton Road, Loughborough Road and David Street which did well, not everyone from other parts of town achieved what one might have expected.

And although Kirkcaldy was hardly in 1948 a land flowing with milk and honey – still less was it anything like a "land fit for heroes to live in", (as a previous Prime Minister had rashly promised at the end of the 1918 war), there was nevertheless an expectation that things were going to get better. Indeed they had to. It was as if the working classes had decided that enough was enough. Wars, unemployment, Victorian repression and economic depression had now gone, and we weren't going to have any more of this! In this, education would play a vital role.

At the very time that Adam became Headmaster of Kirkcaldy High School, a generation of children were being born in large numbers. They were to be called "the baby boomers" and were brought about by soldiers coming home from the war, deciding to get married and settle down and to produce children in large numbers. More and more houses had running water, so there was no excuse for dirt. And because of the National Health

Service, fewer children died due to the horrible and preventable diseases that sheer neglect had engendered before. Little wonder that the ebullient Minister of Health, Nye Bevan went around saying things like "capitalism would wear the new hospitals like medals, but medals of a battle it had lost". He also described that upper class as "lower than vermin", a somewhat intemperate use of language, perhaps, but few could deny that there was an element of truth in what he said. The capitalist press would talk about the horrors of "austerity" that the country was going through. In fact, things were far better than they had ever been before. And although many things were still rationed, you could be guaranteed to get your ration.

Industry now began to boom. Unemployment was a thing of the past, and key industries like coal mining and the railways were nationalised. The hope was expressed, particularly in Kirkcaldy that there would be no more of the horrors of the mining strikes of the past. This turned out to be not exactly true, as the 1980s would prove, but for the moment at least, peace came to the industrial as well as to the military front. The linoleum industry, after an unsteady restart after the war began to boom once again, not least because more houses began to be built, all of which would need floor covering.

And where were the houses to be built? In Kirkcaldy, there was no real choice. They had to be built in the hinterland, in areas like Templehall, the Valley, Sauchenbush and Smeaton. Kirkcaldy may well in 1948, when Adam arrived, have still been the "lang toun"; but by 1960, on any map it resembled a fairly large triangle. Kirkcaldy High School itself, of course, moved upwards to its present site in 1958, a clear symbol of the changing nature of the town itself.

Secondary education was of course very selective when Adam arrived. Critics of this system possibly have a point when they attack its inflexibility in that a decision made when a child was 12 could only, and with a great deal of difficulty, be changed very seldom, and only when a clear and obvious error had been made. They are possibly wrong, however, when they claim that the selection was *ipso facto* a piece of social segregation, and that the middle class children passed their qualification exam and went to a good school in Kirkcaldy High School to become lawyers, teachers and doctors while the working class children were decanted to Viewforth to mark time until they could be used for factory fodder. This made good sort of reading for those who wanted to make a political point, but it was a gross over-simplification – and certainly not 100% true.

And what was Kirkcaldy High School itself like in 1948 when Adam arrived? It would appear that things were not all that it could have been. The previous Rector, Dr FM Earle, is continually damned with faint praise by all those who knew him, and had resigned through ill health at Christmas 1947, having been ill for some time. What the "ill health" actually was, no-one seems to want to specify, but we are pleased to hear that he had recovered by the time that Adam delivered his first ever Prize Giving speech in summer 1948. "The school, as it is now, is largely his creation" said Adam with deliberate ambiguity.

But perhaps the greatest indication that things were not what the Education Committee wanted comes in early 1948. The "vice-principal" or "depute head teacher" had of course taken over as interim Rector. This was a man called Mr J Stuart. *The Fife Free Press* of January 17 1948 contains an account of a bitter political argument because Mr Stuart was not even on the preliminary leet for the job! This would quite clearly seem to indicate that he was not considered to be up to the job.

Stuart's cause was taken up by a local politician called Henry (sic) Gourlay. Gourlay would of course become Kirkcaldy's MP a decade later, although he would be better known as Harry. Clearly, he was at this stage trying to attract attention to himself and felt that it was "most discourteous" not to include Mr Stuart. Gourlay's motion however was defeated by 4 votes to 24. Harry would have been better advised to keep quiet. The Committee clearly had its own views of Stuart's capabilities for the job.

The leet of eight was reduced to four by the day of the interview on Monday February 9 1948. It was a strong leet, consisting of two men who were already Headmasters (such of course was the attraction of Kirkcaldy High School) – Adam himself and William Byres, currently Headmaster of Buckhaven High School, John Robin who was Deputy Headmaster at Dunfermline High School and Leonard White, Principal Teacher of Modern Languages at Ayr Academy. Adam, at 41 the youngest candidate, emerged victorious.

The Fifeshire Advertiser tells us that Robert M Adam, born in 1906 was a native of Paisley, and had graduated with a first class honours degree in Maths and Natural Philosophy from Glasgow University in 1928. He might have gone to Cambridge to do research in Maths, but decided to be a teacher instead. Following his year's training, he had taught at Allan Glen's School from 1929 until 1935 when he was appointed Principal

Teacher of Maths at Dumfries Academy. In 1939, as war clouds loomed he had moved to Aberdeen to become Principal Teacher of Maths and Deputy Head Teacher (until the 1960s it was possible to combine such posts) at Aberdeen Central School, before becoming Head Teacher at the Gordon School in Huntly in Aberdeenshire in 1944. He was married with 3 children (Elinor, Dorothy and Harry), and *The Fife Free Press* adds that he is "keenly interested in school sports".

He took up his position on April 26 1948. On Wednesday May 5, the staff entertained Mr and Mrs Adam to tea in the restaurant of the ice rink. Significantly, perhaps, Mr Stuart who did not of course make the preliminary or long leet was there, but took no important part, leaving it to Miss Christie (commonly known by the pupils as "Dame Christie"), the Lady Advisor to do the official welcome.

The post of Lady Advisor was often one of much ridicule and ribald comments. In the days before women could become Headteachers, the job was a sop to feminism and the growing and justified feeling that as girls were, after all, half the school population, they needed some specialist female help in how not to get pregnant, for example! The Lady Advisor's job, stereotypically, was to advise girls to stay away from boys, not to wear short skirts or revealing dresses and to become "young ladies". In this of course they lamentably failed, but very often when men teachers were reluctant or even forbidden to belt girls, the Lady Advisor would do the needful! It was often vulgarly supposed in male staff rooms that the Lady Advisor, usually a spinster, would now and again offer more than "advice" to the Headmaster!

Dame Christie however was anything but the caricature detailed above. She was much respected in town. Very conscientious and dedicated, she taught Latin and other subjects, and on this occasion welcomed Mr and Mrs Adam to Kirkcaldy High School, taking advantage of the opportunity to talk about the development of the school in recent decades from a small school to the "wide multi-lateral High School that it is today".

Mr Adam meets the Queen and the Duke of Edinburgh in 1958 at the newly built school

So Adam's career at Kirkcaldy High School was launched. The annual Prizegiving in July 1948, (by coincidence a couple of weeks after the visit of the King and Queen to Kirkcaldy and a few days after the official launch of the National Health Service) was a muted, low key affair for circumstances prevented it from being held in the Adam Smith Halls which were being painted. Thus in front of only 500 people in the lecture hall of the school, Adam delivered his first address. In later years things would be different, but on this occasion, Adam had to apologise for his "stock-taking" (a normal practice on such occasions) for he had only been there for 10 weeks and therefore had little chance to review "the stock".

He contented himself therefore with a homily on the need to work hard. He wanted pupils to have sound learning but also to cultivate politeness and good manners, and to do everything at work or play to the best of their ability. He then paid a tribute to his predecessor Dr F M Earle, and to say thank you to Mr Stuart for having done the job in the interval between Earle and himself, before presenting the prizes, the Girls Dux this year being Lilian Haig and the Boys Dux being Robert Fyfe, both of whom also won other prizes.

Adam was of course a great believer in academic achievement and excellence, and in future his Prize giving ceremonies would be lavish and very formal affairs in which he was not above taking a swipe at things in education that were not going well (most Headteachers could do such things!) in front of a large and captive attendance of VIPs and doting, attentive parents.

But of course the Prize giving is merely the icing on the cake. School is, by its very nature, mundane and unspectacular. Hard work and the ability to keep going, to attend regularly and to respond to leadership are essential. Terms are long, examinations come round sooner than one would like, and application is often the key word to get one through a dull, wet Thursday in November or a roasting hot day in June. Children, even the brightest, are not always receptive to learning, and need to be pushed, cajoled, stimulated, bullied, flattered and persuaded as appropriate. Teachers are the same. There are times when they are not working as hard as they ought to be. They too must be directed and managed, massaged and reprimanded, scolded and praised from time to time.

So what makes a good Headmaster? A lifetime in teaching has still not yielded a simple or easy answer to that question, but there is a surprising consensus and even unanimity among those who worked with Robert Adam that he was a good one. In the first place – and this is the vital point, surely – he was always there. His presence was visible and high key. He even in his early days, when the school was where the Adam Smith College now is, was seen occasionally to travel on the school bus from his home at 78 Loughborough Road! Needless to say, the behaviour on these occasions was impeccable. Latterly he would drive his car, usually a Wolseley, an expensive car in the 1950s but one that was very reliable.

He would make a point of haranguing the first year, stressing to them how lucky they were to be allowed to attend Kirkcaldy High School, and telling them the need to work hard. "All homework must be carefully and thoroughly prepared – in 1st year you must do at least an hour, and if you do Latin, an hour and a quarter". He had glasses but didn't always use them or need them, but he did have the ability when sitting in his office to balance his glasses on his brow, then suddenly let them drop on to his nose to read a document which he had in front of him.

On the odd occasion, of course, it is inevitable that a Headmaster has to be out of school for a meeting with the Director of Education or interviewing for a job appointment, for example. Adam made sure that on these occasions he was seen to be at school in the morning, patrolling corridors with his characteristic walk (a rolling gait which has been described as a "waddle"), arms behind his back, noticing everything, saying "Good Morning" to everyone he met, knocking on the occasional door and popping in with some excuse to see how things were going with a notoriously difficult class or with a teacher who had been, for one reason or other, struggling of late.

Occasionally his visits could cause resentment among members of staff who were trying out a few methods which were not in the traditional Adam mould. He once entered a class where a mild discussion was going on about a book that the class had just read. This, of course, is fine 21st century pedagogy but Adam did not approve. He came back several times that day to see if the teacher was doing what he always wanted his staff to do – namely stand up, talk, chalk in hand, near blackboard while pupils sat obediently and deferentially. He even disapproved of a teacher stapling together bits of paper while his class were working. If the class were writing something, the teacher should be walking round, looking over their shoulders and watching what they were doing.

Whenever he entered a classroom, everyone stood up. It was not always very practicable in Art or

Technical for example, but nevertheless some recognition of his being there was required. The pupil who sat nearest the door was sometimes detailed to close the door after him, and it was claimed that he knew the names of about 90% of his pupils, by just talking to them, giving them words of encouragement and asking if they liked the subject. It would be a very brave pupil who would say "No" to that question.

Sometimes his excuses for popping in were rather lame ones. The story is told of how on one occasion a teacher was working in an end room of the top corridor, and Mr Adam very politely knocked on the door, equally politely said "Good Morning" and then said "Just Passing". He could hardly have been "just passing" in that particular area, for he would have been passing through the outside wall, if he had continued his path!

If he had to go out of school for an inevitable appointment in the morning, he would make sure he was back by lunch time, being seen to patrol the Dining Hall and dealing with the occasional misbehaviour in dinner queues and toilets. If his appointment out of school was in the afternoon, he would make sure that he was back by 4.00 pm seeing everyone off the premises, saying "Good Night" to everyone, noticing which teachers were in a hurry to leave and then popping in to the Chess Club or one of the other many extra-curricular activities that he did his best to encourage. Latterly, his Wolseley car was seen leaving the playground at about 12.25 pm every Friday. This was not him knocking off early for the weekend. It was to attend his Rotary Club for the weekly lunch, and in his final year 1970/71 he was the President.

He was Headmaster at a time when it was still possible to get off with a little dictatorship. He realised, from his formative years as a teacher, at an early stage in his Headmastership, that indiscipline stemmed from the staff, and that he had to be tough with them. Once again, the universal verdict from those who worked under him was that he was strict but fair. Just occasionally someone who was not pulling his weight had to be persecuted out of a job – a sad but inevitable occurrence if a Headmaster wanted a good school.

Gradually in the late 1940s and early 1950s, the staff changed. This would happen anyway, but Adam realised that staff changes were vital in the development of a school from a good one to an outstanding one. Some of the poorer staff were gently encouraged (occasionally the encouragement had to be less than gentle!) to leave earlier than they had to, and he realised a great deal of research was necessary for new appointments. He had built up a fairly wide network of contacts and spent a great deal of time finding out just which teachers would do a good job for him, even on occasion finding an excuse to meet a potential teacher in person.

One aspiring Classics teacher was met, under the pretext of Raith Rovers playing against Hibs in Edinburgh, "under the clock" at Waverley Station, talked to very briefly and then received a letter on the Monday offering him a job. That old hanging clock at Waverley Station, often the rendezvous of lovers like the statue of Eros in Piccadilly in London, was thus used for a very unofficial interview. At least one other teacher was "interviewed" over tea in the Station Hotel.

Sometimes it was easier. A student teacher had clearly performed well in his stint at the school. On his last day, he was summoned into the smoke-filled office (Adam was a great pipe smoker, using a bent "Sherlock Holmes" pipe) to say goodbye. Hands were shaken, and almost as an afterthought, Adam said "Have you got a job yet?" The young student said "Not yet" for there was a certain amount of bureaucracy to be gone through at College and with local authorities, as he thought. Adam then said – the real purpose of the occasion – "How would you like to work here". The young student then said "Yes." "OK, I'll see you on August 23". "But, don't I have to fill up a form or go to an interview or something like that?" "Oh, never mind about that!" And a career was launched. Clearly in this case, Adam's judgement was spot on, for the young aspirant would in time become a Headmaster himself.

Adam, although generally well-liked by pupils who all appreciated the fact that he tended to know their names and said things like "Good morning, Mary" in the corridor, had absolutely no compunctions about using the belt on bad pupils. Possibly he regretted its necessity, but nevertheless he knew well that occasionally it was essential to tame a disruptive class or pupil. As he walked round the school, he took his belt with him, hidden in one of the long sleeves of his black gown. He could thus meet visitors, for example, and be absolutely charming, but could immediately deal with any nonsense he saw in the corridors. Normally beltings would be done in the sanctity of his room, but his belt was hidden in his gown "for emergencies".

Modern educationalists are appalled, of course, by this line of thinking, but one really must ask the question of whether the educational system is better now than in the 1950s, and one really would have to come down on the side of the old-fashioned method of discipline, if you want a good school. On the other hand, it certainly could be misused. Many people have bitter memories of being belted by sexually frustrated spinsters or brutal neo-Nazi young men for things like "bad writing". A wise Headmaster made sure that the punishment was only used for things like bullying other pupils, rudeness to teachers or that phrase that covers almost everything "disrupting the teaching situation". He was always able to justify his actions to parents and politicians.

He not only used the belt himself, but encouraged his staff to do so. The thorny issue of men belting girls is of course a difficult one, but when one of his staff, the famous "Bolsh" Brown was asked in a School magazine interview if he ever regretted belting girls, the answer was "No, and I've never known a girl being any the worse for it – rather better in fact".

Another man called Brown provided material for a story about Adam and corporal punishment. This is his most famous pupil called Gordon Brown, who rose of course to dizzy heights of the sort that Adam himself would never have dreamed about. If the following story is true (and one must always be careful about anecdotal stories from schooldays!) then it reflects little credit on Adam and raises a question or two about Brown's naivety as a young man.

It was December 1965. It was the day of a World Cup qualifier, played at lunch time on a Tuesday in Naples, Italy and it was a game that Scotland had to win if they were to compete in the 1966 World Cup finals in England. Most unusually for the time, the game was to be televised live, and a few enlightened employers and even Headmasters of other schools bent a little and made arrangements for their charges to watch the game, which after all was to have vital consequences in the footballing world.

But not Mr Adam. Although a keen football fan himself, he announced solemnly that dire consequences would follow anyone who absented himself that afternoon. But then he said that if anyone really wanted to see the game, they should come to his office to discuss the matter. Displaying a simplicity that was never obvious in his later life as Chancellor of the Exchequer and Prime Minister, Brown with a few others went to see him, hoping that Adam would rig up a television in the Assembly Hall, for example. Adam unceremoniously belted them all! And if that weren't bad enough, Scotland lost 0-3!

This story makes one wonder how Adam got off with that. The boys, after all, had committed no crime other than expressing a wish to see a football match rather than attending lessons. Possibly, however, it was a great lesson to Brown in the future. He would learn perhaps not to trust anything that the Chairman of the International Bank or Angela Merkel or Barack Obama said!

On another occasion, a bright boy who later rose to great heights in Fife Education, becoming Organiser for Modern Languages, decided to absent himself from school to go to the Army Recruiting Office to enquire about a military career. Somehow or other, Adam through his many contacts got wind of this and visited summary punishment on the potential soldier. Possibly Adam did him a good turn in discouraging soldiering as a profession.

Adam took a pride in the progress of his pupils, and was quite open about admitting that success in the Highers and Lowers (replaced in 1962 by Ordinary Grade) were important to the school and of course to the pupils themselves. One of his famous dictums was that in the months of February and March (the exams themselves were held in March until 1961), every day spent in school working hard would see an improvement of half of one percent in the actual mark achieved in the exam. This was not literally true, of course, but it was a useful carrot with which to entice pupils.

Report cards were often issued by him personally. He would come into a class, deliver the reports with praise or blame as appropriate and make his feelings known about the necessity for continued hard work. He was always particularly interested in achievement in History and Geography. These subjects were of course known as the "swot subjects", and Adam believed that anyone could do these subjects if they decided to put their minds to the task. He would sympathise with anyone who could not do Latin or French or Physics or his own subject Maths, but he believed (rightly) that History and Geography told a great deal about the quality and character of the pupil concerned, and a row was frequently given to those who failed to perform in those subjects. He occasionally gave the impression of being less interested in subjects like Art than he was in more academic ones.

On one occasion, he was delivering the reports. One girl had a good report in every subject except German. "Your French is good, Jennifer, as is your Latin. Maths, English, History all acceptable… but your German is not so good. What is the problem with German? Why do you find German so difficult? Have you not been working at your German?" The poor girl, tongue-tied and embarrassed at such a public dressing-down had no answer, so he continued "…and as well as your poor performance in German, I notice that you have been off quite a lot. Is there any reason for that?" he thundered at the poor girl, now on the verge of tears, but she managed to stammer out, "I was ill" "And what was the problem?" he asked without any appreciable softening on his tone. "German measles" blurted the girl.

A few people suppressed sniggers, "the Bod" himself found his facial muscles twitching and eventually he relaxed into a smile as the class burst into laughing. He then enquired after the girl's health, wished her well in her exams especially in German and departed on his way, realising that the ability to laugh at oneself is a vital part of being a Headmaster, even a strict one like himself.

But he was no Olympian character. His strength lay in his permanent accessibility to both staff and pupils. He knew everything that was going on, for he had the ability to listen and to watch – the passive skills of headmastering – as well as the active and the pro-active ones. Above all, he gave the impression that pupils and the school mattered to him. He spent long hours at the school, seldom missed any kind of school function and was frequently seen on a Saturday morning watching a school cricket or rugby match. Most of his pupils will agree that he was strict, honest and fair, but one or two have said that he was occasionally "lacking in the milk of human kindness"

He was however a great believer in formality. Morning assemblies were no half-hearted affairs. The school choir and the school orchestra would be present with the hymn practised beforehand, there would be a Collect (something like the Apostle's Creed recited by the school, for example), and there would be a rota of members of staff and prefects to do the biblical reading (religious diversity was not yet a current political issue!), there would be a short address, possibly a warning about hard work and good conduct, but he would always be particularly careful to read out particularly good achievements by pupils and by sports teams.

The Senior Dance was one of the highlights of the school calendar, and was very formal. Some male members of staff would appear in evening dress, the rest in lounge suits, and the female members of staff and the girls would be there in evening dress. Everyone would be met by Mr and Mrs Adam as they arrived, and would be duly seen off the premises. Alcoholic drink, so often the bane of school functions, would be nowhere in sight. It would have to be a very skilful pupil or member of staff to get off with that. As a result, Senior Dances were much looked forward to and are still much reminisced about.

He himself took charge of the timetable, normally a gargantuan task, but in the very stable atmosphere of Kirkcaldy High School in the 1950s and 1960s, possibly less so than today, for things seldom changed. 1st year would always go to games on a certain afternoon, for example, and there would be very few changes to the curriculum which was stable with hardly any new subjects, for example, and it is difficult not to look back on those days with a great deal of envy.

As he himself was in charge of the timetable, he was always able to ensure that the Principal Teacher of any given subject took the Higher class in that subject, or if there were more than one Higher sections, the top Higher section. This made sure that the best pupils had the best teachers, but it had an unfortunate side effect in that many teachers, particularly the younger ones, seldom if ever, got a chance to teach the better pupils, and thus when asked at a promotion interview "How many Higher classes have you taught?" found it difficult to give an adequate answer. But his method of keeping the best classes for the best teachers meant that the bad teachers (and there were at least two that he was unable for years to get rid of, hard though he tried, with illustrious nicknames like "Fanny" and "Knuckles"), were unable to do a great deal of harm to the fine reputation of the school. Their influence was minimised.

Another complaint about the school was that it was very male-orientated in terms of men having the promoted posts. A look at the Staff lists would give one a certain amount of encouragement to think that, but this perhaps is not so much a criticism of Adam as of the educational system of the time. Women, married women in particular, were subject to the "tiresome processes of biology" (as another Headmaster put it) in that they tended to get pregnant without necessarily giving too much thought to the disastrous effect this might have on next year's Higher class! It is of course very politically incorrect to even mention this phenomenon nowadays, but in Adam's time, it was very definitely one of the reasons why promotion for a married woman was less likely than it later became.

Perhaps a more serious political complaint was about his involvement in the EIS, the teacher's Union. He became President of the Fife Association in 1957, and some members of his staff felt uneasy about this. The EIS is, after all, a Union and occasionally it must represent its members AGAINST a Headmaster! This would surely lead to a clash of interests from time to time, and one of his Classics staff compared this to the way that the Emperor Augustus assumed power – he became the consul (the chief magistrate) and the tribune (the representative of the plebs, the Roman working class) at the same time! So what did a teacher do if he had a grievance against his Headmaster?

Kirkcaldy High School was in his time always seen as a "rugby" playing school, rather than football. This perhaps amazes us, considering the obsession with football that prevailed in the town and still does. It was seen as snobby, but Adam, himself a football fan, did little to change this perception, for he felt that his pupils of Kirkcaldy High School were entitled to consider themselves better than those of other schools. Besides, there were many other opportunities for boys to learn to play football if they so wished.

The 1950s were good years for most people. The Conservatives, returned to power in 1951, thankfully decided not to overturn Labour's Welfare State or National Health Service and the country settled down to a period of benign, albeit aristocratic rule. The Coronation of 1953 induced a "feel-good" atmosphere in the country, and more and more television sets began to appear in people's houses and not a few motor cars as well on the road outside.

For Kirkcaldy High School, a new building was promised, then planned and finally built on the site of the old Dunnikier Policies estate owned by the Oswald family. The choice of site was a good one, for that was definitely the way that the town was expanding as houses were built at a rate of knots to cope with the demand for new housing with running water and other mod cons. "The town has gone north" was the cry as Templehall, Valley and other areas of town were turned from rural to urban with devastating speed.

The old building of Kirkcaldy High School, on whose site at least if not in the actual building itself, centuries of langtonians had been educated, was now beginning to show its age and was clearly inadequate for the now rapidly expanding population of the prosperous 1950s. In his Prize giving speech in the Adam Smith Hall in July 1954, Adam was able to announce that he had already seen plans for a new school and said that it was about time for "if we do not get our new Kirkcaldy High School building soon, we will be bursting at the seams".

The school flitted in dribs and drabs throughout spring and early summer 1958 – something that in itself causes a tremendous amount of disruption and chaos. Adam worked tirelessly during the flitting, never being afraid to dirty his hands and coping extremely well with the multifarious problems thrown up by the new building from electric fittings to dustbins, and in particular the very thorny problem of which Department would be allocated which rooms and store cupboards. Different skills were called for rather than the mundane ones of the day-to-day running of a school. Adam responded magnificently to the challenge.

The Queen was due to visit Kirkcaldy on June 30 1958. It would have been a great idea to ask her to open the school formally. For one reason or other, but mainly to do with the fact that the school was not yet quite ready, this did not happen – a cause of immense disappointment to Adam and his staff, one imagines. In particular the Assembly Hall was not quite ready – something that meant that even the Prize giving would have to be a low-key affair this year with no parents invited – but arrangements were made for the royal party to come and see the school and meet Mr Adam and his senior staff and a few pupils in the playground. This was of course throwing a huge hostage to fortune in terms of good weather, but fortunately June 30 turned out to be a fine summer day.

Security was tight, however, that day – and there was a reason for it. *The Fifeshire Advertiser* of May 10 1958 reports a bizarre story of a bomb being delivered to the house of one of the local journalists, Alan MacKay, with a note saying that a similar device was being prepared for the visit of the Queen to Kirkcaldy. There was even a political point to this – not the obvious ones of communists, Irish republicans or anarchists – but a weird demonstration against the Queen being called Queen Elizabeth II, when in fact she was only Queen Elizabeth I of Scotland! This was obviously the work of a crackpot, and was immediately disowned by the embarrassed local Scottish nationalists, but it was a real bomb and the threat was taken very seriously indeed. It was, after all, only a few years since the Stone of Destiny had been stolen.

Fortunately nothing untoward occurred, and the Queen and the Duke of Edinburgh, after lunch at the Town House, arrived in the school playground to be introduced to a very proud Mr Adam, his Deputy Tom Davidson, and the Lady Advisor Elizabeth Morris before the assembled staff, all wearing gowns and graduation hoods, and pupils in immaculate school uniforms. While Janette Davidson, the "smallest pupil in the school" gave the Queen a copy of "Pet Marjorie" and expressed a hope that her children Prince Charles and Princess Anne would read it, the Duke talked amiably to Tom Balfour the Head Boy.

The Fifeshire Advertiser is duly impressed, even becoming lyrical in its description. "The success of a formal occasion is that it should breathe the atmosphere of informality. And that was the essence of proceedings

277

at Kirkcaldy High School... The vast new building; embowered in trees and with its fresh, green lawns was looking particularly attractive. A beneficent Parks Department had caused geraniums and other plants to blossom, overnight as it were, in the beds of the impressive quadrangle. Brilliant sunshine beat down to give everything an extra sheen..."

Work continued on the school, and session 1958/59 was the first full school year of the new building. Concerns continued however with *The Fifeshire Advertiser* worried about the lack of street lighting for pupils going to and from their new school in the winter months. The area had not yet been built up of course, although a new housing estate to be called the Dunnikier Estate was being planned, and Kirkcaldy High School was, in 1958, virtually in the country. "Even Bright Pupils Will Be In The Dark" was the banner headline, written by a journalist with a mistaken belief in his own powers of comedy, but the Council promised to do something about it.

The school was officially opened on Monday 20 October 1958 by the Principal and Vice-Chancellor of the University of St Andrews, Professor TM Knox in the new Assembly Hall, and the school was then open to the public for the next two nights. The address to the pupils was one of which Adam, nodding sagely, heartily approved, for Professor Knox told everyone to "Be Active" and warned them all of the dangers of indolence and sloth. It was not good enough, he said, to blame everyone else for your own shortcomings – you had to do something yourself. He commended the school's motto "Usque conabor" ("I will try my utmost" or "I will keep on trying") and told a few stories about useless students of his who had come to St Andrews University, done nothing and then wondered why the University had "discontinued their studies" or "booted them out".

Various dignitaries from Fife Education Department then told everyone how the school had cost £500,000 and how it was merely part of the £8,000,000 that had been invested in school building since the war with primary schools also built at Dunearn, Valley, Fair Isle, St Marie's, a junior secondary school at Templehall, and a Roman Catholic one projected "not far from here" in the near future. The future looked bright.

Indeed it did, but no-one could predict just exactly to what heights Kirkcaldy High School would reach. A glance through the winners of Bursary Competitions at any Scottish University will show a disproportionate number of pupils from Kirkcaldy High School. These were the fruits of Adam's selection policy and general running of the school, and as long as that continued, he attracted very little criticism in the town. As early as 1954, he was able to boast that the University of St Andrews offered nine Bursaries for £400, and Kirkcaldy High School had won two of them. He had no Parents Nights in which parents came to school to discuss their children's progress. He felt there was little need for that, in that results in exams, always given to *The Fife Free Press*, spoke for themselves.

Douglas McIntosh, the Director of Education, who became Principal of Moray House College of Education, spoke frequently and often about the qualities of RM Adam. "At weekends, in the evening, day and night, he is ready to work and has worked for the service of this school. Not only that, but his work is utterly efficient". McIntosh would tell of the times that he would meet Adam at say 9.15 am for an important meeting, and have Adam say to him that he had already been in school for more than an hour this morning! McIntosh would even boast that less money per head of the pupil population was spent on Kirkcaldy High School because the school was the most efficiently run!

The catchment area of the school was beginning to spread as well in the early 1960s with the development of the new town of Glenrothes. Until such time as Glenrothes High School opened in 1965, Glenrothes pupils could go either to Buckhaven or Kirkcaldy, and at one point there were as many as 24 school buses that brought children to the school. With as wide an area as all that, there were many good pupils, and there was never the curse of "unviable classes" a phenomenon which affected, in later years, subjects like Latin, Modern Languages and Music where a Headmaster could look at next year's numbers, see that there were only 7 taking Higher Latin for example and say that the class could not run, ignoring quality in favour of quantity. There was never the slightest danger of that happening with the Kirkcaldy High School of RM Adam.

Adam would say things like "We are trying to make the most of the innate ability of our pupils and to send to higher education, to commerce and to industry people who will benefit from their further training, who will find fulfilment and satisfaction in their chosen sphere and who, having acquired the habits of industry, will be critical in the best sense of the word, and who will have been given resources from which to draw in order to use their leisure well."

An experiment took place in the mid-1960s. Often dubbed the "Brown experiment" because Gordon Brown was one of the people who benefitted from it, it was probably the brainchild of the Director of Education,

Douglas McIntosh, rather than Mr Adam, but Adam went along with it. It had its genesis in the realisation that Scottish pupils, even when they attended Scottish Universities, were at a disadvantage against English pupils who had spent two years in their "Sixth Year" at their Grammar or Independent schools.

McIntosh's idea was to give the opportunity to bright pupils to miss out Primary 7, to go to Kirkcaldy High School a year earlier and thus they would be able to spend seven years at secondary school, although they could go to University after six years if they wished. They might have even been able to miss out first year at University, but the Universities themselves would have been less than totally happy about this idea, one feels. The education given to these children would be unashamedly demanding and intensive, and it would be a deliberate attempt to create an elite class, or as the scheme's opponents would describe it "a master race".

There were of course strong educational arguments in favour of this idea. Bright pupils should always be encouraged, because they can become bored and "held back" with the teacher having to give more time to the less able pupils, and many of the pupils in this experiment look back with affection on the educational progress that they were able to make at a rapid speed.

There are also two very strong arguments against. One is the resentment and the jealousy that it causes among other children (sometimes brothers and sisters of the elite) who are made to feel inadequate at this gross selection and creaming off of the brightest children, but the other and stronger argument is the emotional pressure that it put on those selected, and the undeniable effect that few of them chose to stay on for their seventh year, and effectively landed at University a year earlier than they should have, some of them aged only 16. Going to University is traumatic at the best of times, and young people probably benefit from having an extra year under their belt.

In addition, there is the notorious difficulty in assessing children at any age. Some bright sparks at the age of 10 remain just that – bright sparks, without as it were, catching fire. Other children are ordinary at Primary School and suddenly develop intellectually at puberty or later. In any case, the experiment was quietly shelved a few years later, and the jury remains out on whether it was a good idea or not. On the one hand, it created a Prime Minister; on the other it created a disproportionate amount of people who grew up less able to cope with the adult world than might have been the case. The balance of opinion, even among those favourably inclined to selectivity in education, was that it was possibly just one step too far.

Adam, although normally well respected, if not loved, was once the victim of a practical joke of which he, understandably, failed to see the funny side. A few senior pupils, bored as the end of term was approaching, decided to put the contents of Adam's house up for sale. An advertisement appeared in *The Fife Free Press* for the contents of his house in Loughborough Road including a few ridiculous items like "one roller skate" "a nearly complete pack of cards" and "most of the Encyclopaedia Britannica", and his address was given.

The absurdity of this bogus advertisement did not prevent a steady stream of rag-and-bone men, and even a few genuine callers (who perhaps needed one roller skate!), to the house and it was many weeks before they stopped coming. Adam was furious. He knew very well who the perpetrators were – for he knew everything –

but on this occasion he was unable to extort any confessions, and could not prove anything. No police charge could be brought – it is doubtful if the police would have done so in any case – but Mr Adam was the subject of a certain amount of local ridicule.

He would have his revenge, though. Some of the culprits were so persecuted at school, being pursued for trivial offences and conspicuously not allowed to go on school trips, that they decided to leave – they were "encouraged to leave", the phrase was – and years later, when one of them wrote to ask Adam for a reference, the request was granted – but the reference was such that the boy concerned did not get the job. The repercussions went on for some time, and the affair was emphatically not forgiven nor forgotten.

The mid 1960s saw both Adam and Kirkcaldy High School at their zenith, but "the winds of change" were beginning to blow through education, as well as the continent of Africa about which the phrase had been coined. In 1964 the Labour Government of Harold Wilson was elected with a thin majority, and this was confirmed with a more emphatic one in March 1966. This was, of course, welcomed by many in education (and certainly by most people in Kirkcaldy) because it meant that more money would be spent on schools, but there was one side-effect seen by Adam and others as pernicious and even deleterious to all that he had achieved at Kirkcaldy High School.

This was, of course, comprehensive education, already a major issue in England, and slowly spreading to Scotland. It would pose a threat to Kirkcaldy High School in that it might mean the abolition of selection, the very pillar on which Kirkcaldy High School stood. One of Adam's greatest admirers and a lady herself who went on to have a successful teaching career said, perhaps cruelly, that Adam would not have lasted very long in a comprehensive school in that he wouldn't have had a clue how to deal with "the underclass". Certainly his methods of iron discipline would have been put to the test, and his obsession with high academic achievement would not, one fears, have cut much ice in certain layers of society.

Certainly, it would have to be admitted that society, to a certain extent, was unfair and that you got a rough deal if you failed to do well in your "qualie" exam (sometimes, revealingly, called the "control"!) at the age of 11, and found yourself, irretrievably, in a school which was not as good as, and often a million times worse than, Kirkcaldy High School. You had little hope of Highers and basically marked time until the age of 15 when the linoleum factory or the coal mines beckoned.

The social divisions and jealousies that this caused, even within families, was significant, but the real evil aspect of it was its inflexibility. Anyone who has had any experience of schools will know that children develop at different times, and that often children do not show their true potential until the age of 14 or 15. Conversely, some 10 and 11 year olds flatter to deceive for a year or two until they reach the limits of their ability. The old system could not allow for this. Sometimes a school could be "multilateral" whereby everyone from a given area went to the same school but were set or streamed whenever they got there, and a certain amount of flexibility was possible then. But "multilateral" in that sense, Kirkcaldy High School was certainly not. It was rigidly selective. Those who "made it" to the High School had a great opportunity; those who didn't, saw themselves, not without cause, as rejected.

And yet after almost half a century of comprehensive education, there are still those who see themselves rejected by the educational system. The generation of teachers who entered the profession in the early 1970s fervently hoped that comprehensive education would in time eliminate the feelings of rejection and its concomitant evils of crime, unemployment and poverty. But those of us who felt that a generation of comprehensive education would see a new society demanding the end of the excesses of working class life have as yet been disappointed.

Society has not yet found an answer to this problem nor found a way to ensure that high standards can be maintained for the most able, and at the same time that the less able, with their attendant problems of bad behaviour and poor social skills, can get a fair deal. Perhaps there is no answer, but of one thing Adam was convinced and that was that there was no social discrimination in his school. Children from non-academic, working class, backgrounds attended his school and did well. The only barrier to learning in Kirkcaldy in the 1960s was ability, and more important, attitude. He even went further, arguing that strict discipline, far from being alien to non-academic children, was actually craved, for a disciplined environment was in total contrast to the chaotic, inadequate home backgrounds of so many of them. In this, he was very close to the truth.

But it was obvious from Adam's Prize giving address in 1966 that he was beginning to fear the insidious approach of comprehensive education, and there is even a hint that he felt that the writing was on the wall for the "great days" of Kirkcaldy High School. Speaking as he did with the occasional "harrumph" and a characteristic, random shrug of the shoulder, he said "To me it seems that the desire for change is based on social rather than educational grounds. The pupils of this school represent a complete cross section of our community and the reason for change based on the need for democratic equality of opportunity does not, therefore, apply to this school. There is no doubt, too, that pupils must be educated in accordance with their aptitude and ability – that one pupil for example, should study formal mathematics and another only the most elementary facts of computation. In some quarters there is a tendency to deny that such differences exist.

"Unless these differences are recognised and are adequately provided for, a great disservice will be done to the young, and indeed the whole future of the country will suffer. I can only hope that this school will be allowed to continue to give the same service as before…" Brave words, defiant ones even, but, even as early as 1966, the Philistines of comprehensive education and the "common course" (where all pupils of whatever ability studied the same things, including for example, children who could not read doing French!) were already at the gates!

Kirkcaldy High School did indeed go comprehensive immediately after Adam retired in 1971, something that caused a great deal of distress to the staff whose frequent cry was "O Tempora! O Mores!" ("oh, the times we live in, and the habits of people nowadays!"), and the joke was often told about how Adam had died of shock (in fact, he lived for another 20 years) and went up to the pearly gates to be met by, not St Peter as he would have thought, but the Devil. He expressed surprise, but the

Devil said "Haven't you heard? We've gone comprehensive!"

Adam was fortunate in that he always had capable deputies, some of whom went on to become Headmasters themselves. Dr McLaren, for example, went to Bell Baxter, Scott Couper who had been his excellent Principal Teacher of Classics, then Deputy Headmaster, went on become Headmaster at Elgin Acadamy and Hamish Hamilton took over the reins at Harris Academy, Dundee to allow Donald Fraser to take over as Deputy just before Adam himself left.

When Adam retired in May 1971, there also retired with him Elizabeth Morris who had been his Lady Advisor for 18 years. She had arrived in 1953 having been in a similar post at Waid Academy for a couple of years and having taught for 20 years. It was fitting that they should both retire together, for they had recognisably been a team, and the school magazine of 1971 pays tribute to them both with Miss Morris being lauded in the style of Robert Burns over the death of his pet sheep Maillie in a way which although perhaps lacking in the poetical style of the Ayrshire bard nevertheless shows a certain amount of affection for Miss Morris, who was almost universally liked.

Lament in rhyme, lament in prose

Wi saut tears trickin doon yer nose

Oor Lizzie's reign is at a close

And noo awa fae us she goes

Through a' thae years she tended us

Oor cuts and bruises mended us

Frae first year sook to sixth year cad

And so her leavin maks us sad.

Without lapsing into poetry, the same magazine pays eloquent tribute to Robert Adam, talking of his "inspiring dedication and devotion to our school" which he had made into "one of the leading schools in Scotland" and tells us that he had been made Deputy Lord Lieutenant of the County of Fife. This was small reward for a man who had contributed so much.

In his retirement he was a member of the Probus Club, he was a Justice of the Peace and he continued to be an Elder of the Church of Scotland. He died at the Station Court Nursing Home on January 5 1990, at the age of 83. His wife, Mary, had predeceased him but he was survived by his three children Elinor, Dorothy and Harry. Today more than 25 years after his death, his memory is much venerated, as indeed it should be.

Tom Kennedy MP

Until the Labour cataclysm of 2015, Kirkcaldy was generally regarded as a Labour stronghold. Occasionally, it could flirt with the Scottish National Party – and it certainly swung dramatically to them in 2015 - but it has often been a source of wonder that the Conservatives and the Liberals bother to stand at all! Yet throughout the 19th century it was the Liberals who held sway. The change is due to a large extent to the works of Tom Kennedy, Kirkcaldy's first Labour MP, and of course the eponymous hero of Kennedy Crescent. Yet is surprising how few people know who he was, or what he achieved. Even fewer know about Kirkcaldy's famous by-election of 1921.

Tom Kennedy was born in Kennethmont, a small village near Huntly in Aberdeenshire on Christmas Day 1874, (although some sources say 1876, it was certainly 1874) but not a great deal is known of his early years other than that he was a late baby (his parents married in 1857) and that his father was a gamekeeper. We do know that he very soon became part of the radical movement which swept the North of Scotland and affected young men like Ramsay MacDonald, a man some 8 years his senior. Perhaps it was the rough life in the Buchan area of Scotland with its bothies, rich (often absentee) farmers and the appalling poverty and ignorance of the agricultural workers that affected him, and made him and quite a few early Socialists realise that something was wrong, and that organizations like the Church and the Liberal Party (which might, one thought, have been expected to do something to change things) were of limited value in addressing the major social problem of the day.

T. KENNEDY.

But Kennedy did have an education. The educational system on the 1880s and 1890s did indeed have its shortcomings, but for a bright young man who was prepared to apply himself, the rewards would come in the shape of being taken away from the coarseness and brutality of life on the land, and possibly being given something else. In Kennedy's case, after attending Kennethmont Public School and the Gordon School, Huntly, he found employment as a Railway Clerk in the Great North of Scotland Railway Company, a job which was not necessarily well paid (although adequate for the times), but it was clean, secure and healthy. One has the picture of a Bob Cratchet/Ebenezer Scrooge type job with a high desk, an inkwell, an old fashioned pen and an ill-tempered boss. It may have been slightly boring for an intelligent young man, and his mind may well have strayed to left wing politics and other things which might in those days have been considered subversive.

There was of course no Labour Party as such when Kennedy was a young man. The Labour Representation Committee was founded at the very birth of the new century in 1900, but that was merely an amalgam of many splinter groups and parties loosely connected to each other and all believing in some form of Socialism. There were, and would still be for some time, those who believed in working with the Liberals; there were those who despised the Liberals seeing them as mere tools of the capitalists, and as has been the curse of Labour politics for more than a century, it has proved difficult to persuade them to agree on anything!

It was under the official aegis of the Social Democratic Federation that Kennedy stood as candidate in 1906 in the very working class constituency of Aberdeen North. It was already a Liberal seat, and it was no great surprise that in the context of the 1906 Liberal landslide that Duncan Vernon Pirie romped home for the Liberals. Kennedy however surprised a few people by coming second and defeating the Conservatives, and was able to claim that his party was the coming movement. Indeed, the establishment was visibly trembling at the arrival en masse in Westminster of 29 MPs under the Labour banner! *The Aberdeen Press* is sufficiently upset and rattled to attack Kennedy as a "nothing and nowhere" man, "an indeterminate politician vaguely advocating a vague socialism".

Kennedy had campaigned well, tending to focus on workman's lunch time meetings at the Steam Navigation Company and the Corporation Gasworks where he was given a fair hearing. On one occasion his Chairman was "John McLean of Glasgow", almost certainly the future

Red Clydesider. Kennedy stressed his commitment to nationalisation and other Socialist ideals and in a nod to the ever growing Temperance and Prohibitionist movements, stated that he wanted all liquor traffic to be publicly owned as well, so that it could be better regulated. He attacked the Liberals as well as the Conservatives, saying that they were equally to blame for the "Chinese Slave Labour" scandal in South Africa, and on one occasion reminding his audience of a bizarre and, it must be owned, little known incident when the Liberals were last in power of how, when workers in the docks at Hull were objecting to the use of scab labour, a gunboat was sent to enforce the employers' demands!

Kennedy was now bitten by the Socialist bug, and very soon after his defeat in 1906, took a full time post as National Organiser for the British Socialist Party. He also wrote a column for the "Clarion" newspaper. In this he excelled, but like many socialists in the early days, he must have looked upon the Liberal Government with mixed feelings. On the one hand, it was good to see such a clearly talented Government with men like Winston Churchill, Herbert Asquith and David Lloyd George passing welcome and much needed reforms to ease the life of working people, but on the other, it raised the question that if the Liberals could do that, who needed Labour? The 29 Labour MPs wholeheartedly supported the Liberals in the House of Commons, and there would be a danger that the "infant might" of the Labour movement might yet be subsumed under the Liberals.

Kennedy tried again in Aberdeen North in January 1910, but lost again, this time a very poor second and he didn't bother to try in the next Election of December 1910, concentrating instead on his job of National

Organiser for the British Socialist Party. He did this with enthusiasm until, possibly surprisingly given some of his views, he joined the forces in 1914. The Great War, of course, spilt the nascent Labour movement. Some like Ramsay MacDonald were against the war; others still saw patriotism as an important concept. Kennedy at this stage inclined to the latter view. He would soon change his mind.

He was nearly 40 and rightly considered to be too old for active service, but he worked as a Medical Orderly (by no means a cushy number, even though both *The Fife Free Press* and *The Fifeshire Advertiser* would in future years see fit to sneer at him for so doing) and saw action, or more accurately, the results of action, on the Italian Front. A Medical Orderly's job demands its own brand of courage.

He was demobbed in 1919 and came back to live in London (he was now remarried to a lady called Annie Michie after his first wife, one Christina Farquarson, herself a renowned Socialist, had died in 1917) He was now a clerk with an insurance valuations firm, his job with the British Socialist Party having disappeared during the War. He was still very much interested in politics though, having now seen what had happened in the war and having come to the view that it had been caused by too much wealth having been concentrated in the hands of too few people, who had been able to lead so many gullible people to pernicious and devastating mischief.

Meanwhile in Kirkcaldy, people were struggling to come to terms with the peace that had brought so many problems with it. The first inkling that things might be changing on the political front came when *The Fifeshire Advertiser* carried a story on April 17 1920 that

Kirkcaldy's sitting MP of nearly 30 years, Sir Henry Dalziel, might be soon elevated to the Peerage. About a month after that, even without any official confirmation, we find the Labour movement beginning to stir for the first time ever in the town, and Tom Kennedy "of the National Socialist Party" addressing members as one of the prospective Labour candidates in the Trades Council Hall. He deplored the amount of "reactionaries" around and affirmed that "politics and political institutions were inseparable from the life of a civilised community".

Then on May 22 1920 Tom Kennedy, described as "organising secretary of the National Socialist Party" was elected as Kirkcaldy's first ever prospective Labour candidate for the next General Election. He beat two local men, John Nairn of the Scottish Textile Workers Union and Joe Westwood of Lochore, a "miners' organiser". He then spoke graciously and tactfully, hoping that this would be the start of a long and productive relationship with the people of Kirkcaldy.

Little more is heard of Kennedy for a while, but that is not to say that there was any lack of political activity in the town. Diverse characters like the Red Clydeside Socialist John McLean, and then Earl Haig came to town (fortunately not at the same time!), McDonald Ross, the new minister of St Brycedale Kirk attacked characters like "the idler" and (in a denunciation which was unusual in Church circles for the times) "the profiteer", various war memorials were unveiled in Churches but there was no agreement and a great deal of controversy about where the town Memorial was going to be. The major issue however, if one were to go by public meetings on the subject was Drink with Temperance and Prohibition Societies organising meetings and demonstrations, and counter demonstrations being held by "freedom" societies.

But *The Fifeshire Advertiser* in particular is very concerned about the possibility of a coal strike and what it might bring. Bolshevism was a constant bogey and a Leader in the paper saw fit to state (improbably) that "The Council of Action" of the Miners' Union was the "first British Soviet" in the context of a potential miners' strike. Fortunately, those who wanted industrial action failed to get the necessary two thirds majority at a ballot in October, and the threat was postponed. But it would not go away.

In early October 1920, Sir Henry Dalziel who had not been seen in the town for some considerable time; announced that he would not seek re-election to the House of Commons at the next General Election, alleging ill health and exhaustion. He had been the town's Liberal MP since 1892 and had been universally liked until recently. Sir Robert Lockhart, who had been Provost during the war, was chosen, on November 27 1920, to replace him as Liberal candidate at the next election, which was not of course necessarily imminent, as there did not need to be a General Election until 1923. Lockhart's appointment was to the general relief of all Kirkcaldy Liberals who feared that the discredited Asquith might fancy his chances at what was a very safe Liberal constituency and had been for almost 100 years.

But rumours kept reaching Kirkcaldy that there might have to be a by-election before that. It was an open secret that in the New Year's honours list, Dalziel would be elevated to the peerage and would have to resign from the House of Commons. This was, after all, the height of the scandal involving Lloyd George selling peerages or offering them to his friends, or as in this case, where someone had helped him during the War. Dalziel's newspapers, particularly *The Reynold's News* had changed sides from being anti-war in 1914 to being emphatically in favour by 1918, and many people saw a connection between this change of heart and Dalziel becoming a peer. Dalziel's health certainly recovered, and he lived until 1935.

Certainly, there was a noticeable increase in political activity in late 1920. Lockhart, even before being officially adopted as the Liberal candidate had held a couple of meetings in the Beveridge Hall ("women specially invited") to reassure his audience of the welfare of Henry Dalziel, although one wonders what he means when he says that he suggested to Dalziel a long holiday "and that he could do worse than spend a considerable part of it in Kirkcaldy"!

Lockhart assured the people of Kirkcaldy that the continuation of Lloyd George's Coalition Government would be in the best interests of everyone to deal with the problems of industry, foreign affairs and particularly Ireland and Russia where war was still raging. The Coalition of Liberals and Conservatives had been formed as early as 1915, had been confirmed in the "khaki election" of 1918 (Dalziel had been returned unopposed in Kirkcaldy) and was needed, claimed Lockhart, to fight off the problems of Bolshevism and anarchy.

Kennedy too, sensed that there might be a by-election imminent, and appeared at the Pathhead Halls at the end of October to address the Co-operative movement. He said two things that perhaps surprised his audience. One was that he was now no longer associated with the National Socialist Movement (not of course to be confused with a less respectable organisation in Germany in later years!) which had too many links with

Bolshevism, but had re-joined the Social Democratic Federation. Not that it mattered, for he was the Labour candidate for Kirkcaldy and would fully support the Co-operative Movement. The other thing that perhaps raised an eyebrow concerned Winston Churchill. This charismatic, but occasionally erratic and quixotic, character was the MP for Dundee, but had earned some unpopularity there and might try his luck at Kirkcaldy the next time. If that happened, he, Kennedy, would welcome the challenge.

The local press was not in favour of Kennedy. *The Fife Free Press,* traditionally Liberal, had no problem in endorsing Lockhart. *The Fifeshire Advertiser* was in more of a quandary. It was a Conservative paper and did not like Lockhart. On the other hand, it saw the necessity to continue the Coalition, at least in the short term, and in the absence of a real Conservative, it saw Lockhart as the lesser of the two evils. Its Leader writer could be intemperate in his language at times, stating that any by-election which might be called in the New Year of 1921 would be "socialism, communism and bolshevism against all those who distrust extremism".

Nor could Kennedy expect any great help of sympathy from the Church, an organization which was still very powerful in 1921 but which did not seem to be aware of some of the teachings of Jesus Christ about poverty or how it was easier for a camel to pass through the eye of a needle than it was for a rich man to enter the Kingdom of Heaven. The Church in particular did little to differentiate between Bolshevism, an extreme and dictatorial creed which had caused such disruption and bloodshed in Russia, and the milder Labour beliefs of Kennedy, who wanted a more equal society, yes, (and goodness knows, that caused enough distress in Kirk circles!) but would do so only by democratic and peaceful methods.

New Year's Day 1921 did not see (as everyone had expected) Dalziel being elevated to the peerage, but by the end of January he announced that he was "applying for the Chiltern Hundreds" (the technical term for resigning through ill health). His elevation would come, but in the meantime this meant that there would be a by-election in Kirkcaldy. The Coalition had already sent Dr McNamara, their Minister of Labour to speak in the Adam Smith Halls, and Kennedy was not slow to retaliate with a public notice offering to give a "Reasoned Argument and Policy" in place of McNamara's "Coalition Eye Wash".

Lockhart declared that he was standing for the Coalition, and on the day that they had to hand in their papers, the two men were seen to "chat amiably" together in the Town House. Indeed it was a feature of the by-election that in sharp contrast to the extremity of the views put forward by some of their followers (on each side), the two candidates were mild and moderate; Kennedy in particular, with his soft Aberdeenshire accent, charming audiences and particularly the women on the occasion when he held up his baby son in the Adam Smith Hall for them to admire. This son, also called Tom Kennedy, became a renowned economist and political biographer in later life.

There might have been a third candidate, for one David Mason arrived in town intending to stand as an Asquithian Liberal (i.e. a non-Coalition Liberal) but finding that the local Liberal Association were all pro-Lockhart, Coalition and Lloyd George, withdrew from the scene. Kennedy was disappointed at that, for it would have split the Liberal vote, but felt that in any case, he would have enough support in the mining areas, particularly in Methil and Buckhaven which had been added to the constituency.

There were other things going on in Kirkcaldy that winter of 1920/21– notably a smallpox outbreak, and a performance of "The Mikado" by the Operatic Society which attracted a great deal of adverse criticism – but Friday March 4 was the big event in the town with all sorts of musical rallies and marches in favour of each candidate, with Lockhart playing the patriotic card and Kennedy's followers frightening the establishment with their renditions of "The Red Flag".

Kennedy's campaign was against unemployment, against privilege and for the improvement in health and educational services that were so clearly needed if the country were to recover from the war. Nationalisation of key industries was also essential, as indeed was the removal of housing to local authorities rather than having them left in the hands of private landlords. He also revealed an enlightened attitude to Ireland (in 1921 being torn apart by the ravages of Lloyd George's notorious Black and Tans) when he suggested the removal of all troops and the establishment of an Irish Constitution so that people could vote on their future. He was against any kind of partition.

His rallies were emotional ones with banners and singing. His campaign had coined the fine phrase "March Forth on March Fourth", and Kennedy was seen as an educated, clear-thinking, compassionate politician and one who would represent the town well. He was opposed, almost universally by the Press, the two Dundee ones, *The Courier* and *The Advertiser* in particular, who worried about his radicalism, and was attacked by the two local papers *The Fifeshire Advertiser* and *The Fife Free Press* (normally poles apart politically but having made common cause in this case) for not being local. Sir Robert Lockhart on the other hand was very much a Kirkcaldy man.

The emotions involved on both sides are difficult for us, almost a hundred years later, to understand. The poor in Kirkcaldy were very poor, their lot not improved by the aftermath of the war which had brought a slump in trade. The war itself, for all its horrors, had improved the standard of living ever so slightly, for everyone gets a job in war, but now the capitalist classes didn't need the workers so much, and unemployment was the result. For the rich, the Church and the middle classes, there was the ever present fear of Bolshevism (much encouraged by the Press) with the example of Russia in 1917 ever present. Was not Kennedy and the new Labour Party merely a step towards the chaos and anarchy that was currently prevailing in the erstwhile land of the Czar?

There was a novel element involved here as well in 1921, and one of which Kennedy was very much aware. It was the first Kirkcaldy election in which women could vote. Some women had been enfranchised in April 1918, but as Henry Dalziel had been returned unopposed in December 1918, women had not yet had the opportunity to vote at a Parliamentary election. But as yet, only women aged over 30 and who owned property could vote. It did not take a genius to work out that most of them would vote for Lockhart, but Kennedy was very careful on Women's Issues, talking about the need to enfranchise all women, to provide good maternity care (it was in this context that he produced his infant son at the Adam Smith Hall!) and even, without rocking any boats in the Roman Catholic community, mentioning the desirability of some form of birth control. He also made sure that they all saw and met his wife, and even on occasion implied that he believed in God.

The campaign could turn nasty on occasion. Not a great deal of violence was reported but there was certainly much rowdiness and drunkenness associated with the campaign. There was of course nothing new in that, for Victorian elections had traditionally seen a certain amount of revelry, but Kennedy had to work hard to persuade his workers that Lockhart was to be allowed a fair hearing as well. *The Fifeshire Advertiser* says at the end of the three week campaign, that it did not want to see any more of such uproar.

It was a tight call, but Kennedy scraped home by a majority of just over 1,000. His followers were jubilant and he was the hero of the hour, taking his seat in the House of Commons a few days later and joining the increasing amount of Labour MPs. It did not, in truth, make much of a difference, for the Coalition still had an overwhelming majority, but it nevertheless caused a stir and a tremble as the Establishment was forced to realise that the working classes were no longer prepared to turn the other cheek to poverty, deprivation and ignorance while the wealth of the nation was concentrated in few hands. Kirkcaldy had indeed marched forth on March 4th

It was Kennedy's fortune to represent Kirkcaldy in interesting and turbulent times. The problems of labour and Ireland did not go away very readily, and increasingly the country began to see through David Lloyd George with all his scandals in his personal and especially his political life, particularly to do with the selling of honours. The Coalition fell apart in summer 1922, and by the autumn of that year, a General Election was called for the middle of November.

It so happened that such were the vagaries and complications of the British political system of the 1920s, with the Labour Party rising and the Liberal Party falling, that three General Elections were called in successive autumns in 1922, 1923 and 1924. Kennedy fought all three for Kirkcaldy. He lost in 1922, but fought back to win narrowly in 1923 and 1924. The 1922 Election saw a triumph for the Conservatives and a rebuff for Labour aspirations, but then Stanley Baldwin fell out with the Liberals (and some of his own party) over the old issue of Free Trade v. Protection and called another General Election in 1923 which saw Labour, with Liberal help, take power for a short minority Government before it fell at the end of 1924, and the Conservatives were back in power for the next five years.

This political scenario was complicated and perhaps just a little incomprehensible to us nearly 100 years later, but as far as Kirkcaldy is concerned, it marked a seismic and permanent change from being a Liberal stronghold to being a Labour one, a state of affairs that continued until May 2015 as far as Westminster was concerned. There were probably two reasons for this. One was the inclusion of the "coal mining areas" of Buckhaven and Methil in Kirkcaldy and their unquenchable loyalty to the Labour cause in the times of trouble that the 1920s undeniably were for miners and those in heavy industries, but another factor was the sheer presence of Kennedy who worked hard for the town, emphatically did not hide in London (as so many others had done) and by his charisma and charm was able to swing Liberal voters and even the occasional Conservative one to his cause.

He was always polite and charming. His speeches, whether for an Election or not, were free from vitriol and mud-slinging. His approach was a constructive, albeit gradualist, one and he was genuinely shocked at the extremes of poverty that he saw in his constituency, particularly in areas like The Links and Pathhead. He went out of his way to distance himself from what was happening in Russia, occasionally raised an eyebrow or two at the opulence of the British Royal Family, but stressed that he was always patriotic. His war service (as we have seen, he was just a shade too old for active military service as a fighting soldier) had seen him work with the Medical Corps in Italy – a job that compelled him to see an enormous amount of suffering, which he had occasionally been able to alleviate – and he was proud of that, although he never made a fuss about it.

Kennedy shared the views of Ramsay MacDonald and others in the Labour Party that the Treaty of Versailles, brutal, spiteful and vindictive to the vanquished Germans, was not the right way to guarantee peace. Better surely to knock Germany down, (yes, that had to be done!) but having rid the nation of the mad Kaiser, the way ahead was surely to build her up again, and in so doing strengthening the hand of the progressive German Social Democrats against people like the irresponsible demagogue called Hitler who was, even as early as the 1920s, making his presence felt with his seductive, strident, Siren calls for rearmament and another war.

Kennedy's defeat in 1922 did not set him back for long, and when he won Kirkcaldy back in December 1923, he and the country suddenly found themselves with a constitutional crisis with three parties of almost equal strength in the House of Commons but with no working majority for anyone. Baldwin once again refused to do a deal with the Liberals, so the King, in a state of extreme nervousness and apprehension and still obsessed with the recollection of what had happened to his cousin the Czar in 1917, was compelled to send for Ramsay MacDonald.

Ramsay MacDonald! The name, whose very mention brightened up the lives of the working class in 1923! A slightly older contemporary of Tom Kennedy and born in the same part of the world – the north-east of Scotland – and with the same set of values as himself, Kennedy felt that he could do business with this man. Both were charmers and great orators, and both had the same passions about poverty and unemployment. Kennedy felt that things could now change.

It was a pleasant surprise however for Kennedy to find himself summoned into MacDonald's office sometime at the end of January 1924 and offered a job of Junior Lord of the Treasury, or as it was sometimes called Lord Commissioner of the Treasury. Kennedy accepted with alacrity. He was enough of a capitalist to realise that this would represent a considerable increase in his personal wealth, but more than that, he was now to be part of a great reforming movement and at the very heart of it.

He owed his advancement to MacDonald's recollection of his organising abilities in socialist splinter groups before the war, and also to the good job that he had already done as Scottish Labour Whip in 1921 and 1922. The local press, still huffy about the good people of Kirkcaldy having disobeyed their instructions and voted Labour, and still feeding its readers with horror stories about what the "Labourists" (sic) were going to do to everyone's personal wealth – "it will be purloined away by taxations" – nevertheless is forced to concede that Kennedy is a worthy man for this job, and that his promotion is "well deserved".

The Fifeshire Advertiser says that "the new Government certainly owe something to the member of Kirkcaldy for his remarkable victory" and tells everyone that his job as Lord of the Treasury was "once held by Mr Gladstone". It is re-assured to a certain extent that Philip Snowden is going to be the Chancellor of the Exchequer – "as moderate a man as you could get" but then in its sting in the tail hints at the problem that was going to bedevil Kennedy in his relations with his constituency throughout 1924 "the government have in their coffers at this moment money belonging to Kirkcaldy connected with a certain Esplanade".

Kirkcaldy wanted to build a wall along the Esplanade with the laudable aim of reducing local unemployment. Work indeed was in progress. They had applied for a grant to the Unemployed Grants Committee, a 1920s quango. At first they had agreed in 1922, but then some time in 1923 had changed their mind and withdrawn the grant. It had nothing really to do with Kennedy nor indeed the Labour Government, which had only been in power for a matter of days, but it was a fine stick for Kennedy's enemies to beat him with.

Kennedy was a victim of the doctrine of "collective responsibility". Being a part of the Government takes away a little of one's freedom to defend one's constituents, as here. Kennedy worked hard behind the scenes to persuade the Unemployed Grants Committee to change its mind yet again – he would eventually succeed – but for a spell he had an uncomfortable time on this issue, including a bizarre statement from the Town Clerk Mr McIndoe that he was going to sue

Kennedy for defamation or slander. It was hard to see any grounds in this preposterous declaration and the idea was quickly dropped, but it was an indication of the tension between the two sides, the Town Council being still predominantly Liberal.

Kennedy did not hide. He spoke at the Adam Smith Hall, the Hunter Hall, the Olympia Arcade and in Methil to defend himself. He knew that he was being "put through it", but defended himself with dignity and charm. At his meeting in the Hunter Hall, he was forced to speak about unemployment, for the local Labour Exchange had stopped paying dole to about 100 men on the grounds that they were not "genuinely seeking employment".

Without using words like "lazy" or "feckless" to describe the 100 men, Kennedy was able, adroitly, to turn the issue on its head and show what the Labour Government was doing to alleviate unemployment generally. "The stigma of pauperism" he said, must be removed for ever. He was on surer ground when he dealt with the coming crisis in the Coal Industry. The mine owners were threatening to lay miners off, to increase the day and decrease the pay. Kennedy saw, as did most of the Labour movement, that the solution to this problem was the nationalisation of the mines, rather than allow them to remain in the hands of private and selfish owners, a particular jibe at the traditionally unpopular Wemyss family who owned the mines in the East of Fife.

Local issues aside, Kennedy was part of the Labour Government of 1924, a Government whose achievements are often passed over or minimised by even Socialist historians. True, there was no establishment of a National Health Service or Welfare

State as would happen in 1945 – but then again that was never likely to happen with a minority government – but there were important improvements in old age pensions and unemployment benefits, and most importantly of all, thanks to the work of the brilliant John Wheatley the Glasgow MP (whom Ramsay MacDonald grew to distrust because of his success and ability which threatened MacDonald himself), the first steps towards local authorities building and owning houses. All new houses were to be built with the minimum necessities of indoor toilets and running water in kitchens. The fruits of this work, which Kennedy enthusiastically supported, would not be seen for many years, but it was in 1924 that the seeds were planted.

The problem with the MacDonald Government was simply that it could not last. It was not even the biggest single party, and the Conservatives and Liberals could at any time they wanted to, gang up and force them out. They did so in the autumn in one of the dirtiest smear campaigns of all time, linking MacDonald with Russia because of his enlightened policy of seeking a trade agreement with that large and prickly dictatorship, and of granting Russia diplomatic recognition. MacDonald suffered for that in a huge smear about the British Communist Party, and also on the eve of the Election, the infamous Zinoviev telegram, a blatant forgery but which nevertheless seemed to be telling the British Foreign Office that the Soviets were about to take over.

In Kirkcaldy, Kennedy struggled because of this, but in his case, he had an additional burden to cope with – and that was the smear of him being pro-German. This charge had a long genesis, but had been thrown about as early as 1920 when he had been quoted as expressing concern about the plight of starving German children.

Now in 1924, when the Government that he had been a part of had been making noises about the iniquities of Versailles and the need for the Germans to be rehabilitated into the international scene so that they could trade with Britain and France, Kennedy was once again denounced as a "Kaiser lover" a "sausage eater" and even a "Hun" by the ignorant.

Kennedy coped with this with his usual dignity and kept saying things like the job is only just started and that with a working overall majority, Labour would do things like nationalise the mines and bring about the much needed improvements in public health. Once again, he had a good relationship with his opponent, a Mr John Murray, a Liberal as the Conservatives seemed to have given up on Kirkcaldy at this time of their history. On several occasions, the two men shared a platform, embarrassingly once or twice finding themselves in agreement!

Once, it was not a platform that they shared, but a football pitch! This was on Friday October 24 1924 at Bayview, the home of East Fife when the two candidate debated the desirability or otherwise of nationalising the mines. Microphones and loudspeakers were rigged up, and in spite of it being a windy (but fine and dry) day, this novel method of debating was much talked about, even in the national press, not least because the audience consisted predominantly of women. In addition to all that, they raised £17 for a local hospital!

Once again we see the contrast between Kennedy the man and Kennedy the politician. In his moments of weakness – he could never of course admit them openly – he probably realised that the Liberals, at least, and even some Conservatives had some good ideas as well. He could take part in the cut and thrust of political debate, but on occasion he found the House of Commons a little shallow and predictable with no real depth of thought in most of the speeches. Electioneering, on the other hand, filled him with zeal and enthusiasm and he loved making speeches in front of large audiences, enjoying the theatre of it all with the singing of "The Red Flag" and the redemption hymns (with their noticeable changes of words) which so horrified and terrified his opponents who did not like references to "gallows grim" and "lava flame of liberation".

Polling took place on Wednesday 29 October 1924, and the result was announced in the pouring rain the following day. Kennedy had done well to hold Kirkcaldy for Labour, but Labour was doing a lot less well in other parts of the country, so Labour joy was distinctly tempered. Kennedy spoke briefly, shook hands with Mr Murray as they wished each other well, and then he departed to Westminster and a life of Opposition, a totally different experience and a total contrast to the heady days of being in power.

His majority had been reduced from the previous year, but that was perhaps to be expected given the smear campaign so well organised nationally by the national press to discredit Ramsay MacDonald. But Kennedy was (and remained all his life) proud of his part in the first ever Labour Government which had, in spite of its limitations, certainly achieved something.

It had been a short-lived experiment. Labour would be back, and this short interlude of nine months' power had shown that Labour could govern without the country falling to its knees. Ramsay MacDonald had famously got on very well with the King – although the contrast in upbringing could scarcely have been more stark – and much though the establishment had trembled at the appearance of men like MacDonald, Henderson, Wheatley and Kennedy with "people" threatening to emigrate and take all their money with them lest the Socialist would take it all away and hand it all out to the undeserving poor, the country was in most respects the same at the end of 1924 as it had been at the beginning. Winston Churchill, now unashamedly back with the Conservatives, had likened the appearance of the Labour Government to a defeat in war. It rates along with Gallipoli in Churchill's many misjudgements.

Kennedy was hardly inactive in the years between 1924 and 1929 remaining the local MP and from 1927 onwards became the Chief Whip. He appeared at the unveiling of the War memorial in 1925, alongside local dignitaries, but it was 1926 and the General Strike which was to cause him a great deal of grief. It had been coming for a long time. The basic problem was that since the Great War, miners had, according to their employers, been overpaid. A great deal of coal had been required for the War and therefore miners had had to be paid well, cossetted, and kept away from the army, producing the coal which would eventually win the day in 1918.

The end of the war had seen the inevitable slump in demand. Various Government commissions had staved off the problem for some time but eventually in the winter of 1925/26 the owners announced that they were reducing pay, laying off some men and increasing the hours. With their militant leader AJ Cook, a very eloquent and able man (but who, like Arthur Scargill in the 1980s clearly enjoyed himself in the conflict) reeling off slogans like "Not a penny off the pay, not a minute on the day", the miners managed to get the support from the whole Trade Union movement, and after a considerable amount of ineffective bargaining and blood curling rhetoric, a General Strike was called for early May 1926.

The Government for their part stood firm behind the mine owners. In the same way as British Governments in the 1820s had been obsessed with what had happened in France in 1789, so their successors a hundred years later could not help but see Bolshevism and the murder of the Czar in every industrial dispute – a feeling clearly echoed in the Press, both national and local. Voices of moderation, in so far as they existed at all, were seldom heard.

Kennedy and MacDonald might have been one such voice of reason, but their position, in particular that of Kennedy who served a mining constituency and who had won his seat through the miners' vote, prevented them. Naturally Kennedy sided with the miners, both publicly and in his heart of hearts, but he must have wondered whether widespread industrial action on this scale was really the best way of going about it. He would have far preferred to deal with the matter through Parliament, through a vote and through discussion, but the tensions of the time did not allow for that, and Kennedy had to be seen backing the miners, and the other unions as well, in their struggle against Baldwin and in particular Churchill who backed such measures as troop deployment and "starving them out".

The General Strike itself collapsed in less than a fortnight – the Trade Union Council had been less than 100% wholeheartedly behind it in the first place, and certainly quite a lot of fellow workers had been distinctly against the whole idea – to everyone's relief, including, one imagined men like Kennedy who did not the extreme turn that events had taken. But the miners' strike itself went on for months, and Kennedy, in Kirkcaldy and Methil, could not turn his back on them.

He appeared on several occasions speaking on platforms in support of the miners, expressing sympathy with their plight, making donations to their cause – but one senses a certain going through the motions about this and a lack of real sincerity. His hope was of course the settlement of the miners' justified grievances by negotiation, for he felt that otherwise the union would crack before the owners who were, after all, very wealthy and supported by the Government.

Kennedy's private feelings that it was all going to end in tears came brutally true in November when the miners, reduced now to absolute penury and unable to countenance the prospect of the imminent winter without adequate food and heating, were compelled to surrender. The return to work of 1985 did at least have a little dignity, and even pride, about it with Scargill leading his men back to work with pipe bands, banners and so on. Words like "starved back" were freely bandied about with more than a little rhetorical hyperbole.

There was no such dignity about autumn 1926. "Starvation" was far from an abstract exaggeration, and the sufferings of the miners in Kirkcaldy and district were real and intense. They would last for some time, as the owners were able to victimise and refuse to take back the militants and the trouble makers, and there was no redress. "Vae victis" – "Woe to the conquered" was the cry in ancient Rome. The vindictiveness of all this was distressing indeed.

Kennedy watched all this, but what could he do? He could sympathise, he could even make the occasional successful plea for the reinstatement of one particular miner "who would promise to behave and refrain from disruptive activities" but he could not solve the problem. The only problem was long term. The economy must be reflated, he thought, the mines must be nationalised, and the scourge of unemployment, so blatantly used by the capitalists of the 1920s to bring the workers to heel, must be banished for ever. But that could only happen if his Labour party regained power.

There are a few hints, now and again, in the late 1920s that Kennedy may have harboured doubts about his leader Ramsay MacDonald, with all his foreign trips and ill-disguised social climbing, but, when the election was called for 1929, everyone rallied behind this man who still had the aura and charisma, and whose name was still revered with honour in working class houses as some sort of messiah.

Kennedy did form a strong friendship with the charismatic Oswald Mosley. Mosley, of course, is now a demonised, disgraced character and deservedly so for his founding of the British Fascist Party in the 1930s. But it is important to realise that this might not have happened if Ramsay MacDonald had dealt with him a little better when he was an up and coming and very able MP for Smethwick in the 1920s. He had progressive ideas for Government expenditure, for the creation of a Welfare State, for world peace and he saw in Kennedy (as Kennedy saw in him) a kindred spirit. For a spell, Mosley was the blue-eyed boy of the Labour Party, and enjoyed the favour of MacDonald who possibly saw in him some sort of successor material.

But Kennedy too was rising. A very efficient Chief Whip and a man possessed of an integrity rare among politicians and with a certain charm and attractiveness, Kennedy also had the brain to see that although Labour had to be pragmatic, it also had to stick to its ideals. It was in existence to protect the interests of the working classes, and this was paramount, but it was also vital to cultivate a power base among the middle classes who must not be allowed to persist in their belief that Labour was some sort of a threat to their existence. Decreasingly, perhaps, in the late 1920s did Kennedy find himself identified with Bolshevism by his opponents, but there were still financial interests, not least in Kirkcaldy itself who shuddered at the very mention of "Labour".

The Conservative Government of Stanley Baldwin ran its course and called a General Election for May 30 1929. Kennedy was adopted again as the Labour candidate, and to his astonishment found himself opposed not by a Liberal (an amazing turn of events, considering that until about 10 years ago, Kirkcaldy was considered to be one of the strongest Liberal constituencies in the British Isles) but by a Conservative with the unlikely name of Scrymgeour-Wedderburn. *The Fifeshire Advertiser* claims, improbably, that he is a "Fifer, like the rest of us" but the connections between the man who had been educated at Winchester and Balliol and called himself the "Earl of Dundee" on the one hand, and an ordinary Fife miner from Smeaton, Dysart or Methil were hard to distinguish and pick out!

In some ways, the 1929 Election was Kennedy's finest. All women were now entitled to vote – it is sometimes referred to as the "flapper election" in a reference to the fast, young women of the 1920s – and Kennedy fought hard for their vote. He also tried to capitalise on the fact that no Liberal was standing by appealing to the Church-going, Liberal voters with a social conscience by stressing the positive and progressive nature of Labour's campaign. In this he clearly succeeded, for he increased his majority from 1924 and returned to Westminster to find a different, optimistic but more complicated situation.

Labour were back and MacDonald was again Prime Minister, but it was to be another minority Government. They were in a slightly better position than in 1924 in that they were at least the biggest single party, but would still be dependent on Liberal support, for they had no overall majority. They would clearly not be able to embark on the wide range of reforms that were clearly necessary, but they would be able to govern, perhaps passing a few measures that they thought might improve matters. Full blooded socialism, however, would have to wait.

Kennedy was appointed Parliamentary Secretary to the Treasury. He might have expected more, even the Scottish Office but that went to fellow Fifer William Adamson. He was content; however, to serve under MacDonald again, realising that further promotion might yet happen. In the event he was also made a Privy Councillor in 1931. For a while, a very short while, things looked rosy. The Liberals were encouraging, and the Conservatives were not disruptive for the sake of being disruptive and it seemed that with the economic situation gradually improving, Labour might be able to do quite a lot. Certainly it was great to be back in power once again.

But the optimism was short lived. In the autumn of that very year came the event that history has called "The Wall Street Crash". How it happened, no one has really been able to explain to a layman, but what seems to have happened is that shares in the United States were sold cheaply, firms began to lay off men and even to close down altogether, while a few fat cats like the financiers JP Morgan (the creation of the much vilified Pierpont Morgan, the war profiteer) make a huge profit. For a while, it seemed as if the damage could be limited to the USA, but by 1929 world economies were already so interlinked that it was true what they said that "Whenever America sneezes, the whole world catches a cold". The USA may have successfully pursued an isolationist foreign policy in diplomatic and military affairs, but it could not do so in economic terms.

Thus it was that very soon, as early as January 1930, the effects began to hit Europe. In Germany, of course, the depression led directly to the rise of Hitler, in Spain it led to the establishment of the Spanish Republic and its eventual overthrow in the bloody Civil War of 1936, and in Great Britain the effects were, admittedly bloodless, but nevertheless far reaching in political consequences.

Kennedy realised at a very early stage, as he watched with horror the constant dramatic rise in bankruptcies and unemployment in the United States that Britain would not avoid the bad effects, that Labour would have to cut back on some ideas and that there would have to be a (hopefully) short term decrease in everyone's standard of living. He had, from his position in the Treasury, a better view of things than most people did. But he was not prepared (how could he be?) for the political horrors that were to happen.

As early as 1930 and certainly in the early part of 1931, MacDonald kept telling everyone of the need for drastic economies in Government spending. This to Kennedy was anathema, for it was a cornerstone of his Socialist beliefs that a Labour Government must spend money, if necessary raising Income Tax, Property Tax, Corporation Tax and introducing a Wealth Tax to do so. Nevertheless, he was prepared to go along with a certain amount of pragmatic, short-term trimming, if it were to keep the fragile Labour Government in power.

At the same time, Kennedy was aware of the contrary view, as expressed rather more forcibly by people like Mosley. He argued that the banks and other institutions should be nationalised so that they worked in the interests of the nation, that there should be a major increase in Government expenditure on public works like roads, schools and hospitals. All this would help to solve the unemployment problem and the unemployed would then have more money that they could put back into the economy. It was simple, elementary Keynesian economics, but when MacDonald could not accept this, Mosley went mad and left Labour to form the Fascist Party. To Kennedy, this was a terrible loss, and he began to wonder about MacDonald.

The economic situation began to deteriorate badly. Indeed, it spiralled out of control. It may even have been a plot by the international bankers to get rid of Britain's Labour Government, so apparently inimical and subversive to international capitalism. MacDonald was forced to ask the infamous JP Morgan firm (only a decade after he had said that the Great War had been fought "to make the world a safer place for Henry Ford and Pierpont Morgan") for a loan to save Britain. The loan was agreed, but there were a few strings – and one of them was a cut in unemployment benefit.

This was a step too far for Kennedy and many others in the Labour Government who had now lost all confidence in the one-time hero James Ramsay Macdonald. They could not support this – Kennedy was certainly aware that he could not face anyone in Kirkcaldy if he had agreed to that – but others would support MacDonald. They were the King, the Church, the Conservatives and the Liberals.

To the horror of Kennedy, who had now resigned from the Government, MacDonald formed a National Government to deal with the financial crisis. He, MacDonald, would still be Prime Minister, and some of his Labour Cabinet, notably Philip Snowden the Chancellor of the Exchequer, would remain, but it would be a capitalist Government, using the traditional repressive capitalist methods of unemployment and poverty to solve the economic crisis. This, Kennedy could not accept.

Now free from any collective responsibility of having to side with his leader (who was of course no longer his leader) Kennedy now exploded into print in the pages of *The Fife Free Press* attacking MacDonald with a venom normally only reserved for one's enemies in war. And that was exactly of course what Kennedy conceived MacDonald to be – his enemy in the class war. "This I cannot forgive" he thundered before talking about Kirkcaldy's people being "butchered to make a bankers' holiday". The real villains were the financiers who were a "parasitical and tireless gang", and he also hints at hidden pressures on MacDonald who was subjected to "the financial and political pressure of a sordid and mean and therefore very secret nature."

Not a man to mince words in 1931 was Tom Kennedy, but there was price to pay. In October 1931, MacDonald, now the leader of the National Government and feted as some kind of "saviour of the hour" by the newspapers who used to despise him, called a General Election to seek a "doctor's mandate". Kennedy saw that the "doctor's mandate" was no medicine at all; rather it was for the poison of unemployment and victimisation. But the tide now turned against him, his cause not helped by Sir Robert Lockhart telling all Liberals to vote for the Conservative candidate Albert Russell. Kennedy lost his seat, for the first and only time since before the First Reform Act, Kirkcaldy voted for a Conservative, and the broken Labour Party was reduced to an impotent splinter group of 52 MPs.

Small wonder that Ramsay MacDonald is still to this day held in such deep contempt by the Labour Party! Kennedy's career suffered irreparable damage – a shame, for he was clearly of Cabinet material – and in some ways he never really recovered, but he did in 1931 and the desperate years after that, possess something that Ramsay MacDonald never had. This was his self-respect and the love and affection of his family and friends and indeed the Kirkcaldy Labour voters who still loved him.

Now approaching his 60th birthday Kennedy lay low for a spell, the strain of the last few years having taken their toll. Being now perceived as a man of considerable political ability, he was offered a few seats to contest in by-elections by the severely mauled Labour Party, and accepted one of them in Montrose Burghs in June 1932. On paper he did not seem to have much chance in this constituency of Montrose, Brechin, Forfar, Arbroath, Inverbervie and Kirriemuir, where tipping one's hat to the local squire was an unhappy political habit. It would have been difficult at the best of times, but in the circumstances of 1932 when Labour was almost seen as a traitor to their country for daring to oppose the National Government, what Kennedy achieved was almost miraculous.

His opponent Colonel Charles Kerr, a National Liberal, said things like the situation was "too grave for party and factional interests to divert and distract the national will and purpose", but Kennedy worked hard, addressing jute workers at lunch time meetings and fishermen when the boats came in, and to the astonishment of the broken Labour Party polled 7,030 votes, less than a thousand short of Kerr's 7,963, while the Scottish National Party candidate (an odd entrant for the 1930s when Scottish Nationalists were given as much credibility as Flat Earthers) lost his deposit.

Kennedy might have tried other constituencies, even in England, but preferred to bide his time in Kirkcaldy, although he lived in Aberdeen, appearing now and again at Labour functions, being seen occasionally walking along the High Street with his beloved Annie, talking to people and retaining his quiet dignity without in any way allowing people to be in any dubiety about his feelings for the treacherous and wicked Ramsay MacDonald.

By the time that the next General Election came along in 1935, the depression was gradually easing (but not totally in Kirkcaldy where there was still an unacceptable amount of unemployment) and being replaced as the major cause for concern by the sinister rise of Nazi Germany. Kennedy, like quite a lot of Labour people, was in a quandary. He now tended towards pacifism, following what he had seen in the Great War and its aftermath, but how could one stop a madman like Hitler without violence and war? No-one in Britain was really able to answer that question.

He stood for his last election in Kirkcaldy in November 1935, and the times now being a little more normal, he won back the seat from Mr Russell (with whom he enjoyed a friendly relationship, as always with opponents, and indeed they had shared a platform a month previously to protest against Italy's seizure of Abyssinia) by a large majority, his main issue being the reduction and eradication of unemployment. Labour had recovered slightly over the piece as well, but was still the opposition, and Kennedy could only sit and watch the world slide slowly to the abyss.

His record of asking questions in the House was good, and he kept on serving Kirkcaldy conscientiously until in late 1943 when he was nearing his 70th birthday, ill health and general exhaustion, coupled to the strain of living in war torn London with the constant fears of bombing persuaded him that retirement might be no bad idea. In 1943, he "applied for the Chiltern Hundreds" and withdrew from public life to live first of all in Aberdeen and then in about 1948 he moved to live out the rest of his days in Ivy Bank, Lumsden near Huntly among his own folk. He died of arterial sclerosis and angina pectoris on March 6 1954 at the age of 79. He was survived by his wife and his son, also called Tom Kennedy who became a renowned diplomat and economist

He thus lived long enough to see the world returned to peace and a Welfare State established by the Labour Government from 1945 until 1951. Obviously he would have liked to have been part of this, but perhaps the country in Kennedy's floruit of the 1920s and 1930s was not quite ready for it. Certainly they never gave the Labour Party a big enough majority to do the job properly in the 1920s and 1930s. But Kennedy has every right to be regarded as one of Labour's pioneers, and should be recognised as one of those who retained his integrity in 1931.

As far as Kirkcaldy is concerned, having Kennedy Crescent named after him is scant reward for all that he did. His by-election victory of March 4 1921 should go down as one of the great events of Labour history, not least for the slogan "March forth on March fourth!", and the subsequent triumphs of later Kirkcaldy MPs like Tom Hubbard, Harry Gourlay and even Gordon Brown owe a great deal to the foundations laid by the quiet man from Aberdeenshire who did so much for the Labour cause and for the town that he came to love so well. On one occasion in 1921, as we have said, he held up his baby son for approval of the matrons of Kirkcaldy. That son, whom I was once privileged to meet in his house in a small village in Northumberland some 80 years later, was intensely and rightly proud of his father who can rightly be regarded and revered for his work in Kirkcaldy and for the legacy that he leaves.